EUBANK

THE AUTOBIOGRAPHY

EUBANK

THE AUTOBIOGRAPHY

CHRIS EUBANK
with MARTIN ROACH

CollinsWillow
An Imprint of HarperCollinsPublishers

My special thanks goes to Tarda Davison-Aitkins at
HarperCollins for all his hard work and dedication in
ensuring that this book is an accurate representation
of me and my life so far.

First published in Great Britain in 2003 by
CollinsWillow
an imprint of HarperCollins*Publishers*
London

This paperback edition first published in 2004
Copyright © Chris Eubank 2003

A CIP catalogue record for this book
is available from the British Library

The HarperCollins website address is:
www.harpercollins.co.uk

ISBN 978-0-00-712232-5

Set in Photina with Helvetica Neue Display by
Rowland Phototypesetting Ltd, Bury St Edmunds, Suffolk

Mixed Sources
Product group from well-managed
forests and other controlled sources
www.fsc.org Cert no. SW-COC-001806
© 1996 Forest Stewardship Council

FSC is a non-profit international organisation established to promote the
responsible management of the world's forests. Products carrying the FSC
label are independently certified to assure consumers that they come
from forests that are managed to meet the social, economic and
ecological needs of present and future generations.

Find out more about HarperCollins and the environment at
www.harpercollins.co.uk/green

To Ena, Irvin,
Christopher, Sebastian, Joseph,
Emily and Karron

CONTENTS

Prologue   xi

PART ONE **LEARN THE ART**

1   A Hard-knocks Life   3
2   Designer Thief   17
3   Posers, Bullies and Triers   29
4   Golden Boy   43
5   Doctor Johnson   55

PART TWO **APPLY THE PHILOSOPHY**

6   Homesick   67
7   Hate me, but don't Disrespect Me   91
8   It's a Mug's Game   113

PART THREE **ACQUIRE THE FINANCIAL SECURITY**

9   WBO Middleweight Champion   137
10 The Warrior Within   149
11 Godspeed Shattered   165

12	This Spartan Life	177
13	The Showman	193
14	Destroying the Destroyer . . . Finally	211
15	Tyson	225

PART FOUR **ACHIEVE THE FAME**

16	The Sky's the Limit	237
17	Max	247
18	Community Spirit	263
19	Psychologically Challenged	273
20	Luck of the Irish	289
21	Style on the Nile	303

PART FIVE **EARN THE RESPECT**

22	Winning the Lottery	319
23	A Sweet Tooth and Swollen Eyes	333
24	Samantha	351
25	A Heavy Heart	367
26	Just Being Me	381
27	At Home with the Eubanks	391

	Epilogue	405
	Career Statistics	407
	Index	411

Mandela

To whoever it may concern:

There isn't any bigger slavery than the slavery of compromise and acceptance of all the wrongs perpetrated against the African and Africa.

I never thought thoughts to make me otherwise than what I am, so my obliviousness to what you have been taught to think I should be is a statement of my humanity. As a footnote to that, it is a fact that human character is independent of colour and creed.

PROLOGUE

'Ice cream, jelly and a punch in the belly.' Dorothy used to say this to me every time I went round to her house. She was a very old, German Jewish lady, aged 93, whom my mother worked for as a live-in nurse in New York. I was only 19, negotiating my way through life in one of the toughest cities in the world. I had been sent to the Big Apple to distract me from the life of delinquency that threatened to pull me under back in England.

I loved Dorothy; she used to call me 'sonny boy'. She accepted me. She was wheelchair-bound and I used to pick her up to put her into bed. I would sit and talk to her while my mother, a kind and extremely generous woman, busied herself. The house was crammed full of nostalgic bric-a-brac from over the years. There was also money lying around.

In those days, I never had a penny, so I started to take $20 bills from Dorothy's room. This went on for about two years and added up to over $2000. I knew it was wrong, but I assuaged my guilt by telling myself that Dorothy wasn't using the money and my mother didn't notice.

There are certain things you do in your life that you regret but, if you put them right, you feel so much better. I knew I had to give that money back, especially when it became clear Dorothy was becoming progressively more fragile. By now, my fledgling boxing career had progressed quite nicely and I was taking bouts in England, flying back and forth between Brighton and New York. At that point, I was earning a small weekly allowance plus £700 a fight, so I saved up the equivalent of $2500 over a period of months and the very next time I visited Dorothy, I put the money back in her home. If I hadn't done that, my indiscretion would have weighed very heavily on my mind. Thankfully, I paid her back.

Dorothy died two weeks later.

PART ONE

LEARN THE ART

CHAPTER ONE

A HARD-KNOCKS LIFE

My father, Irvin Eubank, was a great storyteller. One of the many anecdotes he recounted described how he acquired his limp. When he was just a toddler, his own father had put some breadfruit in the stove. He was told not to take the breadfruit out and eat it, which, of course, was exactly what he did when he found himself alone for a few moments. When his father found out, he slashed the youngster's lower leg with a machete. My father had a severely hard life, but he would have told this tale to one person one way and told another person a totally different story! Another version had him being cut out of a terrible car wreck and losing his calf muscle in the process. He was such a character, and I see some of that in myself.

He was born on 28 August 1929, in the district of Mount Airey, Clarendon, in Jamaica. He cut sugar cane in the fields for most of his younger years. That is where he met and eventually married my mother Ena who was then, and always will be, deeply religious. She was well known in church circles in Clarendon. She had been married previously and had five children, my older half-brothers and sisters, whom I rarely see. My mother was born on 15 March 1931 in Clarendon. She left school aged 17 and became a nurse's domestic helper. She met her first husband and married him at the age of 25, but unfortunately he died only three years later, leaving my mother on her own with their five children. Then, in 1960, she met my father.

My father saved diligently for many years for the plane fares to migrate to the UK, stuffing his hard-earned cash under a mattress until such a time as the move could be made. They settled in south London and life was very difficult, an endless grind of poverty and hard work. I was born in East Dulwich on 8 August 1966, their fifth child, after David, the twins Simon and Peter, and Joycelyn. My mother told me their main goal was to get their own home and to do so with five kids around was very hard. So, we were sent to Jamaica to be with our grandmother, on my mother's side, when I was still only a baby. My earliest memory is of being pulled on a banana leaf in the hills by my cousin Woodia. Other than that, I have no recollection of my time there. My grandmother was called Constance, but we called her 'Uncun'. She has passed away now. When she was still alive and I had become world champion, I hired and flew in a helicopter packed with supplies of clothes and foodstuffs to Callington, the mountain-top village where she lived. To this day, when I travel to Jamaica, they say, 'You're the man who came in the helicopter.'

My mother visited as often as she could and was always

sending money over too. On one of these visits, she came with the good news that they now had a house in Crystal Palace Road in south east London. Taking fright at how ill we looked, she convinced herself that we were malnourished, knowing as she did how tough life can be in the countryside of Jamaica. She immediately rounded up the four boys, packed our belongings and took us back to England, leaving Joycelyn to stay with grandmother.

I don't remember coming back from Jamaica, but I have clear recollections of my early life back in the UK. We lived in various council estates in London, including Crystal Palace Road, Peckham, Stoke Newington, Hackney and Dalston. My first memory in the UK was of my mother slapping me senseless for pretending I had a stomach ache, when I actually had four packets of Wotsits shoved underneath my coat that I had stolen from a sweet shop while with her in Stoke Newington. I was also quite adept at stealing from the bread van owned by the nearby bakery.

I started smoking at six years old. I used to follow my brothers and go round to Old Ed's house nearby. He must have been in his late eighties and used to give us cigarettes. If he wasn't around, I would make roll-ups by stealing Old Holborn from my father's tobacco tin as he was sleeping on the settee.

Although at times we were desperately poor, I was a happy child. I adored the very ground my mother walked on, still do. I went everywhere with her. Unconsciously I used to follow her every step around the house. Sometimes she would suddenly stop, playfully stick her bum out and *boom!* I'd crash into her backside. I adored her, my mum. She ruled with a firm hand too – in Jamaican households you do what you are told and you do it the first time. That said, she only used to beat me with a foam slipper which weighed about two grammes! It was like being hit with a piece of paper, but I was more concerned about the expression on her face. I was desperate not to upset her. She never smacked me with her hand and my father only ever used a belt.

Despite my father's difficult circumstances, he always said he had a good life. Why? Because he never let it weigh him down, he never had a chip on his shoulder. These are two facets of his personality that I have inherited and are vital factors in my psyche and subsequent success. Like father like son.

At first, life in the UK had been happy and in 1974 my parents were married in Hackney. However, shortly after, when I was eight, my mother left my father and went to live in New York. I didn't see her very often between her leaving and me travelling to New York aged 16. It wasn't until then that I found out one of the reasons why she had left. I kept asking over the space of a year why she had moved away; she broke down and explained the situation to me several times. She told me that when she would come in the front door another woman would leave out the back. He was a womaniser and she had had enough. At least, that's what she told me. That is not what I subsequently found out to be the case, but I will come to that later in my story. Even then, as a 16-year-old boy, I knew that this is what some men are like, and I did not think ill of my father. The laws of morality are expounded by the scriptures but, to some people, actually applying these principles can prove very testing. I understand that a lot of men stray. I know men who stray; that is life.

Back in 1974, however, leaving the marital home was not a decision my mother could have taken lightly, especially in the light of her deeply religious views. I think removing herself from that situation as a wife was relatively easy; what was hard was walking away from her children.

Growing up without my mother, I knew that we had very little money even though my father worked incredibly hard. He took a job at the Ford plant in Dagenham, where he smoothed iron on long shifts, six days on days, six days on nights. He was a hard man, not least because he'd had a tough upbringing himself, but also this was back-breaking work for a pittance of pay. I can vividly recall us all getting up at 5am to jump-start his Ford Cortina so he could get to work. He earned £90 a week.

It is fair to say that my father was a disciplinarian. However, I wouldn't say my upbringing was a hard life; it was *correct*. We got the strap as punishment so often that I began to become quite apprehensive of him. In retrospect, I have no problems whatsoever with him using the strap, even though I would not do the same with my own children (I use my hand on the bottom if I am going to smack them). The strap is not excessive, but the impression this gives a child is not necessarily always good.

Although he sometimes made me feel anxious, he was a brilliant, colourful character whom I loved dearly. My father was a very generous man. Although we had very little money, he was still very giving. He would often buy six or seven mangoes, which he would wash himself, then take the plateful out into the tenement courtyard for his friends and neighbours to enjoy. Whatever he had, other people could have. My father also had a very good sense of humour. He was a character, with his limp, his bald head and his short stature. I haven't known any other man with his degree of charisma and humour. In a Jamaican sense, my father was 'dread', meaning 'magnificently cool'. When I was a teenager, I thought he spoke very good English but in fact he didn't really, it was like a dialect he could switch on at times.

He rarely gave me advice but when he did it was right; he was strict to ensure we behaved in a correct manner. He would talk to us into the small hours, making good points but repeating himself – as drunk people do. I would understand what he was saying the first time but we couldn't fall asleep; if we were close to dropping off he would cut his eye at us, and bang the doors. This again was mostly for effect to get our attention. He was a man of few words but when he did offer advice, it was very telling, and as the months and years went by, I realised just how correct he was.

Dad slaved away, bringing us up on a shoestring; he stayed the course for us. I remember the police coming for my brother Peter one night when he had been up to no good and my father slammed the door in their faces – he would chastise us if we stepped out of line, but he closed ranks when it was needed. He didn't quit on us.

One time I had broken into a games arcade with a friend of mine, stealing about £2000 in ten pence pieces. We were dragging these very heavy sacks of coins along the floor, and needed some help. I called my father and he helped us load the money into the boot of his car and take it to a friend's house. However, the police arrived shortly afterwards and we had to jump across their neighbour's balcony to escape. This may sound like my father was happy to see me carry on in this fashion: he wasn't but he didn't give me a hard time about it either because he was resigned to the fact that he had to help his son. This was one of the reasons I was sent to America, I couldn't stay out of trouble and this was my father's way of helping me break free.

His language was fabulous to hear; he was a yardman, a Jamaican. Ironically, he talked Jamaica down quite often, saying, 'Jumayka a de wors' country inna de worl'. Inglan a de bes' cuntry inna de worl'. Jus' look pon de nym . . . Jumayka!'

He lived his life to the full, for the here and now. He loved women, gambling, drinking and, when he was drunk, cursing. Life was never dull when my father was around. I loved my father. I adored him. I still do, even though he died in July 2000.

Even though my father's behaviour with other women had provoked my mother to leave, it was his approach to life that I drew on to keep myself buoyant in difficult times. He would never allow himself to be weighed down, as I have explained. This had rubbed off on me so much that when my mother left, I just looked at that as having one less person to dodge. With father working such long hours, I was pretty much my own boy, so in many ways her absence was a marvellous thing. I had so much to do and see and get on with. I could let all my rage out, which was good for me.

Problems never lay heavily on my young shoulders, and that was, and still is, one of my greatest gifts. I know that parental splits destroy some kids, but I guess much depends on your frame of mind. Indeed, one of my brothers didn't handle their split at all well and still carries some resentment towards my mother to this day. I have never held a shred of bad feeling towards my mother for leaving. That was the way my life was and I accepted that. She had not let me down because you have to take into consideration her circumstances. It wasn't even a matter of forgiveness, that had nothing to do with it. It was a matter of *acceptance*.

So many people tell me how my childhood must have been very difficult. It wasn't. It was life; it was fun. I enjoyed my early years and had a fantastic time. Yes, those council estates were miserable sometimes, but that never dragged me down. Maybe I don't remember the bad parts because I don't want to, but that is not how it seems to me. People who are always bemoaning their lot have the mentality of those who are losing. The mentality of people who are winning is to adapt and accept. Of course, I did not articulate or even have an awareness of such an attitude when I was young; it was just the way I was. My mother didn't let me down, neither did my father.

After my mother left, our circumstances were naturally affected for the worse. Our behaviour became increasingly delinquent, but that was entirely of our own accord, it was not Dad's fault. I vividly recall one council flat we lived in during 1975, in the middle of the Haggerston slums. We had no heating and no furniture. Not a stick. Father somehow managed to salvage enough money from his measly wages to ensure there were always eggs and bread on the top of the fridge, even if there was little else inside. He would give us 50p each to get some fish and chips, as he was often on shifts and couldn't cook for us. Most of the time we ate egg sandwiches. People talk about hardship – my father had to bring up four boisterous kids on that £90 a week. He was dutiful, which is one of the traits of a good man. He provided as best he could for his family.

The relationships with my three brothers have proved to be of pivotal importance in my life. The central issue that has been a constant feature of my life is acceptance. I seek acceptance in so many ways, from so many people. This is something that has been ever-present for me and I have thought about it at great length. They say that many people spend their adult lives trying to work out their childhood. Well, I have mine worked out. I know why acceptance is such a force for me. It is because of the way I was treated as a child by my brothers, David, Simon and Peter.

I was the youngest, although there were only four years between all of us. I was always keen to be around them, I always wanted to go where they were going, I desperately wanted to get into trouble like they did, smoke the same cigarettes, steal the same sweets. I wanted to be accepted by them and be with them.

However, this was never the case. In fact, far from accepting me, my brothers openly and constantly denigrated me. They used to call me a c**t; one of them didn't even talk to me, he said I was too ugly to be his brother. I was always the belittled younger sibling. It was the most inequitable of relationships, *because I adored them.*

When I was in my early teens, I would sometimes suggest they might have done certain things differently. They would scoff, saying, 'Shut up, you're silly, you are only a fool.' And they were always telling me how to do things, that what I was planning was wrong or how I had reacted to a circumstance was stupid.

I used to fight all the time with David, but I only won once during all those years. That day, he had cornered me and was hitting my arm very hard, when I suddenly turned and smacked him one. I bloodied his nose so he went and told my father who chastised me! Every other fight with David I lost. Sometimes, the television set would get broken because we used to fight over which channel was showing.

Peter never used to hit me, he just dismissed me verbally which was actually more damaging in the long run. Simon was a very hard puncher, which I found out when he knocked me flat in a playground in Peckham when I was only 12. So I kept out of his way and only had a couple of fights with him.

I started to realise that nothing I said would get through to them. Even so, I still wanted their acceptance because I loved them. That became the key issue in my life as I grew up to be a man. In many ways, it was a very positive force, because I had to prove myself to the world, specifically in regards to the business of boxing. However, in the back of my mind, my blossoming career as a pugilist became a way of proving myself specifically to them also. Cheekily, after I had made champion, David once said to me, 'You should be grateful for all those beatings we gave you; it has made you world champ.' He said I owed him. That is the way they were, that is what I have had to put up with.

They were harsh on me, but actually I realised they were also harsh on themselves. Later, as an adult, I still loved them but no longer needed their acceptance. However, this background has obviously had a deep effect on me. I find myself looking for acceptance as an adult, even though professionally I was world champion and personally I contribute, I am kind, I teach by example and I help people. However, the omnipresent desire to be accepted was deeply ingrained in me from my childhood and would indelibly colour the course of both my career and my life.

My primary education was at Northwold Infants School in Stoke Newington. Other children didn't play with me. I was told this was because I was too rough, but I didn't have a problem with that. I was never a kid who played with toys and games, not least because we couldn't afford any. I never liked that, I was more into stealing crisps and sweets.

I was sometimes bullied because of my broad nose. They used to call me Hoover and Shotgun Nose. It used to bother me and I would wish for a slimmer nose. Now, as a man, I like it, it's a beautiful African nose and the only one I have. It also works very well. My feet are like dragon's claws, but they are the only two I have. I have a gap in my teeth but that is just me. As for the nose, it is actually a superb shape, it has made me a great deal of money. Why? Because when you hit my nose, it simply goes flat rather than breaking.

We moved to south London when I was 11 and went to Bellenden Junior School before moving on to Thomas Carlton Secondary. Unfortunately, by now, I had a somewhat boisterous reputation and was suspended 18 times in one school year for misbehaviour. I used to get into fights all the time over marbles. If it wasn't marbles, it was protecting smaller kids from bullies. As a kid, I watched movies like *The Three Musketeers*. I still love watching films. Back then, I wanted to be just like the characters I saw on the big screen. Take D'Artagnan – I was going to grow up to be that guy, swinging into battle from a chandelier, taking on and beating anybody while still being utterly chivalrous and stylish. I modelled myself on characters like that. That is one of the reasons I got suspended from school so many times, going to the aid of bullied kids. I was a loner and drew little influence from my peer group, instead looking towards those sort of movies for my inspiration.

Occasionally, however, it was my short fuse that caused the problem – when you don't know how to express yourself, your feelings manifest themselves in a fashion that is immature and angry. One time, for example, I said to this kid, 'You are chewing your gum too loud,' and that was that – *bang!* I dropped him. My build was only average but I was always 'extra' – namely I was a *showman*. I have never been a show-off, that is a negative word. My intention was always (and still is) to be a showman, to entertain.

I wasn't powerful so I lost as many fights as I won, but I was righteous. I fought at least three days a week with bullies and at least four days a week with my brothers. I then moved to Peckham Manor Secondary School, where such behaviour continued and I was expelled after only one month.

When I was 13, I grew dreadlocks and became a rasta. I smoked a lot of weed too. I eventually cut the locks off, because my father stopped talking to me. He was a Jamaican who wasn't into the rasta lifestyle, so he was very disapproving. However, he loved Bob Marley. The album *Exodus* was on my Dad's record player all the time. I think at one point it was the only record he actually had. Despite being on constant rotation, I never tired of hearing that album, it was my homely feel cut into vinyl. Still today, whenever I hear the record, it brings back floods of memories. Marley was a great musician, and that style of music is in my soul. He has also been a great motivator for me – his words are all about strength of character, rectitude, correctness, righteousness: being an earth man.

Back then, I had so much energy. However, I did not always do the correct thing, I still had a lot to learn. This energy carried over into my behaviour outside of school as well. If someone wanted to steal some sweets, I was always the first in the queue. And, I didn't just take a single Mars bar, I would grab five. I would take the task in hand and do it.

CHAPTER TWO

DESIGNER THIEF

One day my father came back from work and said to my brothers, 'Where's Christopher?' No one knew. At 9 o'clock that evening, there was a knock at the door and it was the police, who informed my father that I had been taken into care. I don't know if the authorities can do that without consent, but they certainly did it with me. I'd had a social worker assigned to me for some time at Peckham Manor. He was called Mr Lord Okine, an African fellow who drove this little white Datsun. I didn't even know what a social worker was, I didn't understand.

Peter was the first brother to be taken into care, then David, then me. Simon stayed at home. It was not my father's fault: he didn't give us up to care, the authorities took us away. It wasn't a complete shame for me because it had become boring at home with Dad. I couldn't stop misbehaving, it was in my nature. I remember thinking, *why is this man beating me so much?* I realised it was because I was getting caught . . . so I stopped getting caught.

The first care home I went to was The Hollies in Sidcup. It was a massive complex made up of 36 different homes, each named after trees, and one called Reception Centre where I was. My brother David was in Larch. I was met at Reception Centre by a member of staff who took me on a tour of the building. He showed me a room which had a table tennis table, a pool table and a communal eating area. The tour continued, revealing a tuck shop, a storage room and the staff room, before finally ending up at my dormitory. They sat me down in there and gave me my briefing.

Being taken into care was almost like winning the lottery. Can you imagine my sense of bliss? The fridge was full of food – beefburgers, sausages, everything. I could play pool. I had a dorm with new friends to meet and, most fantastically of all, my own warm bed – no more four to a mattress! The whole place was even heated! It was such a wonderful experience meeting these kids from Scotland, Manchester, all over the UK, seeing their different attitudes, hearing their different tales. That first term at The Hollies was one of the best experiences of my life – I had three meals a day, table tennis, pool, and there were girls. Heaven! We used to climb down the drainpipes to get into their dorms: it was such good fun.

But just as at school, however, I found myself getting into trouble and was shifted between care homes several times in four years. In 1979 I went to Yastrid Hall in North Wales, which I now know to have been in the midst of the sexual abuse scandal that did not come to light until the mid-90s, when it was revealed that a network of adults appeared to have been involved in abusing children across the country. I wasn't abused sexually or otherwise, I didn't even know there was a problem. It has transpired that certain children were being abused, but at the time I never knew. Admittedly, I was engrossed in my own little world but, fortunately for me, that whole terrible saga passed me by.

From Yastrid Hall, I went to Stanford House in Shepherds Bush for seven weeks in a lock-up for assessment. From there I was sent to St Vincent's in Dartford for a month, before being expelled and taken to Orchard Lodge in Crystal Palace, for another seven-week assessment in a secure unit. From there, I went to Karib, a care home for ethnic minorities in Nunhead, SE15, was expelled again after only one month, then sent to Davy's Street in Peckham.

All this time I was a highly unruly boy. I still had a short fuse, I was a very fast runner (ten miles in 72 minutes when I was 13), quite clever, and my sleight of hand wasn't too bad. I took full advantage of my skills, always breaking into staff rooms and tuck shops or the newsagents down the road to pilfer cartons of 200 cigarettes. Such petty crimes later progressed to shoplifting and repetitive absconding.

Yes, it could be described as a very itinerant childhood. However, my view is this: moving around so much is the perfect way to ensure that an individual continues to have new experiences. You never get stuck in a rut when you're barely at the same place for more than three months at a time. Constantly having to make new friends was not a burden because I preferred my own company anyway; I was still something of a loner. Now, as an adult, I can travel anywhere and feel comfortable in any situation, an ability I put down partly to these teenage years spent on the move.

It was around this time that, despite my antics to the contrary, I started to read proverbs. Although it would be some years before I succeeded in applying (or at least tried to apply) myself to many of the words I was reading, the wisdom they offered always appealed to me. I was always enthralled and intrigued by the wise man and words.

In North Wales, there was a kid in care with me called Timmy Brian, who had this marvellous way of strutting about. I watched him swagger around and noted the effect this had on people, so I started to do my own version, with my own flavour. Timmy was a very courageous black kid from Nottingham who thought of himself as Superman. He used to point his hands skywards like he was flying through the air and I used to roar with laughter. Sometimes I still copy him. If you've watched me on television, perhaps on *A Question of Sport*, you may have seen me doing this. When a show starts, the warm-up man asks the audience to give a round of applause, even though no one has done anything of note yet. I always thought that was an odd situation, so when it happens and the applause starts out of nowhere, I often put my hand in the air like Superman, like Timmy Brian. It is just a fun thing but, of course, some critics say, 'Oh, look at Eubank, assuming they are clapping him.' I'm not, I'm just being a big kid again, back in North Wales with Timmy.

At my last care home, Davy's Street in Peckham, I was always getting into trouble with one particular care worker.

He was a huge man, very tall. It was not his considerable size that was most threatening however – what was most scary was the fact he never treated me for what I was, namely still a teenager. He saw me from day one as an adult and for that reason his obvious dislike for me felt much more tangible and intimidating.

One day we'd had yet another disagreement over something I had done, so he cornered me. He was really angry and breathing heavily with fury. He leaned down over me and said in a truly menacing tone, 'I don't give a f**k about any of this, I will kill you.' Now I had stood up to my fair share of bullies and bigger men in my younger years, but I knew this man was simply too big and too aggressive to mess around with. After this unseemly confrontation, I went to the bathroom and, because the home was a lock-up at the front, I crawled out the window and was gone. I was never in care again.

I had been so unruly when I visited my father on leave from the care homes, he could not tolerate my behaviour and eventually refused to have me back home at all. For the next 18 months, I was homeless. My territory was around Peckham and the Walworth Road, I did not have a permanent roof over my head. Much has been made in the media, and indeed by the public I meet, about how awful this must have been. No, I won't have this said. I lived like a king. I wouldn't say it was bliss, because bliss is not having to work and being at ease with yourself. You can't really be at ease when you don't know where you are going to sleep that night. So it wasn't bliss, but it wasn't far off.

I was a teenage kid, shoplifting daily and earning easily over £100 by 6 o'clock each night. I was young, quick, had good sleight of hand and bundles of courage, so I was never really too compromised. I had girlfriends all over the place and as much marijuana, Special Brew and Treats as I wanted, I went to Blues dances, called Shobins, two or three nights a week and was driven around everywhere by taxi, wearing the finest clothes. I was my own boss, I had no parents to report back to, no school to trouble me. I was lord of my own manor.

During this time, I was part of one of the most proficient shoplifting gangs in the country. On a bad day we would take home £110 per man, but when we were on song we would make £180 each. At the time, the average wage was perhaps £60 a week. There were four of us in the gang: myself (Eu-ey), Sticks, Nasty and Beaver. Sticks took his nickname from the Jamaican term for a thief, while Nasty earned his monicker because he was girl mad. They were both Nigerians. Beaver was the last man to join up. I now realise that this behaviour is foolish, but having gone through it myself I can relate to youngsters and talk to them effectively about getting caught up in this kind of lifestyle.

We worked Monday to Friday, consummately professional, and were very exacting in our standards. We wore suits, shirts and ties and always looked immaculate. Before a job, I would put on my Italian mohair suit, a crisp shirt and tie, and my prized Burberry coat. At the time, Burberry had just introduced these extremely sturdy security tags, so stealing one of their range was not an option, you had to buy your Burberry coat. I vividly recall going to Haymarket to purchase mine: it cost £180 and was a sight to behold. Magnificent. Oh, man, I felt I had arrived. On the streets, how you dress is inextricably linked to how much respect you command, so I was always intimately fascinated by the latest fashions. That may well have something to do with my latter-day passion for dress code.

The purpose of the Burberry coat was twofold. Firstly, you looked impeccable, not at all like a shoplifter. Secondly, if you bought the coat legitimately, you were given a Burberry's bag, which was effectively a licence to steal anything. You would walk into some of the finest clothing shops in the West End and look as if you could afford to buy any item. The sales representatives never suspected a thing, they probably assumed I was some rich African youngster with money to burn. That uniform was crucial to our success.

We had numerous locations to work, including Oxford Street. Of course, things would not always go our way and sometimes we would end up being chased.

That year on the streets was so exciting. We were at the peak of our shoplifting prowess. I had all this money and freedom and never wanted to compromise that by staying at a hostel. Instead, I would crash on friends' floors most of the time, flitting from one run-down flat to the next. I blagged it, as they say. I would go to someone's house and get so drunk I couldn't leave. It was during this time that I started to smoke weed very heavily. I had begun when I was only 12, but by this time on the streets I was a very heavy user. A lot of my shoplifting money was spent on weed, booze and clothes. I must have smoked thousands of pounds of ganja over the years. I still knew quite a few rastafarians and that influenced my attitude towards smoking too.

About once a week I would not be able to get a floor for the night, so I would break into a car and sleep on the back seat. I spent many a happy night napping on car seats in Peckham, Camberwell or the Elephant and Castle. On a few occasions, I did end up sleeping under a mattress but I didn't like that: the cold still got through to my bones. The longest stint I had under a proper roof was at Nasty's. Even then, he got tired of this after a couple of weeks and said, 'Look, Chris, I can't handle it anymore, you need to find somewhere else.'

I was still only a kid but I had been living on my own instincts for so long, my sense of self-survival was deeply ingrained. When your mother isn't there and you live with your father who is doing long shift work, you don't have time to be a child. If you want food, you have to find it yourself. With the benefit of hindsight, it is apparent that my personality was becoming heavily predisposed towards the life of solitude, hardship and suffering that is boxing. I maintain to this day that my childhood never felt like this. I have no complaints, but looking back I do accept that in a sense I was in training for the noble art from almost my first breath.

Of course, however buoyant I kept my disposition, life on the street wasn't all a bed of roses. Inevitably, I found myself in compromising situations from time to time. One night, I had nowhere to sleep, so Sticks introduced me to a chef he knew vaguely. I later found out he was also gay but no one told me this at first. I needed a roof for the night, so I had to keep calm when I went inside his dishevelled flat and saw dozens of machetes and knives all over the house. I said, 'I'll be okay to sleep on the settee,' but he was adamant, saying, 'It's a matter of principle that you sleep on the bed.' I politely refused, but he was insistent. He seemed cool to me, so eventually I said, 'Fine, okay,' and settled down in this bed. At about 3 o'clock in the morning, I suddenly felt this big hand wrap around my waist and start to pull me backwards as he cuddled up to me. I was out of the bed like a flash! Then it struck me that I was with a complete stranger whose house was filled with cutlasses and various other blades, and now I may have offended his feelings. The night before I had burgled a house in Seven Sisters Road and took a camera, which I'd left on this man's coffee table. I tried to say to him calmly, 'I'm not like that,' before grabbing my camera and clothes and hot-footing it out the door! I headed out into the street, but as I was halfway down the road, I got this bad feeling and decided to hide behind a wall, for no specific reason. Seconds later, a police patrol car slowly drove past. I was always blessed with an intuitive street sense that kept me out of trouble so often. Imagine if they had found me, a young black teenager wandering the streets in the middle of the night, out of breath and with a camera around my neck!

People often ask me how it feels to possess the material things my boxing success has brought me, having come from being a homeless delinquent. I do not see it like that. Whatever our individual circumstances, we are all fighting and each person's own individual predicament is relative, it feels like a hefty burden. I always say to people, 'If I have £1 billion and you have nothing, then my burdens are as heavy as yours. I still have things to do, I still have problems, I still have aches and pains. Nature doesn't give anyone more than they can handle.' Everyone's burden is heaviest. I prefer to look at things this way. If I look at it any other way, it gives people who are less fortunate an excuse to say the world owes them something – it doesn't. *The world owes you nothing.* If I had looked at my younger years in that way, I would have suffocated in resentment. I could not allow that, I had things to do. I had to fly, so to speak.

One night, I took a taxi to a gentleman's outfitters in Brighton. We usually hired a taxi to take us around our daily targets, the driver would be paid £70 for the day and was aware of what we were doing. When I got there, the driver pulled up into a side street and I got out with my tool, namely a pickaxe. It was 3am and the streets were deserted. The store had a double set of floor-to-ceiling glass doors. They were alarmed but that was never a deterrent. I took the pickaxe and, *smash!*, embedded it in the top right-hand corner. Then, *smash!*, again in each corner, four very deliberate and targeted blows so that the large pane was weakened. It was then simple enough to kick the glass through and walk into the store.

Of course, the alarm was going off, which in the still of the night always sounded amplified 1000 times. However, I was serenely calm. All the butterflies I'd had before the event had dissipated. This was how I was with any job, whether it was stealing clothes or fighting a contender – as soon as it started I would be at peace.

I grabbed about six suits and then just stood there, stock still in the centre of the store, soaking up the peace. When I was ready, I simply walked to the taxi and headed back to London. Easy. On the M23, however, these two sleek police Jaguar cars pulled up alongside us. I looked behind and another one had taken position to our rear. It transpired that someone had heard the alarm, saw me break in and called the police. I was nicked.

There was no escape. They hauled me up in court and I explained that it was just a matter of money, that this was not my usual behaviour. Things were looking quite bleak, but thankfully the judge granted me bail, which I jumped and headed for a new life which was waiting for me . . . in New York.

CHAPTER THREE

POSERS, BULLIES
AND TRIERS

'They know exactly who you are and what you are doing. They're watching you, don't kid yourself they're not. Wait until you're 17 – you'll get caught, you'll be in and out of jail for the rest of your life. You keep on screwing up.'

This warning shot was fired my way many times by my father over the years, but I didn't change my ways. Unless I was taken elsewhere, he was convinced I was being groomed as Borstal and prison fodder.

It was actually my mother who plucked me out of my life of delinquency. She was hearing all these reports from Dad about my misbehaviour, so she asked him to send me to New York. She even forwarded the money for the plane fare. My flight was on 29 November 1982. I flew in a silk suit, with burgundy Italian shoes, but halfway across the Atlantic I realised this was not a clever choice of garment. I arrived at JFK after seven hours in a cramped seat with my silk suit looking like one big crease. I did a lot of thinking on that plane, though, and promised myself I would stop smoking, go to church and try to start behaving myself. I also thought it would be a good idea to go to a boxing gym, mainly to get fit. I knew that my peer group in London would make it very hard for me to forge a new life, so I was fully aware this was a chance of a fresh start. I collected my bags from the airport carousel and caught a taxi with my father to where my mother lived, at 161st Street on Melrose Avenue, South Bronx.

Being from the street, I was not intimidated with settling into a new environment. One of my first impressions of New York was the culture – I didn't understand how inconsiderate people were with their language and the disrespect they threw around. It took some time to soak in the new terrain – this was, after all, nothing like even the toughest parts of London. My acute sense of observation was to quickly prove invaluable.

Pretty soon, I realised three basic facts that would remain constant during my time in New York. Firstly, it was very, very cold in the winter. Secondly, it was bakingly hot in the summer and, thirdly, I was just as poor here as in south London. In New York, it doesn't matter what colour you are, if you're poor, you're made to feel like an outcast. You can be white, black, Hispanic, Chinese, whatever, if you don't have any money, you don't get any respect. It was very, very hard. I often had a dollar for my dinner and that would get me eight rotten bananas and a quart of milk. I'd put that in a blender with a little nutmeg and that was my dinner. Some days my mother would cook for me so I'd eat decently, but she wasn't always with me as she worked as a live-in nurse for the aforementioned old Jewish lady, Dorothy.

I started straight away on my new less deviant path. I'm not saying that I stopped all my vices overnight, of course not, but that was my intention; indeed, I would drift back into the shoplifting later when I travelled intermittently between New York and the UK, but for now I was determined to start a clean slate. There was no one to tempt me like my London friends and I knew what I had to do. I had one more chance. I wanted to be a success and that meant not stealing, not drinking and not fighting. As I've said, before I flew to New York, I drank very heavily. It was either Bacardi or Special Brew, often swilling several cans before I went out in the morning.

Within three months, I had stopped smoking, no mean feat when you consider the quantity of nicotine and ganja I was getting through in London. Two devastating incidents happened which made me stop smoking cigarettes and joints completely. The first episode was after I had come from Manhattan and stopped off near Yankee Stadium, in the Bronx, to go into a bar that was near to where we lived. There were some guys whom I vaguely knew from playing pool with, and one of them offered me some weed. This was not just ordinary weed, like the weed I was used to in England. This knocked me for six! I walked the eight blocks home but, before I went upstairs, I trudged into the store on the ground floor. This was an amazing shop, a cornucopia of fascinating objects. They used to say they stocked everything from a pin to an elephant. It certainly looked like that, all old boxes crammed to bursting, piled high, teetering with the weight of the weird objects inside.

The store was run by two middle-aged, real African American New Yorkers from down south, Mr Seymour and his sister Norval. This particular day, Norval was serving and as I asked her for whatever it was I wanted, she looked up at me. Now, when you smoke weed, your eyelids kind of shine and droop. I don't know if she knew what I had been up to or not, but my perception told me she did. I could almost read her disappointed eyes saying, '. . . and I thought you were a good boy.' That look, which I am sure she was not aware of, withered me on the spot. My spirit was crushed. I have always had a deep-felt respect for my elders and so this lady's inner dismay really hurt me. I stopped smoking weed there and then.

Some Jamaicans say weed is a herb of wisdom. I agree but perhaps from a different viewpoint, namely that the wisdom only comes if you stop smoking and apply yourself to something. Marijuana helped me because it made me appreciate my focus more when I had stopped.

As with weed, I had always felt guilty about smoking cigarettes, but did it anyway, as you do when you are younger. The incident that stopped this habit was when my mother came down one day and caught me outside on the steps smoking a cigarette. All she said was, 'Jesus Christ!' but that was enough. Knowing how precious her religion is to her, she could not have hurt me more if she had whipped me with a cane. Those two words made me feel like crying. It levelled me and for days I was in despair, so ashamed.

Whatever I did, I would always say to myself, *Please don't say those words.*

I gradually cut back on the drink too and started to get my life in order. Although I had been a persistent offender in London, I was street-wise enough not to steal one thing during my time in the Bronx. Over there, if they catch you stealing even the tiniest thing, they give you a good hiding first before they call the police. New York was a rough place and I was there in the early 80s, when it had one of the highest crime rates of any city in the world. This was not the place to be taking liberties with people's livelihoods.

I was surprised by the prevalence of the gun culture over there. In London there were knives at worst, and even then they were only brandished in extreme circumstances, and actually used even more rarely. Yet in New York it was common for everyone to have a gun. I would find out just how popular firearms were shortly after.

I started attending church and enrolled at Morris High School in the South Bronx, where I studied from 1983 until 1986. I took North American History, Spanish and Geography. I didn't have the same temptations around me as in London, so I became a good student who worked hard towards graduation. My transition was well underway (this period of cleansing, if you like, went on until I fought for the world championship in 1990 – it was constant application).

By the time I was in New York, if I had learned one thing from my teenage years it was this: almost everybody lets you down. My initial impetus to enter a boxing gym was to get fit. However, I soon also realised that, with pugilism, I knew the parameters; no one could let me down, it was all to do with me. The only person who could let me down in the ring was myself. I couldn't help but be drawn to that. There were no false promises any more.

My brothers had previously started boxing – indeed, Peter went on to beat Barry McGuigan in the Irishman's fourth professional bout (McGuigan won the return match). So, I was already aware of the sport before I travelled to New York. I'd actually been in the ring before in the gym where my brothers used to train. However, these few fights were just tear-ups, kids scrapping. In one particular brawl with a kid called Matthew, I'd got badly smashed up: all my teeth were chipped and I was heavily bruised. That early exposure to the business was a very negative experience, which totally put me off boxing.

In New York, however, I was keen to get in shape. I started going to the Jerome Boxing Club, Westchester Avenue, South Bronx. It was a derelict building, so the gym fees were only $15 a month. However, this was money I just didn't have. Fortunately, they let me be the 'caretaker' for the gym, which basically meant I swept the floors and put the buckets down to catch the rain that came through the roof – it was peppered with holes. I had the keys to the place, so I was always in there, seven days a week. Within three months of arriving in New York, I was in good physical condition. I was evolving into a very determined character.

After four months, I was asked if I wanted to spar. By

now, I was very motivated so they put me in with a young man nicknamed Horse, a strong Puerto Rican. I got in there and throughout the first round he hit me relentlessly. The second round was the same, I could barely catch my breath. But in the third round, something important happened – I hit back. My competitive spirit in the ring had been awakened and from then on there was no stopping me.

Adonis Torres owned the gymnasium and was the first person who treated me with respect, like a man. He was effectively my first manager and really looked out for me in those early days. It was quite daunting in a Bronx gym at that age, being a foreign interloper with what was perceived as a peculiar way of speaking. They used to say, 'This guy's weird. He sounds like an English gentleman.' Even though I came from south east London, I had been teaching myself better speech patterns, accents and articulation for some time. How I did that was by listening to the newsreaders on BBC1 and the World Service radio too. I copied them over and over until gradually it just became the way I spoke. I also learned by listening to how the Americans spoke English incorrectly.

So, at first, I was the new boy. However, I gradually became a more permanent fixture. I was there every day and over the next three and a half years, I watched fighters come and go, all the fly-by-nights, the triers, the posers, the good-looking guys with no heart, all of them. I was there throughout. I am often asked if I was 'spotted' as a prospective champion – the answer is no; I never even believed I was a good fighter myself.

I started to be drawn towards learning the art of boxing itself. I began to adore watching other fighters sparring. I loved to see them throw a left hook, take a body shot, go through their moves. The art is a beautiful thing once you can do it. I learned so much by watching other fighters. I don't mean just in the ring either. How their personal lives impacted on their careers always compelled me. Really good fighters who were supposed to be going places would get caught up in complicated personal situations, and before you knew it, their aspirations were in tatters.

Sparring was the gospel of New York gyms. It was their faith. Everybody spars. Sparring is how you become a good fighter. It is far more important than the road work, the bag work, the skipping, the shadow boxing, all of it. The most essential thing you need to do if you want to be a good fighter is to spar four or five times a week without fail. And in New York, sparring was not going through the motions either – these were merciless bang-ups. This was a boxing commandment I took with me when I returned to England and to which I adhered throughout my career.

I started off with one set of three rounds, then over the months that progressed into six-rounders, then eventually full-blooded 12-rounders. We even did some 15-rounders to condition ourselves so that a 12-round fight felt easier. That was how I honed my ring intelligence. There is a *ring* fitness and there is a *road* fitness – if you don't have ring fitness you may as well not even step into the arena.

I started to notice one fighter in particular who inspired me. His name was Dennis Cruz, a southpaw. He had this seductively poetic way of moving, slipping, bobbing and weaving. He was a delight to watch. His jabs were like pieces of art – there was a sign in the gym that read, 'The right hand will take you around the block, the jab can take you around the world.' That's a fact.

I became obsessed with being able to box as well as Dennis. I wanted to be able to weave like he did, to throw shots, to retreat, dance around like he did. I wanted to be as smooth as he was in the ring. This man was poetry in motion. Over the years, I have been asked so many times which boxers influenced me and, to be honest, there was only one – Dennis Cruz. Everyone has 'flavour', everyone has a perception of how something should be done, some people have it much deeper than others. Dennis epitomised it for me.

I have no idea where he is now. I'd love to see him again. The sad thing is that time and hardship have a way of wearing a man down. A young boy has all the possibilities laid out before him, you feel everything will be alright, but as a man things quickly change. For me, I didn't miss my boat, I grabbed every opportunity with both hands. So many people don't do that. They may have a trade and even see a plan before them, but very few people apply themselves and persist. They sometimes fall foul of the easy routes – laziness, drugs, women, squandering – but that's not who I am.

I'm not saying this was Dennis, of course. However, the shame of it was that, as with many fighters, he never made the big time. I have since heard he had personal problems. That was a terrible shame, because he was an astonishing fighter. He was only 135lb but was a grandmaster of the craft. This is not generous credit I am giving Dennis here, this is just a fact, an observation.

The first trainer I had was an older man called Andy Martinez, a Puerto Rican. He was only about 5′ tall. He got me exceptionally fit. He taught me only two punches, which were the straight left and the straight right, no hooks to the body, no body shots. He only worked with amateurs, mainly getting them in shape – which he did superbly. After about two years with him, I wanted to work with Maximo Perez, the main trainer at the Jerome boxing gym. He was from the Dominican Republic and had trained Dennis Cruz: he was our undisputed, sought-after, top man. Maximo had been a fighter himself – for me it is only logical that the best trainers are former boxers, not enthusiasts or observers. You need a brain that knows how it feels to be punched, how to throw punches correctly. Maximo had all the moves and could teach you everything. For me, he was the definitive trainer.

At the time I took a great deal of advice and counsel from the gym owner, Adonis. I said to him privately, 'The time has now come for me to learn more punches and evolve into a better fighter and I can't do that with Andy.' Very diplomatically, Adonis said to me, 'That will be seen as unkind by him because he bought you your first pair of boxing boots, he gives you money for orange juice after training every day. You need to resolve this matter with a great deal of care.'

I acknowledged this point but replied, 'I appreciate immensely all the things Andy's done, the time he's taken with me, the nights he drove me home or gave me money for food because I didn't have anything. I sincerely appreciate that, but am I supposed to hold myself back because someone has been nice to me? I am trying to make this my way of life. I want be a good fighter and to do that I need a better trainer.' I had learned all he could teach me. Adonis was, of course, right, so I thought very carefully about how to speak to Andy with suitable tact.

I was very anxious not to hurt Andy's feelings. I said to him, 'I don't want to upset you, but it is time for me to move on now. I need to work with another trainer and if you don't allow me to then all you are doing is holding me back. That is unfair, I'm sure you don't want to do that. This is not about you, it's about me, I'm not using you, I'm just trying to get ahead. The fact that you've helped so much, I thank you deeply, but I need to move on.' I am proud that, although I was a young fighter, I had the courage to tell Andy. So many fighters do not tell their trainer anything, even in the gym, so they end up stifling their careers with the wrong trainer.

Maximo took me on for about a week and then said, 'You're punching like a girl, I'm tired of telling you the same thing about the left hook – you're slapping the left hook. Go back to Andy.' I told him I would get it right, so I went into the corner of the gymnasium and stood close by the wall for over an hour and a half, throwing the left hook, over and over and over, hundreds of times. Trying to get the pivot right, I had to get the angle right. Over and over, thousands of times in the corner, every day, obsessively for weeks.

This was a routine of my own making – if I was ever unhappy with a particular punch or move, I would stop, retreat into the corner of the gym and repeat, repeat, repeat. Thousands of times. By the end of each little punishment session, I would be drenched in sweat. This was intense, I wouldn't just throw the punch, I was trying to perfect every intricate detail.

So although my training with Maximo lasted only two weeks, I continued to train with him from afar. I had already been watching him work with his stable of six professional fighters from across the gym anyway. I would observe and listen to what he was saying and explaining, then mimic it myself. Even though he didn't have the time to train me, he was, effectively, because I had a very watchful eye, which is the key to success at anything. In the end, I didn't need him to teach me directly, all I needed to do was to watch him teach other fighters and duplicate that.

For example, when one of his fighters was sparring, I would shadow box his every move from across the gym. If he threw a right, I would evade, then counter; it was as if I was physically in the ring with the boxer. I learned so much that way. Some of Maximo's fighters were of an excellent calibre – there was a fellow called Salano who I took a few moves from regarding escape, moving away from an opponent.

So I watched, I listened, I learned, then I repeated, reviewed and revised. Every minute detail of every move or punch was practised thousands and thousands and thousands of times. After a while, I took what I learned from Maximo and started to add my own spice, my own flavour and personality. That was when I started to evolve towards being a complete fighter. This process was equipping me in depth with the skills needed to do my job – the heart, that intangible, unquantifiable, primal factor, was another matter.

People sometimes say to me why do you have to repeat one punch so many times to perfect it? Well, these are not simple skills. It took me two years to learn how to throw the right hand. Then there's the left hook, the right hand to the body, the left upper cut to the body, the right upper cut to the body, the right hook to the body – these punches take years and years to learn. You don't climb through the ropes and just do it.

I was about 19 years old when I first learned how to throw body punches, that's three years after I had first started boxing. Initially, they taught me to punch straight out, 1–2, 1–2, load up and keep on punching. Even that took ages to master, it was very hard. But I applied myself very stringently in the gym. Over months and months of repetition, I observed and criticised my every movement. I imagined taking myself out of my own body then analysing myself in minute detail from the other side of the gymnasium.

People outside of the boxing fraternity do not realise what complexity is involved in throwing just one single punch. You don't punch from the arm or even from the shoulder. You punch from the foot. The wave of movement travels from the toe, through the foot, knee, hip and chest, sears up the arm, forearm, wrist and finally into the knuckles. Then the index knuckle and middle knuckle are the two which need to connect. These two knuckles flow from a direct line straight up your arm. The other knuckles don't have the same support, so if you connect badly with the other two you are likely to hurt your hand. Sometimes you connect correctly with the two correct knuckles and that is the perfect punch. When that happens they just go. Lights out – good night Charlie.

If that is done correctly, which is hard enough, you then have to complete the procedure, which involves getting your fist back into the correct position by your chin, your body is pulled back into form and you are ready to go again. If you can do that meticulously, you will have probably taken two or three years to master it – and now you know just one punch. This was what I was learning all those years. I wanted to know everything.

CHAPTER FOUR

GOLDEN BOY

In my first amateur fight, the referee stopped the contest after only 30 seconds . . . and declared me the loser. The guy wasn't the same weight as me, perhaps only ten pounds heavier, but that is a big advantage in the ring. He hit me in the chest with a perfect punch and I was so startled by the weight behind it that I stuttered back and froze. I couldn't move, so the referee stopped the fight. I won eight amateur bouts on the trot after that, all three-rounders, stoppages or decisions. My amateur career consisted of 26 fights, seven of which I lost and the remainder I won. I was already incredibly focused, but now I was beginning to develop some momentum.

One day after training, I was in the McDonald's on 149th Street and 3rd Avenue, South Bronx. I was carrying two heavy gym bags and was leaning up against the counter where a section is hinged for staff to push up and walk out. I was looking out of the window and didn't notice a man who worked there waiting for me to move so he could get in behind the counter. He tried to lift it which startled me, so I turned to see what was happening. He stared at me and said, 'Move out of the way, nigger! Move out of the way!' I said, 'What?!' His aggression took me by surprise, so I said, 'What are you going to do?' to which he replied, 'Oh, what? You want some? Right, if that's the way it is, I'll go and get my boys.'

At that point, I knew this was a situation that had to be confronted. I pulled my shoulders back and held my head up high, chest proudly puffed out. My arms dropped down by my side and as they did, the bags dropped down my arms and finally fell off the wrists, leaving me standing there in that peacock pose that I later became famous for. If you had frozen that moment in McDonald's, it would have been no different to how I looked in the ring against Benn for the world title in 1990. That was my natural stance. A porcupine puts his spikes out, a dog growls and shows his teeth – this was my stance of protection. I never held my hands up – with my arms so low and open, the message was very clear, 'Let's do this, whatever you've got, I'll have it.' You're showing that person conviction, plus you'd be surprised what you can do from that position, if you know your boxing. I think someone tipped this fellow off about the fact I was an amateur boxer, because he went out the back to get 'his boys' but never came back.

By the age of 18, I was sufficiently skilled to make it through to the light-middleweight final of the prestigious Spanish Golden Gloves tournament, widely seen as a testing ground for future champions. The semi-final was very tough

– for the first time I sensed the flickering of white lights in my head that would have gone on to become a knock-out if I had not eluded further punishment. Fortunately, I went on to get the decision and won the light-middleweight belt. The final was just as tough. I was getting punched left, right and centre. I won because of my aggression; the judges appreciated the fact that I was always taking the fight to him. That was a landmark victory, the first rung on the ladder so to speak.

I had just gone 19 when I turned professional. I was still at Morris High School but the decision to turn pro was simple – I needed the money. I was due to earn $250 for my first fight in Atlantic City. The day you turn pro is not the day you sign the contract, or get your license, it is the day you actually fight: for me this was 3 October 1985, at the Atlantis Hotel, against Timmy Brown. I was absolutely petrified. You are taught to exude confidence in boxing, but that is something which you don't possess at first. You hear about all these great fighters who have 35–0 records, but all you want to do is have yourself respected and win your first fight. At the time, Thomas Hearns had this awesome record and I was just astounded that anyone could be so phenomenal. He was a great champion. You're not thinking of being champion, you just want the first win and to pocket a few hundred dollars.

They left me in a room in the Atlantis Hotel by myself beforehand for probably only half an hour, but it seemed like an eternity. I went through a searching, emotional self-examination. I really put myself through the mill: *Are you going to do this or are you going to bottle it? Are you going to have courage or are you going to be a wimp?* My heart was pounding almost out of my chest. I was going into the unknown, something that has always made me uncomfortable.

The hardest thing about boxing is the unknown. Before every fight you get extremely nervous; there's the pressure of the fight, the ring entrance, everything that comes with a bout, so you are naturally terrified. That only ends when the referee says, 'Box'. At that second, I always had pure peace, blissful, sweet peace. Once he said that, I knew the territory, everything was a reaction, he made a move, I reacted, he made a wrong move, I scored a point. The chess game had begun and I knew I played exceptionally well. I always savoured that word, 'Box': it brought such serenity.

It was a four-round fight and I won on points. That first purse was $250, which was a lot of money to me, but I had already spent it! I had been calling a girl in the UK called Carol Chevanne on the school phone and had racked up quite a bill. The school authorities found out and I apologised, explaining that I would pay back every penny. It was a serious enough offence to be expelled but they gave me the chance to keep my word. I won the fight and so paid the bill. So even when I did slip up, I was doing all I could to make amends. This first success was later followed by four more four-round points victories against Kenny Cannida, Mike Bagwell, Eric Holland and James Canty, all in Atlantic City.

In the summer of 1986, I graduated from Morris High. I had been a good student in as much as I didn't have any friends, not even any acquaintances really, to distract me. My personality in regards to succeeding in church, school and boxing was very focused and I suppose that alienated people. I always felt like my school mates were just kids – in England I had been living like an adult for years, feeding myself, earning my own money, looking out for myself.

Succeeding at school hadn't been easy, especially as my academic life in the UK had not been well spent. However, as I was training to box in parallel with my studies, I very quickly found that the same principles of application, repetition, hard work and perseverance paid off in the world of academia too. Boxing is like that – its philosophy is a blueprint for so much in life.

Immediately after graduation, I began a course at SOBRO College of Technology in the South Bronx. I was on a course for six months learning on a Wang word processor, aspiring to become accomplished with computers.

To bring money in, I also did various jobs. One year before I was to leave New York permanently, my mother introduced me to Alan Sedaka, who owned a building company called Durite. One job I took was on a building site run by Alan's firm. I looked after this office block in Long Island and was paid quite handsomely. My father was in New York at this time and was working on the job with me. He used to wind me up all the time.

Another part of the job was to make van deliveries, even though I had never driven in my life. One day I was given an automatic – which I tried to think of as just a go-kart! I got in this van and was doing okay until I hit the town and began to feel a growing sense of panic as the congestion built up. I stopped at some traffic lights but overshot and found myself in the grid where people walk across. So I reversed back – the van had no rearview mirror so I was only looking in my wing mirrors . . . *Crash!* There was an almighty bang as I hit a motorcyclist. This angry guy wheeled his motorbike round and parked it in front of my van so I couldn't move. 'Look what you've done to my bike!' he snarled.

Already I was thinking about what on earth to do. I was an illegal immigrant without a green card, no driving licence: we were talking deportation if the police got involved. The guy said, 'Listen, what are you going to do? You hit my bike?' So I said, 'Yes, I've got my insurance papers and everything in here, let me just pull around the corner, we're holding up the traffic, everyone is beeping, this is ridiculous.' At first he wouldn't hear of it, but I persisted and eventually after about five minutes he got on his battered bike and began to wheel it out of the way . . . *Screeeccchh!* I zoomed off into the distance!

I was doing well at my studies, I had money from jobs and the fights I was winning, but this was all keeping me very busy. Alan Sedaka was always very keen to see me do well. His brother Maurice was also a kind man and one day he took me to one side and gave me a priceless piece of advice. He told me to choose studies or boxing. To use his words: 'Put all your eggs in one basket or risk being mediocre at both.' I thought about what he said and knew that he was right. So I made my decision. It was a relatively easy choice when it came down to it: one was safe, one was dangerous. I will always go for the danger: my grain has always been to take the riskier, harder route. I have always lived in black and white, hot or cold, violence or silence. If you just want to exist you have to just stay in the grey area. Easy is just existing. I don't want that. I want to make a difference. Boxing was an extreme but fulfilling life. Plus, the potential earnings far outstripped any wage as an office worker. My mind was made up. Boxing it was.

People often ask me what my mother thought of what I did for a living. She accepted it and prayed for me. She would have prayed for me whatever trade I had chosen, that is the way she is, intensely spiritual. I remember coming back from my seventh amateur fight.

'How did you get on?' she asked.

I told her I had won.

'Well, what about the other boy?'

'Well, I beat him,' I said.

'What is going to happen to him?'

I explained that he had lost the fight and that I would move onwards and upwards as a result. She just quietly said, 'Well, remember he has a mother too.' That is how a mother looks at the world. There's a quotation by one of the great philosophers which goes like this: 'The tragedy of woman is that they become just like their mothers. The tragedy of man is that they don't.' I have become like my mother in many respects and that I believe is a strength.

Shortly after graduation from Morris High, I had started travelling back and forth to the UK. I had lived in New York for three and a half years straight, but for the next 18 months I bounced back and forth across the Atlantic. I found that because of a lack of money, I sometimes started to get pulled back into the old lifestyle of shoplifting.

Ironically, one day back in New York, where I had always managed to steer clear of trouble, I had a near-miss when I was playing dominoes at a club in White Plains Road. For this particular match I was on song and winning. There were four of us playing cut-throat, it was very tense. This one onlooker was looking at my hand and said, 'This guy can't play, he just happens to be pulling it off, he's making lucky money.' He was jealous of me making cash because it was a Friday and everybody was losing their hard-earned cash to me. Deliberately confrontational, he said to me, 'You can't play,' so I replied, 'Rather than talking, why not just play and put your money on the table.'

He obviously didn't have the money so this was embarrassing for him. They all knew I was boxing at this point and he said to me in Jamaican, 'Yu kyan fight wid yu fis' dem, but . . .' – at this moment he pulled out a ratchet knife – '. . . yu kya' fight dis. Gwaan a Inglan, Inglish bwoy.' I said to him, 'Where I come from in England, if you pull a knife you should use it, otherwise put it away. I haven't done you any wrong, you have no reason to be pulling a knife on me.' Fortunately, he bottled out and that was that. Or so I thought.

A couple of weeks later, I went back to the same club. I started down the stairs and, as I did, I noticed the man who had pulled the knife on me and one other man. When I got to the basement, there was no one around so I headed back up to street level. As I emerged, one of these men blocked my path in between this Space Invaders machine and the bakery next door. He said, 'Eh bwoy, yu a eedyat. Mi a go kill yu bwoy!' He said he was the brother-in-law of the fellow with the knife and it was clear he had taken our little confrontation as a slight on his family which, of course, it wasn't.

Being as righteous as I am, I explained, 'Listen, he pulled a knife on me, I didn't do him any wrong,' but he was totally disinterested and as I spoke to him he pulled out a .38 calibre gun, calm as can be, right in the middle of the street. I immediately ran around this Space Invaders machine to try to get into the bakery. The lady who worked there had seen what was going on and said, 'Leave 'm alone. Him a good bwoy, let him go!' He cornered me and grabbed my T-shirt, ripping it in the process, and thrust the gun under my chin. 'Mi wi' kill yu bwoy!'

I knew the law of the streets in New York, so I was well aware that people got killed when they were not remotely in the wrong, it was just a matter of violent ignorance. I pulled myself away and started to walk across to my cousin Woodia's house. I was not strolling, I was walking as fast as I could while still keeping my dignity and not looking spooked. The first time someone pulls a gun on you, you're shaking, you're genuinely terrified. With typical Jamacian humour though, these two big ladies in their 30s were watching this scenario play out down below and as I walked very quickly across the street they were laughing. 'Look 'ow faas' 'im a waalk!' New York . . . boy, it can be a tough place to live.

A year later, I was in the same dominoes club playing a game with a man I was quite friendly with. He had heard of my close escape and knew the chap who had thrust the gun in my face. He told me that about three weeks after he threatened me, the same fellow had been killed in a shoot-out. The lesson to take from this was simple: if you are a bad guy, an inconsiderate ruffian or a bully, there is always someone nastier, more malicious just around the corner. That's what happened – he got killed. You reap what you sow.

My cousin Woodia, who had pulled me on that banana leaf all those years ago in Jamaica, lived in and ran his business from New York. He sold drugs. That was his trade. My business was training, succeeding at school and keeping out of trouble. These had been my obsessions. Despite my substantial dalliances with the criminal life, I could never have been involved in selling drugs, it wasn't part of my make-up. Shoplifting I could do. Selling drugs was just killing people and bad karma, totally different. One was preying on the weak, the other was stealing to feed yourself.

Although these were the very circles I was trying to avoid, Woodia was family: I loved him. After I had made a different life for myself and my family in England, whenever I was in New York I would always go and visit old friends, some of whom were still wrapped up in the darker side of life. On one trip I went to see Woodia at the house where he lived and from where drugs were sold.

It was a basement apartment with a wire mesh covering

the streetside windows. I rang the bell and noticed several faces peering through the meshed glass. The door buzzed and I started to work my way down the dark stairs, but halfway down Woodia's friend, Freedom, met and escorted me towards the thick door at the bottom. He knocked twice on the door and I went in – next thing I knew, I had three guns pointing at my forehead, an Uzi, a Colt 45 and a .38 calibre pistol. I said, 'Hey! Woodia! It's Chris, I'm your cousin, man, what's all this?' He said, 'That doesn't matter, Chris, this is my business.'

Woodia died prematurely, aged 27. The word was that one of his girlfriends had poisoned him. One night, while eating a Chinese take-away, he died where he was sitting. One of the regrets in my life is that I didn't go to his funeral. Forget a man's wedding, they come and go, people get married several times. Always see a man off, it only happens once. I thought, wrongly, that I was too busy to fly to New York for his funeral. I was wrong: you can never be too busy for the people you care about.

CHAPTER FIVE

DOCTOR JOHNSON

I met many people through Alan Sedaka, one of whom was Benjamin Aryeh, not a nice character. He didn't do anything illegal, but in business he was very cold. None of the people who worked for him liked him and I could see why. The first time I met Benjamin, he offered me a job as a gopher. I really needed a job at the time, but I didn't take him up on his offer – this is because I asked him about his footwear. 'Nice shoes. Those are crocodile, right?' He shrugged his shoulder and said, 'I don't know, someone bought them for me. Are they crocodile?' From that second, I was not interested in him or the job, it was not for me. He had played down something which was just a simple compliment. That first impression sealed it. Even though I needed the money. I wanted the right kind of money. The going rate would have been fine. *It's respect I need.*

Benjamin had a brother, a lovely guy called Nathanial, whom I used to bodyguard for in New York. I would go to casinos or clubs with him and watch his back. It was a bit silly really, because I didn't have a gun and if you are going to bodyguard someone in New York, you have to carry a firearm. However, my aura was one of psychological dominance. My presence was imposing, so people would instinctively back off. I looked very dangerous – my eyes burned with savage focus. Plus, I always dressed impeccably, even back then. I always had my designer clothes from England and snake-skin shoes; I was probably the city's best-dressed bodyguard.

In places like New York, if someone is thinking of attacking they will first survey the terrain and weigh up the risks. Even though I did not carry a gun, my presence was sufficient to nullify any threats, because Nathanial's terrain was perceived as too risky to attack. I never thought about being unarmed, and the courage and presence I displayed meant that no one ever did pull a gun, thank God.

In hindsight, Nathanial gave me the bodyguard job just to make himself look good with his girlfriends. Occasionally, he would ask me to go to a club with him and a girl, but mainly to watch her. If the couple separated, I would be following the girl through all the darkened rooms and labyrinthine passages of somewhere like The Tunnel (an underground station converted into a club) while she would play games and try to lose me. I got paid $200 each time I went out with him. This wasn't a scary job, after all I was a fighter, but also he wasn't a bad guy looking for trouble. He wasn't a flash man, although he had his little Porsche. He wasn't courting danger. He was just a nice guy.

Nathanial was landlord of a building in a middle class

area, a really run-down slum of a place, near 17th Street and Chelsea. One day in 1986, I went with him to collect some rents that were a little overdue. At this stage, I was 4 and 0 as a professional boxer. One of the tenants we went to see was a gentleman called Walter Johnson, whom I now know as 'Doctor'. Nathanial had brought me to this property as the heavy guy. He said to me, 'Look mean, be very quiet and menacing, and get us paid.'

Doctor lived in a little studio flat with all his belongings which he shared with his daughter Kali, whom he had brought up. Nathanial left me for a while when he went to see someone else and, although I had this very hard exterior, Doctor was not fazed at all. In fact, after a few moments he quietly said to me, 'Come back another time, I'd like to talk to you.' Nathanial had introduced me as this ultra-hard, up-and-coming boxer. What I didn't know at first was that Doctor was heavily into the martial arts, having studied them since he was ten. He had been coached by his own father and become exemplary at jiu-jitsu and many other forms. That day we met, he relished the opportunity to talk to someone about his passion for such skills, how deeply he had studied and how much he knew about the philosophy behind them.

Two or three months went by when, one day, I found myself in that same area of New York, so I decided to take Doctor up on his offer and drop in for a chat. Even though he is 17 years my senior, the relationship just took off from there. In fact, this older element of his wisdom was part of what fascinated me. He would come to the gym and just watch, he never said anything. I had trainers with me and he always stayed and observed the workout. He struck me as someone who had an innate and vastly experienced sense of the street – obviously his colossal knowledge of martial arts bestowed that upon him, but even little things made me smile and warm to him. For example, one especially cold day, I asked him if he had a hat and he pulled off his own, tugged another hat out of that one and gave it to me. I called him Doctor in reference to the combination of his knowledge of Eastern medicine plus his philosophy of life and martial arts.

Despite our strange first meeting, we got on very well. When I moved to the UK in 1988, we kept in touch by phone. When I travelled to see the Mike McCallum–Steve Collins fight in Boston and stayed at the Plaza Hotel in New York, I met up with Doctor and we immediately continued where we had left off, reviewing martial arts techniques, ideas, diet and strategy.

He eventually joined me in the UK and we are still great friends – I've known Doctor longer than anyone in this country, longer than my wife even. He was to be an invaluable presence during training and in my corner at many of my future professional fights.

Initially, we were not exactly friends, though; it is more accurate to say that he was teaching me the martial arts; that was the common ground. As I was mastering the art of pugilism, the noble art, I wanted to hone it to near perfection. So, actually to incorporate the martial arts was a necessary evolution of my learning curve. As I have mentioned, Doctor had an expansive knowledge of internal and external martial art forms such as aikido, jiu-jitsu, karate, tai chi and Chinese boxing, and at first it was very difficult to incorporate this into my style. I found it very frustrating. For example, martial arts like pa-qua are open handed, but obviously boxing uses a closed fist. Doctor's martial arts were about holding, striking with your palm and fingers, whereas boxing was about striking only with your knuckles. He was trying to teach me these forms, but because I liked him so much I couldn't tell him that I was struggling to incorporate them into my boxing. This went on for perhaps three years.

What I did extract from everything I observed about martial arts was the foot movement, which was all about positioning and escape. The stance and poise in martial arts is 98% on your back foot and 2% on your front. Boxing is 50/50, unless you go into a position to strike, at which point you vary the weight distribution. I took that and spliced it into my boxing style. People often ask me how the martial arts and boxing mix. The point is this: boxing is actually the highest form of martial arts, because you have to learn how to absorb punishment before you can initiate it.

Another aspect Doctor brought to my game was stretching. Obviously, as a boxer, flexibility is vital, but many fighters only have flexibility in one dimension, namely that of the direction of the punch. So another aspect I took from the martial arts was to develop all-encompassing flexibility, or amplitude, and by that I mean agility in every direction. For example, I learned how to do the Japanese splits, which is where your legs are completely flat, then you roll your abdomen and chest to the floor. This is an excruciating skill to develop and can only be achieved by constant repetition. A fight is not just about strength, it is also about flexibility. These extraordinary skills, when taken into the ring, proved to be very powerful tools. Doctor could enhance the stretching I was doing, and did so right the way through my career. Some smaller elements also crept in, such as doing Doctor's jiu-jitsu wrist exercises, which were very useful for extra strength – no matter how much you bandage that joint, it can still get damaged. Sometimes he even made me wring out a dishcloth or play a guitar for extra wrist and finger strength! I never did much weight-training – lifting weights and boxing never go together, it tightens you up. Boxing is about being loose and relaxed.

Another factor I studied intensely was the philosophy of fighting, the art of war, psychological dominance and the like. Due to my passion for this aspect of the business, I became an exceptional adversary, because I was born with an intellect and the courage to actually apply that intellect. This gave me the character to manipulate situations before a fight, dealing with the mental strain and terrain.

What martial arts allowed me to do was get away from the conventional. The conventional will see you beaten sooner rather than later, because people will be able to work you out. People cannot beat you if they don't know what you are going to do next. If you box with your hands up, then no fighter will be scared of you, because they know that stance – they have been training for that all their boxing careers. Box with your hands down and it unsettles them; they haven't seen it before, it is uncommon, unconventional, extraordinary. The opponent has to work out the terrain from scratch and while he's doing that, you are hitting him. If you can think alternatively, you can go on to be champion for a long time. As I did.

It has been said by some observers that it was quite advanced for such a young boxer to integrate the martial arts into boxing as I did. I don't see it that way. When I met Doctor, I just thought, *Here is a man who understands the philosophy of life and that can be applied to everything*. He has applied that in medicine too; he was always giving me herbs, ginseng and all the oriental teas. I was always the type of person who was interested in the older man who knew something I didn't. Doctor seemed to know so much and seemed almost mystical. I was the one who took certain aspects of the martial arts philosophy and applied this to boxing and that is why people said that I had a very unusual style. I had learned the skills in the gym, then I put my own flavour in there with the martial arts, the stances, the angles. It was a complex hybrid of all the arts with regard to the foot movements and my personality.

I must reiterate that the actual striking did not draw from any of the other martial arts, because boxing has it all in its own manual. Plus, how you deal with punishment is essential to your success. Absorbing punches without telegraphing pain is another skill that only comes with repetition and training. You stand in front of a fighter and leave your abdomen exposed, allowing him to punch it time and time again. Initially, it is agony and your face contorts with the pain, but over the months and years of doing this you learn to absorb the punch and not even flicker when contact is made. It hurts your stomach, but you learn not to hold your breath because if you do that you'll get tired. You've got to learn how to breathe and be tense at the same time. You see a heavy shot coming in, you brace into it. It is instinct gleaned from repetition in the gym. You condition yourself; you mask the gut instinct to grimace or wince, because otherwise your opponent knows you are hurt and will come on harder. If you show pain, you will probably lose the fight. The best boxers are those who can absorb punishment; being able to give it out is only half the equation.

This philosophy of fighting extends to your mental attitude as well as your physical conditioning. People assume you go into the ring prepared to take a life. Incorrect. You have to go into the ring fully prepared to *surrender* your life, if that is what is required. In fact, not only did I go into the ring thinking: *you may damage me, you may even kill me*, but I used to think: *if you can do that to me, I will appreciate it*. But know this: you are going to have to take me because I am not giving up, ever.

If this sounds extreme, let me clarify my position. It is not that you consciously think you will die every time you step into the four-cornered circle. It is not that prevalent. Your strength of mind and resolve of character are prepared to face this possibility. You don't think you will die, because you have a faith in your ability and because it is all about a positive mental attitude. You must always think positively. As will become apparent from my story as it unfolds, it all comes down to one deep-rooted factor: integrity.

PART TWO

APPLY THE
PHILOSOPHY

CHAPTER SIX

HOMESICK

I returned to the UK in January 1988 to make my home there. I came back principally because I wanted to be with my brothers, whom I still adored. My first fight back in England was on 15 February of that year, against Darren Parker in Copthorne, whom I stopped in the first round. Then came a fellow called Winston Burnett, who was target practice, but he would have beaten me if I hadn't known what I was doing. The next fight was a mismatch, against Michael Justin, who was supposed to have ability. He was hard and willing but did not have the ability to deliver shots. He showed lots of heart coming forward, swinging at me, but it was no contest. Two more middle-round stoppages against Greg George and Steve Aquilina and suddenly, I was 10 and 0. Over the next 24 months, I was to fight 11 times on my long haul towards a title shot.

At first, however, it was tough. I had no money and lived in a tiny bedsit. Perhaps inevitably, I found myself occasionally drawn back into a life of shoplifting. Before I had left for

New York, I'd been in many amazing chases with the police, but perhaps my finest was a two-day pursuit in mid-1988. It was an absolute classic. We had hired a taxi as usual to take us around our targets and he then escorted us while we took the gear around all the pubs in the Walworth Road or the Unity Centre in Peckham. That morning, the car that arrived was a big burgundy Granada, driven by this fat Turkish man, aged about 27. He picked me up at around 8 o'clock in the morning and we set off to collect Beaver. We drove to south London and headed for a large department store. On this particular occasion, I didn't take anything but Beaver stole a leather jacket. As he walked past me he said, 'It's hot,' meaning we were being watched by store security. So we started walking briskly (but not without style, even under pressure) towards the exit. It seemed at first that we had succeeded in not drawing attention to ourselves, but suddenly Beaver flicked his fingers in the air, which was the sign for us to take off.

We split up instinctively. Beaver ran off in one direction and I headed for the car park, running up to the top floor where the Granada taxi was waiting. I said, 'It's hot, it's on top, we're being chased. I'll get in the boot.' The Turkish driver said, 'No, don't do that, just sit in the back seat and act normal.' I should have gone with my gut instinct but instead I sat in the back. We started to descend the spiral ramp that led to the exit, down and round, down and round, all the time waiting for someone to stop us. We pulled around this final corner just before the ticket barrier, thinking we were going to escape when, dismayed, I saw two policemen stopping all the cars and checking the occupants. The taxi driver said, 'Just stay where you are, you will be alright, they won't know it's you.' I waited anxiously for our turn in line and decided to lie down on the seat. When the policeman stopped us, he looked in the back at me and said, 'That's him.'

'Step out of the car, please,' he said to me. I got out and immediately started explaining to the senior officer, saying, 'Listen, you've got the wrong man. I haven't got anything, look in my bags.' Unfortunately, the security guard from the store confirmed that I was one of the culprits. At that point, I played an old trick I'd learned from my brother David, which he always used to great effect. I began to act frantic, severely agitated. 'I've got heart problems, I've got stress problems, this is making me unwell. I'll take you to court.' I started shouting and ranting at this officer, trying to work my way out of the predicament. After about ten minutes, I just started to think I was getting somewhere when the officer, in a truly disparaging tone, said, 'Will you just shut up!' So that was that, nicked.

I sat down in the police Rover and slid my way across the seat. Already my mind was racing – it was a Friday and I knew that I would spend the weekend at the station and it would be Monday morning before I'd see daylight. I had a blues to attend on the Saturday which was going to be fun: good music, lots of girls, drinking and 'crubbing' (close dancing). That, I wasn't going to miss.

More worryingly, I knew that as soon as they put my name in the central computer, it would alert them to the fact that I had jumped bail from the gentleman's outfitter's theft, where I had been caught on the M23. Then it would be prison and who knows what future for me. This was a desperate predicament. I had to escape.

The obvious thought was to jump out of the car, at high speed if necessary. As we slowed down to drive around this flyover, I tugged on the door latch but the child-lock was on. So now I was really in trouble. A change of tack was needed. I started to apologise to the policemen in the car. 'Officer, sorry about my behaviour earlier, I was out of order.' I continued being Mr Polite all the way back to the station, in full charm mode. They were very much more relaxed by the time the car pulled up.

Don't forget, I am an unbeaten professional boxer at this point and training almost every day, so I am the fittest man on the planet – and I do not say that in jest! The police officer's grip on my arm had slackened just a little, so that when he turned away from me to unlock the over-sized lock on the door to the cells, I pulled free and I was gone, off like a bullet. The only problem was, I was wearing my cherished £140 snake-skin shoes, which I had bought from Panache in Walworth Road. As stylish as they were, they were not best suited to sprinting, not least because they were dress shoes with smooth, wafer-thin soles.

The officer was, of course, coming after me, so I ran around a car. He stood one side of the car, hands on the roof, staring at me. He said, 'Now don't be stupid, son,' and, voice brimming with confidence, I replied, 'Let's see who's stupid,' and ran off across the yard away from the officer and security guard. Because of my fitness, within a few seconds I was twenty yards or so ahead. After all, I was running six miles every morning before I even opened the gym door, so these fellows were never going to keep up.

At this point I banged past a middle-aged man who then joined the chase. He was wearing one of those army jumpers with shoulder and elbow patches. By now, though, I had built up a good speed and dived through a subway, then dashed up this long flight of steps to bring me back to street level, deliberately choosing the steps instead of the ramp to make their chase tougher. I can picture to this day the sight of this man, panting desperately for breath, face all reddened and flushed, skidding through the subway and coming to a stop at the bottom of the stairs. He looked up and I was standing there, grinning at the top of the steps. My heart at this point was barely beating above resting rate. This guy chasing me was so exhausted he was barely conscious.

We stood there looking at each other waiting for the next move, then I heard another officer shouting, 'Don't stop! Get him!' I calmly reached down and took off each shoe, held them up in the air triumphantly, before turning around and setting off at speed towards a street full of market stalls. As I weaved my way through the stalls, out of danger at last, I could just hear a faint voice shouting, 'Thief, stop!' I was so fit they never stood a chance. Once I was sure I was safe, I caught the train back to my friend's house and slept there for the night.

I was awakened at 7.45am the next morning by a knock on the door. I heard someone's voice saying, 'Is Christopher here?' before being let in. It was the police – no, it was the 'cozzers'. I know cozzers is a generic term for the police but real cozzers only come from certain police stations. This particular cozzer was like a huge bulldog, 6' 4" with a furious scowl. He didn't care very much for me because I was wrong. He came into the front room where I was sleeping and said, 'Christopher, get up now.' I was half-asleep, squinting through my eyelids, saying, 'What? What are you talking about?'

I got up and stood in front of him wearing only my socks and underpants. My clothes were hanging up in the wardrobe but I knew I had to delay getting fully dressed because at that point they would cuff me, especially after my escapology of the day before. I couldn't believe my bad luck; this chase had been going on for two days now!

I surveyed the terrain and noticed that the sash window was too near the officer to offer a realistic chance of escape. So I asked him if I could brush my teeth. He wasn't stupid, so he followed me into the bathroom where they knew there was a window. They watched me brush my teeth. I had acne at this time, so while I was standing at the mirror, I squeezed a pimple and the pus and a little streak of blood started running down my face. I turned to the disgusted officer and said, 'I've got to clean myself up.'

'Fine,' came the reply, and he continued to stand there.

'Can I use the toilet now?' I asked.

'Sure,' came the reply but he still stood there.

'Can I have some privacy in here?'

'No.'

So he stood there and watched me use the toilet. Or rather, pretend to use the toilet. After a short while, I played out the charade, did a fake number two, used the toilet paper and so on, pulled up my underpants then came back into the front room.

'Right, officer, I'll get changed now.'

He was standing leaning against the door frame and had started talking to another officer and a girl who lived in the house. Alternately he would talk to them then turn around to keep an eye on me. Then, for one moment too long, he had his head turned away from me. That was all the opportunity I needed. Like a flash I was through the sash window, in only my socks (silk, mind you) and underpants.

The estates around Walworth Road were real rabbit warrens so it was easy for me to lose anybody who would take up the chase. However, it was cold and drizzling so I was absolutely freezing. As I ran into one courtyard, this little kid, about 13, saw me and looked surprised to see someone wearing only socks and underpants running around at 8.15am in the rain. I went up to his front door and said, 'I'm being chased by the police, I need a coat, I'll bring it back.' There was absolute sincerity in my eyes. I could see his brain thinking it over, while I'm standing there shivering, half-expecting the cozzers to come round the corner at any moment. Eventually, after what seemed like an age, he timidly said, 'I'll just go and ask my dad.' As soon as he was out of the hallway, I grabbed a coat off a hook and ran off. Poor kid. I eventually made my way to Nasty's flat and finally, after two days of being on the run, I was safe.

I don't have a problem with people who steal things. Well, don't get me wrong, stealing is wrong but shoplifting at the time was justifiable to me, I was a kid. Anyway, I knew that the mark-up on some of those clothes was 400%, so I just thought of it as stealing from the rich to give to the poor, namely me. People need to make a living, it's nothing personal, it's not you they want, it's just the money. However, if someone steals and hurts a person in the process, that is totally unacceptable, and against everything I stand for. I abhor that.

After Maximo I trained myself. When I started working in the Jack Pook gym in Brighton, my brothers, who were boxing themselves, introduced me to a trainer called Ronnie Davies. He had been Southern Area Lightweight Champion himself in 1967, so he knew the business. I was constantly in the gym, but Ronnie worked as a site manager for a building company. He toiled a long day on site and would come to the gym, back bent double, and work with me. I used to say, 'Come in from the cold, stick with me, I'll take you to the top.' And I did.

He said to me, 'You only need to train four days a week.' I replied, 'You can come in four days a week, I will be here *seven* days a week.' Ronnie wasn't training me. I knew how to box, all I needed was someone to be my eye outside of the ring, because there are certain things you can't see. I would come back to my corner and his perception and observation would be very enlightening, because he could see things I was too involved to catch.

Ronnie was also a brilliant bodyguard. By that, I don't mean personal security, rather a man who knew which fighters were dangerous, which ones were under-rated or over-hyped. Plus, he could protect me from the litany of problems, situations and liabilities that boxing exposed me to. There would be so many people trying to get to me, hangers-on, charlatans and takers, and Ronnie had a fault-less radar for that, he sniffed them out immediately. He always watched my back against things like that. He was a very good companion. I will always love Ronnie Davies.

Ronnie also made me laugh. His humour was so cutting, so dry, that he would regularly have me roaring. Over the years, we had so many hilarious times, nights when our sides would ache from laughing, where we would fall asleep still sniggering. One time, we were planning to fly back from Portugal to Heathrow via Dusseldorf, but I had lost both the passports at the airport in the Algarve. So we had to dis-embark in Germany and wait overnight for the passports. I have never laughed so much as that night. From the moment we walked off that plane, we cried with laughter.

We went for a walk around the streets of Dusseldorf and I was telling Ronnie, 'You mustn't eat pork.' I have always had a love-hate relationship with pork and had recently been listening to certain people who would not touch it. I was saying, 'It is not a clean meat, Ronnie, never touch it again, if you know what's good for you!' He was laughing at me about it but I really wanted to win him round to not eating pork. They'd offered us pork on the plane and I was saying, 'This is a very dangerous meat, Ronnie.' As we were strolling past all these shops and restaurant windows, we stopped near one which had this big spit roast of pork going around on a skewer, crackling skin and juices sizzling. I walked in, got their attention and, said, 'Yes, sell me all that's left of the pig!' Ronnie was doubled over in stitches.

A few more shops down the road, we were walking past a kebab shop and there was this big German guy shaving slices off the revolving meat. Despite this being Germany, as he saw me a bright light of recognition lit his face up and he immediately struck up my peacock pose, complete with kebab knives in hand. Yeeaahh!

That night we were sharing a twin room and we took this Haagen-Dazs ice-cream back for our night-cap but it took hours to polish off because we were laughing so much. Eventually I said, 'Quiet now, Ronnie, we need to get some sleep.' I switched the lights off but after about ten minutes he just burst out laughing again. Another twenty minutes later I went to get some water out of the mini bar, but dropped the bottle, so more hysterics. My sides were aching more than after any body shot! Ronnie took the monotony out of boxing – that scathing sense of humour sliced the tedious side out of my spartan life.

The public perception was that Ronnie was my trainer, so as soon as I could, it made sense for me to have Ronnie styled to suit my team image. He had his hair cropped very closely and began wearing immaculate suits too, no more training bottoms. When I went on to win the title, I insisted he bought a Jaguar too – it was far more stylish and made for a better show. This was all part of the business plan. It was about showmanship. All my team had to be well turned out, not just Ronnie.

I had hooked up with a local promoter by the name of Keith Miles and he started to help me get fights. I worked two jobs, in Debenhams and the other in Wimpy, because the money I was earning from fighting was simply not enough. However, this was very tiring and coupled with my obsessive training, I knew it could have detrimental effects on my performances. So I voiced my fears to Keith Miles, who agreed to pay me £120 a week as an allowance.

It was at this time that I first met my future wife, Karron. Her sister, Phillipa, used to go out with my brother, Simon, one of the twins. One day I glanced through into his kitchen, saw Karron and thought, 'What a beautiful woman. It would be a dream to be with a woman like that.' But this was an impossibility. She was, and is, a gorgeous woman. What was I? Nothing. I had no self-esteem, other than my belief in my boxing ability. Back then, no one else knew that either. So, at first, to be with her was just an impossible wish.

By coincidence, Karron had actually seen my seventh fight, against Winston Burnett at Hove Town Hall, back in March 1988. She'd come to watch with a male friend of hers. She wasn't dating him but I still had not even spoken to her at this point. I had seen her since in a supermarket but couldn't pluck up the courage to speak to her.

I didn't have a car as yet, so I used to walk everywhere. People began to notice me walking around Brighton, strutting even back then. Jack Pook used to train my brothers at the time and he said that I walked, 'as if I owned the United Kingdom.' I walked everywhere like that. I was always very, very proud, no matter how difficult my circumstances. One day I had walked about three miles into Brighton and as I was coming back past my brother's house in Portland Road, I saw Karron talking to Peter. I was wearing a nice black cloth coat and went up to them and said, 'Hi Peter,' before turning to Karron and saying, 'Hi, would you give me a lift please?' She said, 'Well, I am talking.' I said, 'Well, when you've finished, if you don't mind, would you give me a lift back to my apartment? I'll be in the 7–Eleven, buying a Lucozade.' She looked stunning.

Shortly after, she came and picked me up from the 7–Eleven in her old black, banged-up Fiat and took me to my apartment in Trafalgar Street. When we pulled up outside, I turned to her and said, 'Did you come to my last fight?' to which she said, 'No'. So I said, 'Would you like to see it on video?' I was delighted when she said, 'Okay'.

She came up to the apartment, but while we were watching the video she began to have a severe headache and neck spasms. I gave her some painkillers but the headache just got rapidly worse. By now I was thinking: *Okay, I'm a minority in this country, and where I've been living in New York, this kind of thing happens all the time, people get blackmailed or conned.* I called an ambulance and they took her to hospital, where it became apparent that, fortunately, she was being genuine. At that point, Ronnie walked in and said, 'What have you done? What did you do to her?' to which I vehemently protested my innocence. What had happened was, unbeknown to her, she'd suffered a trapped nerve the previous day when, during a scuffle at the jewellery shop where she worked, one of the owners had accidentally hit her on the back of the neck as he was grappling with a robber.

Keith Miles found out about what had happened and assumed the worst, so I had to tell him too, 'I didn't touch the woman, she broke down.' They were all very suspicious. The next day I was walking through Brighton's Norfolk Square, past where Karron worked, so I went in to see if she was better. She said she was fine now and gave me a 'Thank you' card. I said, 'Thank you, it was not a problem. Would you like to go out for dinner?' She said, 'Yes' and I was elated.

We started to go out and, with my £120 per week allowance, we had some good times. All I did was train, so that money went a long way – we went out quite often. I would train first thing in the morning, about 5.30am, finish at about 7.30am and then start gym work at 2pm or 4pm depending on how I felt. At this point, I was touched with it, I was on heat to train. It was a passion that I could feel within my solar plexus, an inner passion. At first, the people around me were sceptical that I could keep this focused and have a woman in my life at the same time, but it was never an issue. I know it is for some fighters, but it never even started to become a problem for me. I've always remained my own man.

In a sense, because Karron was so easy to get on with, it eliminated the complication of having a difficult girlfriend. I knew this was the woman for me, so I started the relationship off correctly. I hadn't been out with many women seriously up to this point. I had a girlfriend in England before I left for New York, and over a period of three and a half years, I only had two girlfriends over there. I was so focused with my training and also with the church. The scriptures taught me that you shouldn't fornicate and I did the best I could! The thought was constantly in my mind but I took that energy and channelled it into training. Karron and I became close very quickly and moved into a flat together above a garage that Keith Miles owned. Bear in mind, I was not famous or wealthy at this point, so to this day I know Karron is with me *for* me, which for a celebrity is priceless.

My relationship with Keith Miles, however, was not working so well. He used to talk down to me, like I was an idiot. He would say, 'Do as you are told.' I must state that at times he was very nice and a real character, but when he spoke to me in a way that wasn't dignified, I couldn't accept that. I said to him, 'When you disrespect me, I'd rather starve than accept your disrespect.' So that business relationship ended, and with it went the flat above the garage.

We moved into a room in Karron's mother's house in

early 1989, during which time Karron became pregnant with our first child, Christopher. We had all our belongings in this one little room, with a fold-up futon to sit on and a little kitten for a pet. I was training very hard by now and some of that time was spent with the superb boxer, Herol Graham.

That first fight that Karron had watched before we were even dating was the only time in 47 contests that she came to see an actual bout. I would never have my wife, mother, father or children at the fight. Boxing matches are a desperate situation and I could never understand how fighters wanted their family present. I realise some say it motivates them, but I could never understand that. I wouldn't even allow my father to watch (mind you, he wouldn't have wanted to), he would have had a drink and torn the place down in excitement! When I later had a gym upstairs at home, my kids occasionally came up to watch me train but never saw me sparring.

While we had been trying for our first child, I said to Karron, 'It is not possible that we will have a girl. It will be a boy and his name will be Christopher.' There was no more than a 0.001% chance of having a girl. Karron didn't see it that way, but I was convinced. I spoke about this in the press (I was starting to attract media attention with my lengthening unbeaten record) in a very blunt fashion and they made a big headline out of it, but that was not fair. Sure enough though, Christopher arrived on 18 September 1989.

I felt the same when we had our second child, Sebastian, on 18 July 1991. By then, I thought it would be nice to have a girl and I honestly feel that by relenting in my mind, we had Emily, who arrived on 19 April 1994. Since then we have also had little Joseph, on 23 October 1996. I was very proud to be present at all their births.

Some boxers are affected for the worse when they have children but I was not softened towards the boxing business. Remember, I learned to fight in New York, and as the saying goes, if you can do it there you can do it anywhere. This was my job and I now had young mouths to feed and provide for. I always wanted to be successful, so I didn't need a family to make me more motivated. Yes, they all have to be fed, clothed and put through school; with any child comes a responsibility which you have to attend to, your duty is to provide. However, I have always had a very strong sense of satisfying *me*, of becoming an accepted individual, something I am still chasing to this day. So, my drive for success in boxing never wavered one bit when the children arrived.

As mentioned briefly before, people in the fight business worry about the effect a relationship might have on a boxer's heart. There is a saying which goes like this: 'After a personal quarrel between a man and a woman, the former suffers chiefly from the idea of having wounded the other while the latter suffers from the idea of not having wounded the other enough. Thus she will endeavour by tears, sobs and discomposed mien to make his heart heavier.' Marvellous. Fortunately for me, this was not the case with Karron.

I am very aware that my conduct in my private and public life can impact very heavily on my children's lives as youngsters. Having a well-known father will mean that if there is a problem, everybody will know and they will have no refuge. So I must ensure that this never happens. You can't get any closer than your family. My children are me, my children come before me and as an adult you come to realise that.

Christopher is very intelligent but doesn't let me know. When I listen to him talking around other children his age, you can see and hear the intelligence. All his reports from school say he is a clever child, he always gets good reports, all Bs, the occasional A. Away from his studies, he is slightly absent-minded. He handles who his father is very well and whenever he stays around other children's houses, I always get good comments from the parents. He is very well behaved outside of our house, but inside he is always fighting with Sebastian! Everybody likes him and speaks well of him.

I remember saying to him when he was only nine years old, 'Don't try to be like me, you may reach where I am, you may fall below or perhaps rise above, but just be who you are. Look to words, to passion, grow up to be a man. Remember this – if I can do it, so can you. Be the best you can be.' He asked me once what dignity was and I said, 'If you lose it, it is sad,' and then explained why that was. I said if I ever tried again to become what I once was, namely champion, so long after retiring, then not only would I not be the father I once was, but also the public would recognise the fact that either I needed the money or still craved the fame. They would then laugh at me or say, 'How sad.' On hearing this explanation, the tears welled up in Christopher's eyes, even though he was only nine years old.

Sebastian is going to be the black sheep. He is his own person. Whereas Christopher will be influenced, Sebastian has his own mind, his own common sense. When we are on holiday, he goes off with a group of other kids without us. He is clever, a good kid. He is the one who will take a stand, which is good. He is more daring – for example, he will fight with me and I will hit him in the arm with a hard blow and he will go, 'Ow!' but come back at me! Christopher is not interested in all that. Sebastian likes shells, fossils, books – he's read all the Harry Potter books. He is his own boy and will be his own man.

Emily is a really lovely girl. If she takes after her mother, she will do very well. I don't know if her arrival made me more tender, I think perhaps that I had mellowed more with age anyway. I wasn't brought up with any girls (as my sister stayed in Jamaica), so I didn't see how my father would have treated a daughter but, suffice to say, Emily gets away with a lot more. The boys get away with NOTHING. I often let Emily get away with small things, although never the important stuff. That may be wrong, but I am yet to find out. I am tougher on the boys.

The youngest, Joseph, doesn't understand fear, he is boisterous and has fight in him. If any of the children could be a fighter (and I vehemently don't want that), he could. His character is already without fear, it is in his grain. He

Left: As a 15-year-old, with staff member Johnny, outside the Karib care home for ethnic minorities in Nunhead, from where I was expelled after only one month.

Below: With my brother Simon, in Peckham, in 1981.

Above: A cool 20-year-old attending a blues dance.

Right: What I considered fashionable in my early twenties.

Left: With my friend Lukey.

Below: My grandmother Constance.

Above: Experiencing all things new in Manhattan, in the summer of 1985.

Right: On one of my regular train journeys from Brighton to London during the period 1986–87.

Left: I was keen to get into shape while in New York, so I started going to the Jerome Boxing Club in the South Bronx. I was in there training seven days a week in 1984.

Below: In my best attire on the streets of New York.

Left: A proud winner of the Spanish Golden Gloves trophy in 1984, with Adonis Torres, my first manager. He treated me with respect.

Right: With my cousin Woodia (on the right) and his friend Freedom. One of the regrets in my life was not attending Woodia's funeral after he died prematurely, aged 27.

Left: Battling through a tough amateur bout (the semi-final of the Golden Gloves tournament, Madison Square Gardens, NY), as an 18-year-old, which I lost.

Below: Womenpower. My grandmother flanked by Aunt Clare (left) and Ms Annie.

Below: At 19 I had the poise, got the pose later.

Right: In Peckham Park with my friend Julian.

Left: Alongside my manager Adonis Torres (left) and Pat Vercase at the Jerome Boxing Club in 1985.

Above: The day before my first professional fight in Atlantic City.

Above: My first born, Christopher, 18 September 1989. I was a proud young father. *Above right:* Early 1991, with baby Christopher.

Right: Yeessss! I knew beating Anthony Logan would eventually lead me to the fight I wanted – Nigel Benn.

Right: Benn with his manager Ambrose Mendy at the press conference weigh-in (which I didn't attend) for our first fight. The animosity that was directed at me was unreserved.

Left: I had closed Benn's eye in the fourth round of our first WBO Middleweight Championship bout in November 1990 in Birmingham – now the fight belonged to me.

Right: The final blows before the referee intervened in the 9th.

Right: The moment I won the WBO World Middleweight title from Nigel Benn. In so doing, I honoured the years of my life I had spent learning the art.

Left: I was the ecstatic World Middleweight champion and so happy that I proposed to Karron by way of the TV cameras after the fight.

Left: Watson 2, White Hart Lane, September 1991, Round 11. The moment my knee hit the canvas, my body completely recovered.

Right: The extent of Michael Watson's injuries after our explosive second bout had a devastating impact on me.

Below: In beating Watson for a second time, I had triumphed in a bout I seemingly could not win. That night at White Hart Lane in 1991 was by far the most special fight of my career.

Right: The Ultimate Gladiator – and with a special dedicated showcard to all the fans who support me.

has watched how I deal with the other three children above him, so he can surmise how much he can push things – he looks at me, raises an eyebrow and tasks me! He will be like me. His devil-may-care attitude will only be contained when he sees that it doesn't work and only gets you into trouble. Joseph reminds me very much of myself when I was a kid. Back then, I had my own agenda and was always busy. With Joseph, if you tell him something, he will have forgotten it within seconds – he has other things to think about.

I am quite strict with my children but only to discipline them about what is correct. I will not smack any of them for being naughty. If they do something that requires punishment, they will have to collect 20 bags of leaves from the lawns, or maybe write out 30 sentences using the key words I give them. Very often, I will not punish them at all in such a fashion. Joseph once scribbled on the wallpaper, so I said to him, 'Did you do that? Don't lie and there will be no punishment.' He sheepishly nodded and so that was that. He knew not to do it again. You have to draw that sort of behaviour out of a child. The only time I will smack one of my children is when one of them has bullied one of the younger ones. That is not acceptable but it does not happen very often either. Some parents believe that the law should be involved if a parent smacks a child. If that is so, not only would I be prepared to go to jail, I need to go there.

When I was in the *Celebrity Big Brother* house in early 2001, I had a discussion with Vanessa Feltz about how to bring up children. It seemed to me that she was advocating the politically correct way to teach children. I could not agree with her on that. The politically correct way to bring up children means they will call their mother a cow and tell their father to piss off. That's the end result, in my opinion. I've seen this, I grew up in this country around certain people who did that. In a Jamaican household, there is no disrespect whatsoever: you do as you're told.

For parents, the best thing to do for your child is to have them exposed to the world. The problem is, the hardest thing for you to do also is to expose them to the world. Nevertheless, let the child go. Because of my background, I was given no choice, I was thrown in at the deep end. As a parent, I'm too much of a coward to put them through that. I don't want to expose them. I want to protect them. My eldest child said to me one day that he wanted to hang out at Churchill Square in Brighton. I said, 'No way, I will go to prison first. Do something, achieve something, don't waste your time down there.' Fortunately, I pulled myself back in time and did the clever thing, which was to let him go.

I am somewhat like my own father when it comes to the children. I don't have much time for playing with toys and such like. I never played with toys as a kid myself, largely because I didn't have any. So I struggle to sit down with them for hours on end playing children's games. I have to go out there and provide for them all. I was never that type of kid, so now I'm not that type of father. I'm more into teaching my kids reason, wisdom and discipline. Yet, I agree with Nietzsche's thought that, 'Women understand children better than men. But a man is more childish than a woman.'

Society, or the media, cajoles people to think that you should try to understand your child. But your child will be alright if they understand YOU, the parent. When they do, you will understand them. I say to my little ones, 'What? Am I supposed to understand why you jump around making noises and ripping the wallpaper up? I'm supposed to understand you weren't thinking? Well, no, think. I don't like that.' They have to come to understand you.

Think about it. When I became a man, I thought how right my father had been and that I wish I had listened to him much more than I did. There is a natural chronological evolution at work here: my father was a complete loser when I was 15. At 17, he was just trying to hold me down, he didn't understand anything I did. Yet at 21, he was all right. He still wasn't for me, I couldn't keep his company that much, but he was okay. Then you get to 30 years old and the only person you want next to you is your old man. Well, let me say this – *he hadn't changed*. It was never that he didn't understand me. It was me who misunderstood him. One shouldn't make that mistake.

With me in this experience of bringing up the children is Karron, and I am immensely fortunate to have such a wife. Karron is a good woman. She is an exceptional mother who doesn't really allow anyone else to look after the children other than her sister. She sometimes burns herself out, though, as four children are a handful. My philosophy is this: my job as a fighter was by far, without any doubt, the hardest business or way of life in the world, bar none. The pressure, the solitude, the physical demands, the media attention, it was so demanding. My estimation is that to mother children is 15 times harder.

We had little money, I was trying to get on the straight and narrow, plus I was constantly training. Karron used to work in the jewellery store for two fellows called Kevin Douglas and Burt Wilkins. They were into boxing and knew all the old boys of the business, like Mickey Duff and Jarvis Astaire. Kevin and Burt were very kind to me, they literally used to feed me and take me around to show me a good time. Even then, I was aware of what was correct. For example, one day I was in a car with Kevin and Burt, when this man took a parking space that we had been waiting for. Kevin was known as a hard man, a very streetwise Cockney, who was into his antiques business. He didn't want to confront this man because of his size, 'He can't do that, it is a matter of correctness.' So I got out and said to the man, 'Move the car!' He said, 'I will only be a minute,' but I firmly said, 'Move the car now, not in a minute!' He moved the car.

Karron and I knew we couldn't stay in that one room at her mother's forever, so we managed to get a mortgage and bought a small three-bedroom maisonette in Hartington Road for £64,000. During this time, I met someone who would become one of my closest friends, a man by the name of John Regan. Ronnie was working for him at the time and kept reporting back about my developing career. John started coming to fights and gradually we became very good friends. He has been with me through some of my finest and darkest moments. John is a man of integrity whom I would trust with my children, my mother and my wife. I would trust no one with my own life. I wouldn't put myself in that position.

Money was still short, so I went looking for a new promoter. I would travel up to London on the train, dodging the fare each time, and visit many promoters to discuss working together. My father had warned me about promoters and managers, saying, 'Don't watch the ones who take hundreds or even thousands of pounds. Watch the ones who take hundreds of thousands.' So I was wary of who I wanted to work with.

I had sourced the names of all the big promoters. One such man was Frank Warren, who had me come up to London every day for two weeks and kept me waiting every time. One time in his office, I had waited for ages then went out to get myself an orange juice. When I came back, the secretary said that Warren had left. This was the type of treatment one had to put up with from some promoters, Warren being one. It was only a matter of one-upmanship though – which failed.

CHAPTER SEVEN

HATE ME, BUT DON'T DISRESPECT ME

As a professional boxer, it is vital that you keep your skills confined to within the ring. Used on a normal man in the street, they could be very dangerous, potentially fatal, even with smaller fighters. This is the reason why I haven't had a fight outside of the ring all of my career. There is only one instance where I used my fists away from the business, not in a fight, but as a necessary action in a very specific situation.

I was walking along Meeting House Lane in Brighton one afternoon. The streets known as 'The Lanes' are very narrow indeed, perhaps only five feet wide at some points. I was strolling along when I heard a commotion up ahead. I looked up to see a man running down the lane, carrying in his hands a tray of gold rings that he had just stolen from a jeweller's window he'd smashed. He was shouting, 'Get out of the way! Out of the way!' and running very fast towards me. This was a power play, I had seen this all the time on the streets. I was walking in my usual precise fashion, but stepped to one side so this guy could pass by when he came level with me.

When this man was about 30 yards in front of me, I could see he was quite large, about 6′ 2″ and roughly 190lb. I was ready to stay out of his way. However, just in front of me there was an old lady. She was in her mid-50s, only small, maybe 5′, immaculately dressed with grey pleated trousers and a grey top. She wore circular horn-rimmed glasses, and her hair was 75% grey, 25% black, cut into a smart bob. To me she looked exactly like Miss Marple. She couldn't have noticed this big man coming behind her but as he approached her, he shouted, 'Get out of the way!' and then *BANG!* he barged into her, knocking her heavily into the nearby wall. If the Lanes weren't so narrow, she would have been thrown across the ground.

Now I had a problem: *take but do not hurt*. He was now level with me so without hesitation I moved into him with a three-punch combination: left uppercut to the ribs, *BOOM!* Left hook to the chin, boom! Right uppercut to the head, *BOOM!* He folded. I held him on the floor with my knee while the police were called. I wasn't famous at this time, I was still a promising local boxer. As he struggled underneath me, he turned his face to mine and snarled, 'Do you know who I am? I'm going to kill you!' I said, 'Well, I'm Christopher Livingstone Eubank,' and, *crack!*, I kicked him. There was a man watching who objected and said, 'There's no need for that,' and, to be fair, there wasn't, but that was just my boisterous nature at that time. The police took him away and I was later given a 999 Award for my actions.

Had he not hurt that old lady I would have gladly let him pass by. Once he hit her, however, I had absolutely no regard for his well-being. I never considered that I might hurt this guy. I knew how to punch correctly so my hands were undamaged, but then I never thought about hurting my hands even in the ring, I've always had faith. He was hit with three very hard punches, all thrown correctly, with complete resolve. If I had hesitated I might have got into a fight with the guy. As it was, I just thought, *you're going to sleep for a little while*. And he did.

In August 2002 I performed a citizen's arrest outside the Hilton hotel in London. This man had introduced himself to me as a prince and a businessman and I in turn had introduced him to a friend of mine, Rory McCarthy, who was keen to invest some money with him. After the money (the significant amount of £500,000) had been exchanged Rashid could not be found anywhere. My friend lost many assets and money because of this man and I felt partly responsible, as it was me who introduced them.

One Thursday night I was at dinner with Rory, who I had not seen in some time, but had to return to the Trader Vic's restaurant, when I bumped into this man, who was coming out. I was shocked as I had been searching for him for over a year. I said, 'Hello,' not wanting to scare him, 'Don't move, I've been looking for you for a year. If you move I will have to restrain you.' Despite my request he tried to get away, but I threw him to the ground and pinned him there. I called to some passers-by to call the police and when they arrived I handed him over to them. It was quite an ordeal and I suffered some minor injuries as he punched, kicked and attacked me with keys while attempting to escape.

With my 10–0 record, I had begun to attract attention from boxing insiders. I was well aware that the fights I wanted would not just present themselves to me. So I had let it be known that my eye was on a fight with then Commonwealth Champion, Nigel Benn. Benn was a vicious fighter of huge power, who at that point was undefeated in 20 fights. Moreover, the ferocity and venom of his victories had made him one of boxing's most awesome new talents.

I was saying, 'I can beat him, give me the fight.' But so far, no one was giving me the credit I deserved, so my remarks were just laughed off. Part of their problem with me was that my style was very unconventional, no matter where you came from in the world, so they thought I would lose to Benn – indeed, most thought my statements were far too premature to be even taken seriously.

Some snipers even laughed at my lisp and ridiculed me for that, as if that had anything to do with my boxing ability. I did see a lady once, Melanie Bloor, who taught me how to pronounce my 's's more clearly. After a fight, though, your mind and body are so ravaged that you often talk very fast and my lisp would become much more pronounced. Throughout my career, my feelings on the matter were like this: if you want to ridicule my lisp, okay, but that's me, you're letting yourself down. Some journalists quote me in articles using 'th' instead of 's', but that is such a cheap, puerile, unsophisticated shot, school-yard stuff, not very clever. That type of criticism doesn't really bother me, because I feel I can be understood when I talk and that is the most important thing. If anything, I prefer to think of it as an endearing quality. Plus I would say that they are the ones with the speech impediment because they don't get across any view and I do.

Despite these petty criticisms, I had realised that I had a lot of flavour and that is what makes you 'box-office'. It is fair to say I had only fought ten times thus far, but I knew the capability within me. My eleventh fight was against Simon Collins at York Hall, Bethnal Green. This fight was actually taken at six days' notice, despite the fact that I had a very tough bout against Anthony Logan the following week. This Jamaican boxer was very hard; he came to the fight to load up and punch very hard. When you are faced with someone who wants to use their strength to beat you, you have to use your skill to beat them. Don't try to match them with your own strength, even if you are stronger. That is not the way to progress.

I beat Simon Collins on a technical knockout in round four. I was always in control, but what interests me about this fight when I watch it on video is the remarks of the commentators. They showed that they had no understanding of me as a boxer or as a person. As I have said, I broke him down with skill, used the jab, moved around, stayed out of the way, then moved in and took him out. I did talk a little bit in this fight, sometimes you can't help yourself, but it was not something that was deliberate.

Charlie Magri, who was commentating for ITV, was critical of my performance. You could hear the disregard in his voice, but he had to stop himself because he was quietly impressed. However, he made two major observations. Firstly, that I had my hands down too low and that Nigel Benn would mercilessly take advantage of such an exposed defence. I guarantee you that any man who had gone in with Nigel Benn at that time, in his prime, with his hands up in an orthodox defence, would have got knocked out. That stance means you're not ready to fight, you're ready to block. That was using too much of a textbook defence and, largely against the consensus of opinion in the game, I knew that you couldn't fight Benn that way. I believed you would have to fight him in an unorthodox fashion: check and counter – everything would have to be unconventional because Benn was so vicious. Benn fought many opponents who had their hands up in a perfect boxing manual style. He knocked most of them out.

Magri made his second observation of note when Collins had just been stopped in the fourth. He pointed out that Benn would have taken Collins out in round one. My answer? Exactly. Benn would have steamed in there and probably finished it in less than 60 seconds. The point was this – what use is a bout like that for a fighter? If a boxer has no control, that is what happens. I preferred to gain more ring experience, work my moves, draw something positive from the match. I wanted to play chess. I needed to entertain the public and enhance my own abilities at the same time, and the only way to do that was by a prolonged contest.

I would bring the opponent to the brink of being stopped then, just as people were craving for the stoppage, I would pull back to the ropes, look at the crowd and gesture. It used to drive them crazy! *That was my flavour, that was box office.* A first round win is very explosive but all you have achieved is a missed opportunity for target practice. First round wins are just headlines. Substance is more important.

At the same time, if you choose to take your time, you must be careful not to humiliate the man. If you do that, you can awaken the warrior in him and that, as I later found out in Watson 2, could be a dangerous scenario for both combatants. If you humiliate someone, you will only make yourself look bad. There is nothing the crowd hates more. So with Simon Collins, when the time came, I finished the fight. The end of this fight is a good example of the way I would move backwards in preparation for the finish. It is almost like a cobra recoiling before the fatal lunge. You know the end is near.

After the fight, I was interviewed on television and I said, 'My trainer said if you have him on the hook, take him out. This is a nasty business, it's not a game, we are in this as professional businessmen. It's sport to the spectators, but not to pugilists like myself.' This was the most public expression to date of my supposedly controversial views on my profession.

I was so sure I could beat Benn by now that I took on a world-class, highly-rated fighter in Anthony Logan. This was only my twelfth fight, so I was still classed by many observers as a novice. Logan had fought Benn for the Commonwealth Middleweight title and almost knocked him out. Then, just as Benn was teetering, he'd thrown a shot from down by his left ankle, a left hook that knocked Logan out. Even though it would be another 13 fights before I would come to finally face Nigel Benn, I was already aiming at getting that shot. With Logan, I knew that if I could win, it would eventually lead me to Benn. Everybody in the boxing fraternity thought I was taking the wrong fight, saying to Ronnie, 'We're surprised you're putting the boy in.' That's how they talk. Even Ronnie asked me, 'Are you sure?' to which I replied, 'Don't even question me.' My resolve was like stone.

Previous to Logan, the calibre of the fighters I had been in with was journeymen, mainly seasoned fighters. That said, I was a novice and they still needed to be beaten; after all they were professionals too. When I took on Logan, I stepped up into the big league. It was only an eight-round fight for contention, not a championship bout. Don't forget, I had boxed only eight days before against Simon Collins, but to take the next fight on so swiftly never troubled me. Boxing was my way of life, I was always fighting, it was a constant feature of my world. I had to make my name, so I took whatever fight I could get. I had to earn money. Never forget, this was a living. The idea was to earn money and win titles. I was relentless.

In the actual fight itself, Logan tried to bully me from the outset and, indeed, throughout the bout. He kept putting himself on top of me, holding and hitting, holding and hitting. Previously in my career, I had never been held and hit like that, and they were really painful, very annoying shots. He also kept hitting me on the side of my ear, which again was a really annoying and painful punch. However, I knew quickly that I was a technically more refined fighter, so I had this one under control. As usual, I had studied many tapes of Logan's previous fights, and I deduced that I could jab better than he could, I could punch better than he could and my style was more artistic. I was fully charged and irrepressibly enthusiastic.

If you watch the Logan fight now, you can see that my style is still novice-like, my elbows and arms are positioned differently to my more accomplished later stance, where my elbows were much more tightly tucked in. So it was a tough fight, even though I knew I had the measure of him. I needed to win this fight so I was firing on all cylinders, with everything. People in the crowd were shouting for me to punch myself out because the pace was very fast, but I knew what I was doing. In one of the early rounds, I got caught with a solid left hook. It was a good shot and I wobbled from a slight twitch from the nervous system, then I planted my feet, reset and carried on relatively unscathed. That was my constitution showing even back then. I wasn't going anywhere, even though it was a good shot.

In this fight I was completely obdurate and Logan knew he had his hands full. Sometimes, you can break a fighter's heart with your spirit – I have seen many good fighters give up on bouts they were winning because the opponent simply wouldn't go down. It broke their spirit. One of the best tenets I learned in New York was, 'When you are feeling beaten up, exhausted and you want to quit, remember that your opponent will feel exactly the same.' That is a slice of boxing genius that must be remembered at all times and should be applied to all situations in your life.

The Logan fight was the first time I was being vicious, raining blows left and right, followed by upper cuts. He was tired and I was unforgiving, ceaseless, I had my focus. By the middle rounds, when he was continuing to hang on to me, I picked him up and threw him off me so I could start attacking again.

In round eight, I clipped him on the chin with a perfect shot. It didn't look like it was that powerful, but as he came forward I caught him with a glancing shot. The reason it was so forceful was my feet were placed ideally, they pivoted at precisely the correct instant, and so all my body weight was behind the left hook. He wobbled badly and would have fallen over if I hadn't been in front of him to hold him up. I sapped all his power and because of that almost subversive punch he was desperately holding on.

I was now fully in charge. At the end of the fight the referee had to look at the colour of our shorts, because when there's two black men, mistakes can and have happened. I was looking at the ref, thinking, *Give it to me, I know I've got this fight*. I got the decision, of course. Because I had been talking up a clash with Benn within the business, certain insiders gave me this fight to shut me up, they thought I was just a pretender. Plus, as I hadn't made my name yet, there were bigger money fighters for them to chase than me. They all thought I was a big-head. I wasn't big-headed, I just had faith in my abilities.

Logan was a good example of my method. I had applied my plan, it had all come together. On paper that guy was a far better fighter than me, but all those cynics who said I was naive to take the fight were categorically wrong. I took the fight, I won it. You need to trust yourself. I had to win this bout to get to Benn, I did so with true resilience and I showed I was a genuine candidate. The people who had wanted me silenced now had to reassess me. This was a pivotal fight in my career.

After the Logan victory, people began to sit up and take notice of me. One of those was Barry Hearn, the sports event promoter. Initially, Ronnie Davies was my manager but then I started this relationship with Barry. We met at the 1989 World Snooker Championships – Barry knew of me but had not seen me fight live, only on the television. We met again at the Grosvenor House Hotel to agree our deal, and he later told me I was 'a vision of sartorial elegance.' My first words to him were, 'Mr Hearn, I am an athlete and I know my worth.' I signed a contract with him which paid me an allowance of £1200 a month to support me while I was training. To this day, that contract is incorrect. There were clauses in there that made provision for my career developing. One such point said the terms would be renegotiated if I won the British, Commonwealth or European title, by which time I would be earning enough from fights to not need the allowance. Another clause said the allowance would stop if I was injured for more than two months. This was not an eventuality I considered, I was never injured, at least not in a manner that I allowed to interfere. The third and most significant clause of note, and the one that I never agreed with, said that the monthly wage would stop if I lost two contests. I told Barry that I wanted that to be if I lost one. He was surprised, and said, 'Yes, but Chris, what about cut eyes, freak accidents? Come on . . .' I replied, 'I'm not interested, Barry. If I lose once, you rip that contract up.' When it arrived for signature, however, it still said two losses.

At first, Barry had me work with a manager called Darkie Smith, but it didn't really work. He tried to train me but I was never listening, because he wasn't the calibre of trainer that Maximo was. From what I had witnessed in New York, I knew what I was doing, it was already in my head, it was just about repetition and streamlining to get it perfect. Darkie Smith stopped working with Barry shortly after.

You need someone like Barry Hearn on your side. I knew he was a promoter who could get me the fights I needed. It goes beyond being about fights, it begins to start being about getting the championship fights. I had grand ambitions and Barry Hearn had the know-how to get me the shot I wanted, which was Nigel Benn.

Promoters and managers never really have your interest at heart, or at least not before their own, of course. From 1990 to 1995, Barry Hearn was a huge promoter, the No. 1 in the United Kingdom. Why? Because he promoted Chris

Eubank. You are only as good as the fighter you have. Don King was only as good as he was because he had Ali, Holyfield, Tyson, boxers like that. If you own the heavyweight champion of the world, then you will be the best promoter in the world, everyone will have to come to you. I was to become the biggest name in world boxing, other than the heavyweights, and Barry Hearn became the kingpin. He was the best promoter by far at this time.

A lot of fighters complain about the politics, the underhand strokes that so many people pull in boxing. I was never interested. Ronnie was a great bodyguard against much of that and Barry was a master. I let them resolve those sort of issues. As a professional fighter, you have to be very careful in striking the right balance. Yes, it is vital you are aware of what is going on with your career path, but at the same time do not become trapped in the quagmire that underpins the business. My view was always this: I ignored all of that because it was like having a boulder on my back. I would be told there was this difficulty, that obstacle, but all I ever said was, 'Get me the fight. I'll keep training, you just get me the fight.'

After beating Logan, I won a couple more points decisions, both at Bethnal Green's York Hall against Frankie Moro and Randy Smith, both awkward journeymen, slippery veterans who made for rather dull fights. The Randy Smith bout was Barry's first with me, although there were only about 100 people there – unfortunately. But at the time I was a no-name boxer so wasn't in a position to pull in the crowds. Then I was scheduled to fight Canadian Les Wisnieski at the International Centre in Brentwood. There was a good undercard of local fighters and my bout was top of the bill. He was a journeyman boxer who, to me at this stage, was just there to make me look good. He was willing but his ability was limited. However, you must never waste opportunities that come your way and, knowing that influential people were keeping an eye on me now, I used this bout to show my command of the art, the repertoire, the refinement. This was a truly stylish performance.

I was on song from the very first bell. This was my artistic licence on display, pure exhibitionism. If you watch this fight, you will appreciate the dexterity and complexity of my moves and punches. I was catching his punches as easily as catching a ball thrown by a child. That allowed me the freedom to shine. All these seemingly silly little shots were so impressive and inspiring to the judges, it was all very deliberate. The objective is to catch the eye of the judges and the people.

However, although some of these moves look small and relatively simple, they are the result of all those thousands and thousands of hours of repetition in the gym. This sort of poetry in the ring does not just happen by accident. For example, when I circled the ring in this fight, this was not me playing, this was all method, this had all been premeditated and done time and time again. That deft sleight of foot is not from the road work, it is more the product of circling in the gym hundreds of thousands of times. If you don't do it in training, you can't do it in the ring. Even when you are using footwork like that, you need to take care, you are still fighting a professional.

Out of 52 professional fights, I have probably been on song, and by that I mean poetry in motion, maybe 15 times. This bout was one of them. It was vital that I looked impressive – this was my second fight with Barry Hearn and they were building me towards a world title fight. I had to show my pedigree.

I stopped Wisnieski in the second round. Afterwards, the commentator Reg Gutteridge said, 'The referee pointing his finger probably caused more damage to Eubank than Les Wisnieski.' Inevitably, the people who said I was not good enough to fight Logan, now said I was not taking on fights of sufficient calibre, they would always find a negative angle. For me, it was an ideal opportunity to scintillate and I made sure I did. After this bout, they all knew I was serious. And just as importantly I thought yes, I have a future in this sport. I had put in a very good performance and got well paid for it. It was the richest I've ever been.

Next, I comfortably beat Ron Malek in five rounds at the Festival Hall in Basildon, before stopping Jean-Noël Camara at Bethnal Green with a two round demolition. I was flying, even my worst critics had to admit this was an explosive yet refined performance of poetic beauty. Now they knew I could box. *So bring me to Benn.*

Two of the next three fights were very tough. First up was a fellow called Johnny Melfah, a fighter of average ability, at the Royal Albert Hall. When I got in the ring with him,

Melfah was playing rather excellent cat and mouse. He was repeatedly getting to me and landing some big, hard shots. Naturally, I had all the style but he was just out of range and cleverly used this to his advantage. In my career, I was never knocked out, but I did sense what I call 'the white lights of unconsciousness' three times. Once was the near-miss in the final of the Spanish Golden Gloves I mentioned previously; another time was in the Watson 2 fight (more of which later); and the other occasion was, remarkably, against Johnny Melfah. I knew I was substantially more talented than this man but, credit where it is due, he landed an enormous right hand that made me sense the white lights. I circled around the ring and got myself back together but he had definitely hurt me. It was a big, powerful shot.

Then he made a mistake – he dislodged a tooth I had chipped and I really didn't want to lose this particular tooth. In training for the Melfah fight, Errol Christie, who was a superb sparring partner, had dislodged a front tooth with a hefty punch. I had it splinted with dental cement and it seemed to be secure. Then, at the end of the third, Melfah hit me with an average jab, but for some reason this repaired tooth, which had already withstood some almighty bombs, was dislodged again. This really niggled me, I didn't want to lose that tooth. That put me in a devastating frame of mind – if a fighter isn't skilled enough to use raw aggression, then you can come on against him with feverish power. I did that, like a man against a baby. I forced myself upon him like thunder. In the fourth, I hit him with a shot that left him concussed. When he hit the ground his leg bounced.

That tooth really niggled me. In my opinion, this fighter had nothing on me. Although he had fought at the top level of British Middleweights, he was never in my class, and it made me angry that this cumbersome spoiler had nearly cost me my tooth. At the finish, I was like a lion after him, breaking his jaw in the process. *Don't dislodge my tooth, it will cost you.*

I then travelled to Kirby where I beat José Da Silva in six rounds. I entered the arena with a much more extravagant show and vaulted over the ropes as usual. Then I stood there, stock still, tapping one glove on top of the other, effortlessly serene. It was quite a show. However, bearing in mind I was supposed to be kept away from southpaws, imagine my shock when Da Silva comes out in that exact stance! My first reaction was to stop the fight, *Hey! No one told me he was southpaw, I don't want this fight!* Of course, I didn't stop the bout, but instead I slid around the canvas, used my ring craft and surveyed the territory. I circled away from his right hand jab, controlled his tactics and hit him extremely hard with every shot. It caught up with him in the sixth round and I stopped him. I had beaten him with intellect – you don't box just with your fists, you box with your mind. Mind and fists are better than just fists.

In January 1990, I fought a fellow called Denys Cronin in Splott, Cardiff. You always look forward to seeing your opponent for the first time to try to size him up, see what sort of job you have ahead. When I saw Cronin, I turned to John Regan and said, 'Wow, if he fights half as good as he looks, I'm in trouble here.' He was a Caucasian with an incredible physique, the best body I have ever seen on a boxer. He was exactly like a full-size Action Man.

Before the fight, I was in the men's washroom when Cronin walked in. I had already used the urinal and was washing my hands. Cronin relieved himself but made to walk out of the bathroom without washing. I said, 'Hey! Wash your hands!' He swore at me and walked out. I knew then that I had won the fight.

That bout was the perfect example of my relationship with a hostile crowd, a tense interconnection which I made much use of throughout my career. In that arena in Cardiff, the hate that poured my way was so fierce, you could almost reach out and pluck it from the air. They were salivating for my demise. Apart from my small camp, I'm pretty sure everyone else was against me. If I had hit the canvas, the place would have gone ballistic.

However, this is what I loved, what I wanted, no, what I craved. You see, let me tell you something about boxing. There is a great deal spoken about fighting 'in your own back yard', as they say in the business. Get the crowd behind you, lift yourself with the support. I always reversed that psychology. Let me come to *your* back yard. It's not even that I want to come, I *need* to come. I didn't mind people being against me. Please, all of them, at the same time, viciously.

I drew so much energy from hateful crowds, I soaked it up like a human sponge. The problem for my opponent was that I sucked all the venom in, allowed it to well up inside me, transformed it into positive energy, then unleashed it back against him. This was a martial arts philosophy that I used to my advantage throughout my career. When you think of the negative vibes thrown my way over the years, you can imagine how useful that was to me. The more they hated me, the more energised, devastating and arrogant I became in the ring.

The tangible power source that hateful crowds provided me with was so palpable when I was hitting Cronin. They were getting hit. They winced physically at every single punch that connected. Imagine all that negative energy being channelled on to that unfortunate fellow. In hindsight, he was never going to win, the crowd just made me more focused.

Years later, when I was at the Mike Tyson–Julius Francis contest, the crowd were booing Joe Calzaghe and David Starrie. They were interviewing me on the arena microphone and asked, 'What do you think of Joe Calzaghe being booed?' and I answered, 'Oohh, do you remember the days? When they booed and hissed, those were the days.' Golden times.

Stopping Cronin took my tally of opponents for the previous 12 months to ten, seven of whom I had knocked out or stopped. I was keeping very busy. On 6 March 1990, I was lined up for my first title fight, for the WBC International Middleweight belt against the durable Argentinean Hugo Corti, again at Bethnal Green's York Hall. I was in tremendous shape and very confident, plus my focus to earn this first accolade was fierce – that said, I have always thought, 'A belt is only as big as the fighter who wears it.' Corti was always going to be in trouble. I knocked him down a couple of times and looked to the referee to stop the fight, which he did in the eighth. Winning the WBC International Middleweight belt was a good step up the ladder, but I was not about to be flattered into complacency. I had bigger fish to catch in Nigel Benn. A shark in fact. After the Corti fight, Doctor arrived in the UK and we resumed our close work in the gymnasium together, providing me with a welcome colleague technically and a great ally emotionally.

The next two fights were both in my home town. The first opponent, Eduardo Contreras, to this day took the hardest punches I have ever delivered to anybody and never went down. He had this curly hair and every time I landed a perfect punch, he just shrugged it off, shook his locks and danced around. He soaked up everything I had, but fortunately he never came at me with anything of note, so I beat him on points.

This fight was significant for two reasons. Firstly, it was shown on ITV, whereas previously my bouts had only been screened on Screen Sport, with highlights elsewhere. Secondly, although ITV only usually showed a fight from the bell for the first round, the ITV executives in the crowd that night saw my entrance and understood what superb television that would make.

Although the Contreras fight was on my territory, the boxing crowds were not automatically behind me in Brighton. Nevertheless, the next fighter, Kid Milo, was despatched with aplomb in the eighth. Milo had lots of heart but limited talent and ability. When an opponent is obviously in trouble, or bleeding from cuts, I used to always ask the referee to step in and save them from any further damage.

CHAPTER EIGHT
IT'S A MUG'S GAME

There is a saying that advises, 'Patience is bitter but the fruits of patience are sweet.' When I received the news I had been waiting for, that I had been given a shot at Nigel Benn, I knew my fragment of opportunity had arrived. After much negotiation, I eventually had to accept a lesser purse (£100,000 compared to Benn's £800,000) but I just wanted to do whatever it took to get him in the ring. I saw it as a matter of honour, and the point was what I really wanted was Benn's title. I knew the big money would come later. People were already talking up a fight with the winner against Michael Watson or even the astonishing Thomas Hearns. All this chatting, playing, let's get to the brass tacks here – the fight.

I have always used a points system for my opponents, marking them in advance on a scale of one to ten. Benn got a ten. I would then train with that number in my mind. You go through identical routines and regimes, but subconsciously I would somehow think harder for a ten than for a five;

I was always more focused, although my work was more or less the same.

My foremost thought was obviously to become champion of the world and therefore honour the life of solitude that had dominated all my adult years. However, I have always found extra mileage and motivation in placing material or emotional goals in front of myself during the preparation for a fight. While I was working towards the Benn title fight, Karron and I went to view a lovely four-bedroom detached house, with a nice garden, in Old Shoreham Road. I thought at the time, *Wow! If we can have this, that will be it. We will have arrived.* It cost me £190,000, which was big money at the time. Simply put, the mathematics of the situation were that if I did not beat Benn we would lose the house, it would be repossessed. That was a sure-fire motivator.

Closer to my heart, however, was Karron. We had talked about marriage for some time but, for me, there was no possibility of getting wed until I had proven myself, in other words, made champion. Karron didn't see it like that, she was with me *for* me. However, that was my way of look-ing at our relationship. So what I actually did, although I didn't realise this at the time, was use marrying Karron as an emotional incentive to win the fight against the Dark Destroyer.

As usual, my pre-fight preparation was meticulous. I had seen Michael Watson's sixth-round victory over Benn at Finsbury Park and some people suggested that would provide me with ideal knowledge on how to beat Benn. In fact, what it taught me was how to beat Watson. Benn had punched himself out, but I learned how to cover up properly. If you cover up and keep your hands clenched, you'll get hurt. Watson covered up but kept his hands open around his head, fingers on his forehead. His defence that night, as I would find out when we later fought each other, was staggeringly exceptional.

For the last fight before Benn, I was up against the Brazilian Renaldo Dos Santos. We came out for the first round, I was in my zone that night, very focused, I poleaxed him with a huge right. He went down and that was the end of that, I knocked him out in 20 seconds – including the count. One punch. I was devastatingly accurate and very, very cool. There was a scary moment in the next fight on the bill, when a boxer called Jim McDonnell was knocked out and was unconscious for about 20 minutes. While they were trying to revive him I got into the ring and started talking to him saying 'Jim, Jim, wake up, wake up', over and over. They tried to get me out of the ring but I refused. He was a friend and an up-and-coming fighter like myself. They took him to his dressing room and I followed. I was still talking to him when he opened his eyes, just like that, and was absolutely fine.

Although this one-punch knockout had the welcome effect of hyping the Benn fight substantially – after all, Benn was supposed to be the big hitter – I hadn't intended to make such a bold statement. I was not so gifted that I could go in and knock a man out intentionally in 20 seconds. As I've said before, I liked to work a fight longer than its natural life to gain practice, but that was a strange one, I didn't mean to end it that quickly. You never know how a fight is going to go, but that was the most fantastic advert for Benn–Eubank at Birmingham's NEC, on 18 November 1990.

From the first public announcement of the Benn fight, billed as 'Who's Fooling Who?', it was my perception that almost no one outside of my own immediate circle wanted me to win because Benn was the people's champion and I was almost universally disliked. Even if I had been more popular, Benn was the public's golden boy. However, I had caused much consternation and received some quite belligerent criticism for some comments I made about my profession: namely, 'Boxing is a mug's game.'

These were to be the five most controversial words of my career. So many people within the sport, fighters, promoters, managers, even enthusiasts, were incensed. I was accused of hypocrisy, biting the hand that feeds me and condemned as traitorous. I was talking for the fighters, yet I was ostracised by so many of them. That I could not understand. For me, it was crystal-clear common sense. They may not have been the prettiest words I've ever used, but the sentiment behind them was completely indisputable. Let me explain why I said such a thing and then it is for you to make up your own mind.

Let's start with a simple fact: 99.9% of boxers get disfigured, used, abused, manipulated and ultimately discarded. Yet, 100% of boxers are the single most important element of any fight they compete in. They are the nucleus. The problem is, promoters and managers will have the boxer believe that he is working for them, because they pull a lot of the strings in the business. This is totally wrong, the fighter employs the promoters and managers, he is their boss, without him there would be no fight business. That is a fact and I will not accept any argument against that basic statement. A boxer's position of primacy is irrefutable.

Issues are immensely complicated behind the scenes in boxing. Suffice to say, the best man does not always win. As I have said, Ronnie was a superb 'bodyguard' to me, in the sense that he understood the intricacies of the boxing politic, he knew how to guide me through the minefield. When I was being particularly outspoken, especially in the earlier days before I was champion, he used to say to me, 'Be careful Chris, if you talk too much, they will have you bumped off.' By 'bumped off' he meant that arrangements would be made so that I would lose a bout. 'Fight well, but don't talk too much,' he used to say.

Am I saying some fights are fixed? Absolutely. If you ask for too much money, or you're behaving like a primadonna, they'll have you bumped off. Judges can be indirectly influenced by nice hotel rooms, champagne, women, backhanders and the like. It goes on. However, fighters would do well to remember this: *the politics is only an illusion put in place to hold you down.* If you keep winning, you can still have your voice. An unbeaten record empowers. If you suspect that arrangements have been made against you, you will simply have to knock the man down before the end of round 12.

I always used to say, 'The judges had a job to do and they did it.' It never worried me that they might have been influenced. There were several controversial decisions in my career in my favour, which I accepted with gratitude. There were also several suspect decisions too: Collins 1, both Thompson fights. They were all, in my view, questionable decisions. However, just as I had been happy to accept the judges decision in my favour, I wanted only to do the same when the cards went against me. That was the way my cookie crumbled. To moan about it would have been undignified and wrong. *You must never be a bad loser, take your beating and subsequent defeat with dignity.*

If you lose a fight, then you are no longer in a position to be so outspoken; if you believe circumstances have 'conspired against you', they will have effectively silenced your forum. If you are a strong-minded individual and speak up for what you believe in, then there are people in the business whose interests may not be best served by your opinions. If that is the case, your path will be a tricky one. For me however, regardless of obstacles, it was the only path because that was my truth.

Many a fighter is told that the promoters can make or break his career, constantly conditioned that he is 'only a boxer'. Although it is vital to get a great promoter working for you, and in Barry Hearn I had one of the best, this assumption denigrates the importance of the fighter. So many pugilists just go along with these people, they accept that chain of command. I never did. I was the most important person involved and if people didn't like me saying so, hard cheese. Many great fighters have fallen by the wayside, not through lack of talent, but by having the wrong people around them. Also, if you accept someone talking disrespectfully to you outside of the ring, then your integrity is compromised and thus you will probably show the same flaw in your character in the ring.

It was not just the wrath of boxing insiders I had to face for saying boxing was a mug's game. The media berated me for this statement too. However, when I tried to explain my reasoning in press conferences, they weren't interested. I never had the experience of sitting down with them and explaining it at length, to an audience who may not have agreed but at least had given my opinion a fair hearing. At any one of my press conferences, 75% of what I said was philosophy. The Fleet Street mob used to get quite riled by this, shouting out, 'Chris, no! Don't go on about philosophy, talk about the fight! Chris, please don't!' I understand that pure philosophy can be very dry, but even when I tried to tag my theories to an event inside or outside of the ring, they still wouldn't listen. They just wanted tabloid.

This is another reason why boxing is a mug's game. You are supposed to fit one of a very few stereotypes. You can be the animalistic powerhouse (Tyson, Benn), the thinking man's fighter (Herol Graham, Marco Antonio Barrera) or the arrogant self-certain upstart who needs to be brought down a peg or two (me, Naseem). That is not my opinion, that is the type of neat compartment they allocate for you. And if you do something that does not dovetail nicely into the stereotype you have been allotted, they will generally choose to ignore or ridicule it. 'Eubank talks to school kids in deprived areas and makes everyone feel more positive.' This sort of headline does not sell newspapers.

If you don't provide them with enough tabloid material, they will quite often make it up. One quote attributed to me was that the four best things in life are 'sex, champagne, chocolate and cocaine'. That I would have even acknowledged this last vice is absolute nonsense. They said I hated Nigel Benn – as I will explain, that was simply not the case. This was tabloid manipulation of the public.

To take all this manipulation, disrespect and abuse, then to step into the ring and put yourself in a physically very vulnerable position, how else can you look at boxing but as a mug's game? No one talked like that, I told it as it was.

Critics would say to me, 'But Chris, don't you love the business?' I would say, 'I beg your pardon? Love? There is no love here, I am earning a living. I need the money.' In the United Kingdom, you are supposed to work in certain livelihoods, like sports, because you love them. Well, sorry, but I didn't love my job. At least that's what I would tell the media so they couldn't stereotype me. The truth is I did love the life.

Boxing also allowed people to cast aspersions about my character that were not correct, I was a finer human being than they were all making me out to be. I tried to let the people understand that I was just like them, this was just a job of work, I had my hobbies outside of boxing. What you see me do in the ring is just how I earn a living and feed my family. It is barbaric, I am just being honest.

It wasn't that I had no love for certain aspects of the business. I loved, and still love, the philosophy behind the noble art, learning to move, learning the restraint, absorbing pain, winning a fight, even a dirty fight, with nobility. I wanted to learn how to do it just right – as I learned in school in New York: 'Always try and do it the right way the first time, because if you don't you're only going to have to do it again.' That is so true of life, I have striven to be a good observer, to see my mistakes and to endeavour not to repeat them. That part of boxing I did indeed love. Unfortunately, my critics never listened to me qualify myself like that. They just said, 'Oh, Eubank hates boxing.' Never.

The *Independent* once ran an advert that quoted the Marquis of Queensbury talking about the 'noble art', in which they quoted me as saying, 'Boxing is a mug's game.' When I first saw that piece, I was disappointed, because I felt my choice of words seemed base when compared to the subtle language of the Marquis. However, they also ran a byline at the bottom which said, 'Great minds don't think alike.' When I saw that, I was satisfied. Boxing *is* a mug's game. What I didn't realise was how many people didn't know that.

In any other profession, they would have made me their trade union leader.

Looking back, I can see why people sided with Benn, because they didn't know the real me, but at the time I just thought, *why don't you accept me?*

Much was made of how verbally aggressive I was during press conferences. This was largely untrue. I am not denying for one second that the word hate was mentioned, but not by me. That sort of language was simply not consistent with my frame of mind. Take the famous television studio interview on ITV's *Midweek Sports Special* with Nick Owen where I was seated next to Benn, Ambrose Mendy (Benn's Manager) and Barry Hearn. I sat with my back turned to Benn and would not look him in the eye – indeed, at no point before the fight did I do that in public, which really annoyed him. There was no need for me to look him in the eye, because that would have been giving him an advantage to which he was not entitled. There is a fellow called Samuel Johnson, author of the first dictionary in the 16th century, who said, 'Treating your adversary with respect is giving him an advantage to which he is not entitled. Sir, treating your adversary with respect is striking soft in battle.'

When questioned by Benn on my refusal to make eye contact, I said, 'I will look you in the eyes when I get in the ring. When I finally do look in your eyes it will be when I am caning you.' That was me being a person of truth. I was not intimidating him, I was just standing my ground.

So the atmosphere in this television studio was somewhat tense, to say the least, some might say bristling. However, if you listen carefully to my answer when asked if I hated Benn, it was very clear and utterly consistent with my stance throughout: 'I don't hate the man, I just want his WBO title.' I openly stated that I had a great amount of respect for his punching power. For his part, Benn said,

'I personally do hate him.' That was part of his tactic which was good for the hype, I guess, but those sentiments had no place in my world. It was tense in there, of course, but that was the game he played, talking about hate, staring you down. It was his way of trying to aquire a psychological advantage. I was not being so personal. I just needed some money and the title. He had a method of fighting and living which wasn't mine. My method was more sound and psychological.

Different fighters employ different tactics before a fight. Many will try and intimidate you, scare you or at least unnerve you. Benn's approach was pure, venomous intimidation. And, yes, it was terrifying; it felt very real. He was without doubt the most terrifying man I had ever met, still is. He was aggressive in that televised press conference, but I have seen him much more aggressive than that. We were at the Café Royal in London in the build-up to the fight and I was heading into a room for a meeting. I opened the door and there was Barry Hearn, Ambrose Mendy, some trainers and Nigel Benn. I am a polite man, so when I saw they were busy I said, 'Oh, sorry gentlemen, I can see you are doing business,' and I went to close the door.

'Get the f**k out!' Benn shouted. 'Get out, f***ing get out!'

'What?' I said, astonished.

He repeated the abuse. 'F***ing get out! Go on. C**t!'

'Listen,' I said. 'Don't talk to me like that. If we're going to fight, let's do it in the ring.'

He just stood there. 'F***ing get out!'

Immediately he jumped up from his chair, marched out

from behind the table and squared up to me, inches from my face.

'What? You want to do it now? You want it now?'

I was faced with a monumentally important situation. If Benn had won this little skirmish in that room, in doing so he would have sealed the fight. Without a doubt. I was dressed in a pristine suit, so I stood my ground, imposed myself on the situation and said, 'Listen, if you want to get it on now, let's do it, but I didn't come here to fight, I came here for a press conference. Let's do it in the ring.'

By this point, Barry Hearn and Ronnie Davies had got up and stood between us and was saying, 'Now, come on boys, come on.' 'Barry's body was actually shaking, throbbing, that's how much tension there was between me and Benn. That was the type of fear that Benn put into people. He was that vicious. A terrifying man.

That was a severe experience. However, all Benn was trying to do was trick me, but I wasn't going to be intimidated by him and his hostile antics. He was intimidating but I would never let him know because that would have awarded him the victory. This was my outlook on that whole situation: *This man is truly terrifying but where's your courage? Are you going to let him talk down to you in this manner, are you going to allow him to get into your head before the fight?* No way. I could stand up to that. Logically, it was a simple fact that, as we had never fought before, he could not know for certain that he would beat me, so therefore I assumed it must be bravado, intimidation tactics.

It was in situations like these that I was able to draw

heavily on all my painstaking studies of the philosophy behind the art of war. Being terrified of another boxer is not a weakness if you recognise it. If you can articulate that fear and have reasons for and against that feeling, then you can defeat the person who terrifies you. It was vital for me not to lose sight of the fact that this was only a trick by Benn, something that people constantly do to make you feel inferior. One helpful way of stripping him of his aura of fear was at home – whenever Karron and I mentioned him, we called him 'Benjamin'. I relished this psychological battle – remember, where I came from on the streets, hostility was the faith. I actually suggested that it was Benn who was petrified, because I was so unpredictable. He didn't agree, obviously.

So having come to accept and rationalise his intimidation within myself, the next battle was the fight itself. It was perfectly evident to me what this bout would be all about – resolve. With someone as brutal as Nigel Benn, you can only go in there and win by having complete, absolute conviction in your skills and an omnipresent and unerring resolve. I had both and I was ready. I went to the fight thinking, *You may be able to beat me but you will not knock me out. It doesn't matter what happens, I know you are NOT going to knock me out.* I knew I could outbox him before long. I wasn't even necessarily thinking about the win, it was more about the impossibility of him knocking me out. From the moment I started training, that was my train of thought.

This was an historically awaited fight. The gate receipts alone at the NEC were over £1 million for what was the first all-British World Middleweight title fight and the richest bout ever in the UK. Unbeknown to the public, Ambrose Mendy had nominated himself as the WBO observer for the taping of my hands. This was something I would obviously have objected to, if I had known in advance. There were also poor facilities in my dressing room, no ice or towels. Then, as I walked into the ring, my entrance music was sabotaged. Barry was absolutely furious and said to me, 'Let's go back to the changing rooms, Chris.' I remained serenely calm and said to him when we were back in the locker room, 'They've screwed up my dressing room, they've done everything to unnerve me, but the only thing that can beat me is Benn, nothing else.

I vaulted into that ring, and stood static, calm cool and collected and performed the pose. I knew that 95% of the population thought I would get my head knocked into the fourth row – that was the kind of rhetoric that was going around. What's more, most of the 12,500 people there wanted to see that too. They were booing me from the moment I walked in until when I got to the ring – even some people in the £200 ringside seats were hissing. I had a crowd of about 40 or so up from Brighton.

As an adult, my favourite movie is the stunning *Once Upon A Time In The West*, starring Charles Bronson and Henry Fonda. It is billed as a hard-nosed Western but for me it is sheer romance. The tale is of a man (Bronson) who waits years to avenge the sadistic murder of his brother (which

Bronson's character witnessed as a young boy) by a psycho-pathic killer played by Fonda. Bronson's character appeals deeply to me. He played his harmonica, I recite my poetry, he was an expert gunfighter, I was an expert boxer. In one scene, he is in the corral, the soundtrack is so stirring and he stands there in the face of a terrifying individual in an extremely cool way. Bronson's character was emotionally clever too, he wasn't going to kill anyone who didn't deserve it and he wanted to kill that man in a fair fight. In Benn 1, he entered the ring like an uncaged tiger, a wild animal off the leash. I just stood there, cool. It reminds me of those movies, I am following Bronson's lead. Like him, this was the moment I had been waiting for many years.

The bell for round one rang and, instantly, Benn's pace was berserk, demented even. I could not believe that he was so frenzied, he was clearly trying to blow me out of the ring within a few rounds. I had expected him to come out hard and fast, but even then maybe at, say, 60%. His first attack was at 100% and he never let up for three rounds. So in order not to get extinguished, I had to match that pace, this was a desperate predicament and nothing less than 100% was essential from me also. Now I knew the force that had wiped out the impressive Iran Barkley in one round in Benn's previous bout. I had rated Benn as a 'perfect ten' for power and aggression – I was finding out to my cost that I was exactly right.

I gladly admit that such was the ferocity and power in his attacks that by round three, I said to myself: *if he keeps this up, no matter how much resolve I have, no matter how totally abhorrent the idea of going down was to me, I may not be able to withstand it.* It was inhuman, incredible, vicious and almost too much. It may not have looked that way from the judges scorecards or to the spectators, but those first three rounds were a veritable tempest.

People used to talk about Benn as being, pound for pound, one of the hardest punchers in the game. I can vouch for that – in my opinion, he was equal to what Tyson is reputed to be. Benn's power was simply astonishing. Fight fans ask me which punch of Benn's was the hardest – I say, 'Simple, all of them.' Every shot. The jab to the head was like a huge battering ram, his left hook was devastating. When Benn hit you, you stayed hit. Most boxers hit you and even if it is a good shot its damage is fleeting; it's just a punch. When Benn hit you, it was a lucid, lingering punch; it was almost like a living entity whose sole purpose was to wreak havoc inside your skull. That degree of shocking power cannot be trained into someone, it is just within them. The equation is speed + strength = power, but there is a natural factor as well. Benn had the lot, he was so strong, so lightning fast. He is by far the hardest puncher I have ever come across.

Some people start dancing when they are hit hard, some people fold and some people smile, almost as if to say to the opponent and the judges, 'I'm okay, no problem,' when there is. My tactic was to say, 'Come on, hit me more, harder. Give me some more.' The harder Benn hit me, the more I was resolved to attack back with the same kind of power and passion. I may not have punched as hard as him, but I was always coming back with that resolve.

Fortunately, as with Benn's gift of power, a granite constitution was my natural inheritance, so my body was capable of taking severe punishment. In the corner, I regularly asked Ronnie to slap me as hard as he could across my face (although I also used to say, 'No talking during the exam'). I needed to stay focused, remain sharp, pull back from the abyss that Benn was trying to batter me into. Ronnie never slapped me unless I asked and he could never slap me hard enough, but it helped keep my focus.

So, up until round four, Benn was on top. Then things got worse, much worse. In that round, he landed a punch which I have spoken about at times over the years. We were in a clinch and I had dropped my head on to his shoulder. When you do that, your jawbone automatically opens. My jaw relaxed and my tongue slipped in between my bottom teeth and my top gumshield. At that exact second, Benn nudged me off his shoulder with a jolt and *BOOM!* He hit me with a mammoth right uppercut. The seismic impact guillotined my tongue with my own teeth, opening a deep, half-inch long laceration that immediately started bleeding heavily down my throat. I was drinking copious amounts of my own blood from that moment on. When you swallow blood, it can curdle and choke you, so I didn't tell my corner because Ronnie may have told the referee, who then may have stopped the fight. That was not an option for me. If the referee came too close, I kept my mouth shut. That uppercut was later highlighted in a documentary called *Clash Of The Titans* where they froze the moment of impact. It felt like my tongue had almost been severed.

My resolve was total, and in the face of such an onslaught, my goal was now not about winning the fight, it was about carrying on until the last bell rang. After all, some of these punches from Benn would have hospitalised many fighters. Yet, at this lowest point of the fight for me, my pre-fight prediction was starting to come true. I had said to him, 'I have a surprise for you. When you hit me, I am not going anywhere. I am staying there and coming right back at you.'

From that moment, I have almost no recollection whatsoever of rounds four to six. I assume that I was just dealing with the dire situation – watching the video confirms that. I cannot recall clearly any of those nine minutes when I was in the ring with a manical, mindless fighter. I was kept alive only by gut instinct, integrity, resolve. The sole memory I have from those forgotten rounds was when he dropped me with a body shot that felt as though it had ruptured my being. He had been hitting my abdomen with body shots from the opening bell, but this one particular punch had a near-calamitous effect on me. He had hit me low and I'd gone down to recover, as he had disturbed my genital area. When the referee said, 'Box on' as I came in Benn slipped to one side and BOOM! It was a body shot that nearly broke me in two. I can see on the video that I went in to evasive mode, but continued to use short sharp jabs and chopping rights that he was running on to, while his corner men were shouting, 'Get him to the body, he can't take it!' That is the single memory from those three rounds that has forced itself through my amnesia by the sheer power of the punch.

My memory returns fully with round seven. I started to

notice he had blown himself out. You cannot keep up a pace like that – perhaps understandably, he had thought no one could withstand such a barrage, but he had not reckoned with my resolve. I was still there. Still fighting. Still standing upright. Suddenly, he was no longer coming on ferociously without regard, he had regard and this changed everything. All the time he'd had no regard for my punching ability and ring craft, there was nothing I could do but weather the storm, face the tornado. In doing so, I eventually forced him to treat me with regard. Now he was in my zone. I had closed one of his eyes and that was a substantial handicap because this was no longer a contest of brutality, this had evolved into a cat and mouse game of strategy. That was where I was king, that was my speciality. I had studied this part of the art form intensely, in this type of fight I had a Ph.D. Now the fight belonged to me.

That said, I did not suddenly think I could win, not least because you could not control how the judges were scoring it. It was still a matter of staying in there. The emphasis had changed though, and I was always going to counter-punch him better. I would strike, get out of range, strike again as he moved in, back out and so on. I started to pick him off, his eye was badly swollen now and the tide had turned my way. Unlike earlier fights, like Simon Collins, when I mentioned earning ring time and honing your craft, with an opponent as dangerous as Benn, you have to finish the fight at the first opportunity. Benn had, after all, beaten men almost at the moment that he himself was teetering into unconsciousness. You can't play with people like that, you have to finish it. The end came in the ninth when he hit me with a shot that kind of landed on my bum. I went down, off-balance, then got back up and brushed my gloves off. Then I hit him with a string of jabs, then a right hand, and his legs went. Now it was my time to bombard. I was on overdrive, auto-pilot, raining the blows in. With fighters as awesome as Benn, you cannot deliberate, you must take him out when you can.

The actual moment in time when the ref intervened and stopped Benn, thus making me world champion, is very hard to describe. I turned to the centre of the ring, gloves clasped together and screamed skywards, head turned towards the glaring lights above the ring. My whole body was tensed, and in that feral roar I unleashed eight years of training, of learning the art, of isolation, of punishment and of pain. The moment was captured by a photographer and won him a 'Sports Photograph of the Year' award.

For me, I had completed the first stage of my journey, I had honoured all those years of work and application. I had done it. The feeling was overwhelming. Watching the fight now, the words of Rudyard Kipling spring to mind, almost as if he was commentating on the fight, telling me to, 'force your heart and nerve and sinew to serve your turn, long after they are gone and so hold on when there is nothing in you, except the will which says to them "hold on."' The poem goes on to say that if you can do all these things, then 'Yours is the earth and everything that is in it.' I was to hold a world title for over five years.

There were practical benefits of winning the Benn fight,

such as being able to keep the house in Old Shoreham Road, but in the highly charged, ultra-emotional aftermath of a battle like that, these material benefits are not on your mind. When a fighter has been in a really tough fight, he bares his soul, he reveals what is on his mind. All I could do was talk honestly and my truth was the desire to marry Karron. As I have said, my view was that unless I had made something of myself, namely champion, I did not deserve her hand in marriage. When I was interviewed by Gary Newbon, this realisation filled my mind. It wasn't premeditated but I turned to the camera and said, 'Karron, can we get married now? Can we get married? Marry me Karron.' That question may have been transmitted into millions of homes but it was purely a private affair between myself and Karron. Remember, I was still a loner, I didn't really keep any other company, the only person I really knew was Karron. She has since told me she was shouting, 'Yes! Yes!' at the screen. Gary Newbon asked me another question and, as I was in excruciating pain, I said, 'I have to go to the hospital now.' As I said those words, the years of craving acceptance from my brothers and never receiving it welled up in my soul and as I turned from the camera, I said, 'Peter, Peter Eubank, I did it. I told you I'd do it, man.'

PART THREE

ACQUIRE THE FINANCIAL SECURITY

CHAPTER NINE

WBO MIDDLEWEIGHT CHAMPION

For all my detractors before the Benn fight, the aftermath saw the bout recognised by many as arguably the greatest ever to take place in a British ring, certainly the best all-British contest. Some observers said it was the start of the modern era of British boxing. This was all a tribute to both fighters, but it was rewarding for me that I was finally recognised for the skills and application I possessed. In my opinion, I had shown myself as the ultimate boxer for what I achieved that night. The better opponents always make you win with more style or integrity, and vice versa with the poorer men. Even Benn acknowledged that I was the better fighter on the night, although he said weight loss problems had not helped him. Ambrose Mendy later told John Regan that he felt it was Benn's best fight ever.

That fight was a landmark for my career – Benn was a man who the country felt would beat me, yet he had not even finished the fight. I did not go to the after-fight party, I just wanted to get home to see Karron and talk about the marriage proposal. The next day I spoke to the media in Brighton and explained how Benn had broken my body, but could never have beaten my mind. At one point Ronnie had to help me out of bed and put me in the bath. For a week after that fight, I was urinating and excreting blood. At one point, there was some concern for my welfare but I slowly started to recover. Normally, I would be back in the gym training within two days of a fight, but this time my body had to be rested for two weeks. The tongue injury was agony, I couldn't eat easily, I couldn't drink anything hot. That took seven weeks to fully heal. Ronnie was typically scathing, offering me bags of salt and vinegar crisps after the press conference!

Of course, being world champion is a magnificent feeling. In the weeks after the victory, people would come up to me in the street and congratulate me, which was rewarding. Many of them said, 'We always thought you were better than Benn,' but that was never the point. You win and raise your standard of living and profile. You lose and you don't, you have to go back to the drawing board.

There are other aspects to such a victory that may not be so apparent. I had lived a life of personal isolation for many years and lifting the championship belt honoured that path. However, in many ways, it only served to reinforce or exaggerate my solitude. Sure, the media attention was intensified, the fan mail swamped me; prestigious invites and requests filled sacks of mail every morning. People in the street shouted my name; it seemed everybody knew me. To outsiders, it might appear I was in the middle of a social whirl.

In fact, success only exaggerates your loneliness. No one was running with me at 5am along the beach front. No one was with me doubled up in pain from a torrent of sparring. No one was sitting with me speaking to the twentieth interviewer that day. People think world champions don't have burdens, that you are some superhuman. Plus, you are no longer the underdog, you are the champion. Immediately, you have your first defence – will he lose? If he does, then maybe he was a fraud all along? I could not have that being said, so the training, that homage to solitude, intensified. The road work became even harder, the need for abstinence was even more absolute, my loneliness was compounded. To succeed in boxing, you have to be alone.

If you are doing the extraordinary, then you are out on a limb, people watch you put your dreams in front of the crowd, risking ridicule and failure. Some people want you to keep winning and keep the dream alive; others crave your demise. Of course, there were those who disliked me before the Benn fight who really disliked me after! People distance themselves from you, but perceive that detachment as of your own making. They say, 'Who is this guy? He is not like me. I have no empathy with him. He lives in a big house, he is always well-dressed, he goes to the right parties, this is no ordinary man. He can't be like me.' As Friedrich Nietzsche says, 'The higher we soar, the smaller we appear to those who cannot fly.' That can be a very lonely existence. Being famous is lonely.

*

I had started opening my training sessions up to the public to raise money for charity but also to get across to anyone who was willing to listen, that I was not arrogant. The charge was a nominal fee. Once I had flung open the doors, floods of people came in and I just poured out all this philosophy and advice. Ronnie used to complain, saying, 'You're talking more than you train, kid.' However, I explained to him that I had refined and streamlined the art so well, that to speak to these people *was* training. As I place so much emphasis on the philosophy behind boxing, a man's integrity and frame of mind, by passing my views about life over to people, I felt like I was honing my own approach. I was training philosophically.

Don't get me wrong, you are not going to get in the prime physical condition needed for a world title fight by talking. You have to train relentlessly. Plus, until you have studied the philosophy yourself, learnt the skills flawlessly and perfected the entire package through years of repetition and practice, then you should not be spending energy advising others. However, certain parts of my fighting mechanisms were so well oiled that by offering such advice, I inspired myself and in so doing I became more vibrant and positive. In the face of the brutality of a bout, that could only be a good thing. Ronnie never understood that and neither did anyone else.

So what advice did I offer? All sorts, everything. I would present analogies with the practical art of boxing. So, for example, I would espouse the beauty of the right upper cut to the body. As in life, go straight to your target. That doesn't mean there will not be obstacles in your way, there probably will be. You still go straight for the target, just disregard the obstacles, do not let them distract you. Do not lose your focus. There were so many snippets of advice about actual boxing technique or thinking that could literally be applied to almost any general part of life. Boxing is the great metaphor.

Fortunately, Karron accepted my on-screen proposal on that night of 18 November. We were married only 36 days later, on 23 December, in Brighton. Karron was four months pregnant with Sebastian and later told me she was even having morning sickness in her wedding dress! We were married at St Peter's Church, then drove across to the reception, which took up the entire ground-floor atrium of the Ramada Hotel on the seafront. We had boxing gloves on the invite and a layer of cake for each of the nine Benn rounds. Barry Hearn was Best Man and made a great speech, it was a momentous day. I was so lucky to have married this girl – remember, when I first glimpsed her in that kitchen, I had shook my head thinking she was out of this world.

We honeymooned in Barbados, but even there the intrusion of the media was hard to escape. A photographer had been following us around all week, which was fine to begin with, we said it was okay, but then he just would not stop. At one point, we were relaxing on the beach and he actually stuck the lens pretty much in our faces. I said, 'Hey, enough!' or words to that effect and pushed him away. I was arrested for assault. I was taken to a wooden hut which was the courtroom and given a small fine, although they also banned that photographer from ever entering the country again. So, was this the life of a world champion?!

My first title defence was against Dan Sherry. Although he was only ranked at No. 10 contender, I had rated him a seven as a fighter. He was unbeaten in 17 bouts, which meant he was relatively inexperienced for a title shot, but his record was strong, so I knew he would have inner strength. He was managed by Sugar Ray Leonard and had been sparring with lifers at a US prison in the build-up to the fight. Also, being trained by Pepe Correa meant he would have certain qualities I needed to be wary of.

Sherry was very respectful to me beforehand, but I knew this was only a trick. Boxing is rife with such things. He was all smiles, like the clean-cut North American hero, calling me 'Mr Eubank' and all that. That nicety was even more of an insult. Why? Because I knew he was a fighter who taunted opponents in the ring verbally and physically and would use rough house or underhand tactics to get a result. The big smile was a transparently thin façade. He said I thought too much, suggesting that perhaps I didn't know my craft as well as I thought I did. Before the fight, my view was, 'Well, Sherry, can you walk it like you talk it?'

The Brighton Centre was full for the fight, and almost as soon as the bell for the first round sounded, my predictions were proved completely correct. He quickly began taunting me verbally. That was stopped briefly when I dropped him with a hard jab in the opening round.

He got himself up and jabbed his way to safety. He was good at hitting and running. This was bad news for me because I was low on energy. In those days the weigh-in was on the day of the fight and I had come in a bit over the weight limit, so I needed to go for a run on the beach to sweat off the excess.

Sherry was a competent boxer with a good jab, but this was never going to be a classic bout. In fact, I told the media after that he was punching like 'a light weight.' At one point, Ronnie felt I was treating Sherry with too little regard. However, Sherry really started some silly antics about half-way through the bout. His verbally snide remarks increased and then he started to mimic my moves! In the seventh round, he struck one of my own poses and started to showboat.

When he started this parading, I began to get frustrated. He wasn't bringing me any kind of test, so I said to him, 'Come on, come and fight!' In the ninth round, I caught Sherry with a vicious uppercut which badly sliced his mouth. The blood was flowing fairly freely from the wound. Interestingly, at this point, the media boys who were so often against me were at the ring apron shouting, 'Chris, stay on him! Go on, Chris!' Although they made no secret of their feelings towards me, they wanted the title to stay in the UK. They misunderstood me as a human being but recognised the importance of me keeping the title. They knew my value, I was good copy.

Unfortunately, what happened next was something I deeply regretted as soon as I had done it. The next round,

Sherry was verbally abusing me, using racist terms and deriding me abhorrently (he denied this after the fight). As we got into a clinch on the ropes, I had somehow come to have my back against his stomach. At this second, Sherry kissed my neck, two or three times. I could feel his breath on me and that, combined with the racial abuse, made me lose control. I flicked my head back instinctively to move the offending kisses away. Sherry took the opportunity to over-react, making as though I had headbutted him with venom, when in fact I had hardly made contact.

The problem was, what had started off as play-acting nearly cost Sherry his life. In flailing around the ring, he swallowed enough of his own blood to cause himself to collapse (Barry later said, 'the boy deserved an Oscar'). The ringside doctor, Tony Buckland, rushed in and had to administer hasty preventative treatment. Initially, one of Sherry's eyes was not reacting to light, a sure sign of con-cussion in a fighter. He had also been choking. There was chaos in the arena while all this was going on. Fortunately, to my great relief, Sherry was back on his feet in no time and made a full recovery. However, my impulsive head jerk was to cost me dearly, in more ways than one.

I was deducted two points for what they called a head-butt, but still won the fight on a technical knock out as Sherry was not in a position to continue. The referee, Frank Santore Junior, said Sherry had not been 'fighting like a gentleman', so my own indiscretion was treated with more leniency. Although some observing members of the British Boxing Board of Control said they might have disqualified me, this fight was not under their jurisdiction so the decision was given to me.

The media reaction to this decision and the fight in general was very poor for me. Many said they felt I had lost on points, something I could not agree with. They jumped on this unsavoury conclusion to my first defence as a chance to angrily berate my character. One reporter said my 'carefully constructed image' had been badly tarnished. Still others belittled my WBO belt as 'a cardboard crown'. Let me tell you, it hadn't felt like that when I was in the ring with Nigel Benn.

The media coverage missed the point. I was wholly apologetic for my actions. I was fined £10,000 by the BBBC whose 22-man hearing, led by former police detective Leonard 'Nipper' Read, had found me guilty of bringing the business into disrepute. That figure rivalled the biggest fine to date in Britain, which was levied on Errol Christie and Mark Kaylor for a press conference punch-up. Their penalty was later reduced on appeal, but I personally had no intention of protesting (Ronnie called the fine 'disgraceful, a diabolical liberty'). The panel also issued me with a reprimand about my future conduct. The thing to note is this: yes, I had acted impulsively and in so doing broken the rules and regulations of the business. To make matters worse, it had been watched by millions of television viewers in over 30 countries. For that error of judgement, I had to be fined. I agreed with that premise and accepted my fine without complaint. Indeed, I said, 'It was unprofessional and it won't happen again.' I could not have been more accepting. Of course, the press dwelled on the so-called headbutt and the subsequent fine, seeming to be less interested in the £5,000 I had given to Comic Relief that same week.

Around this time, Henry Cooper criticised me heavily in the press, saying I was too serious and had an attitude. I have always looked upon him as a good role model who teaches by example and is a very well-behaved man outside of the ring. When Henry Cooper criticised me, it was unfair and harsh, but each to his own, you have your views, I have mine. I will give him credit as a gentleman though.

Everyone wanted to get rid of Eubank. Gary Stretch is a great looking man, there was a lot made of this 'boxing male model' in the press, but I wasn't really interested. One of my first encounters with him was at the Benn press conference, when he had interrupted proceedings, pointed at me and said to Benn, 'Leave a piece of him for me!' He was quite personal in the lead-up to the fight, saying he did not regard me as a world champion, and his corner were similarly derogatory. I knew this was all just business. However, John Regan believed Stretch was totally psyched out by me beforehand.

He may have looked pampered, but Stretch fought with great heart. I myself had, somewhat reluctantly, gone along with Barry's big fanfare and was accompanied to the ring with Union Jack-waving girls in a gesture Barry said was for our fellows in the Gulf War. I wasn't entirely comfortable with all that razzmatazz to be honest, but I always had an eye on what would sell and this was the first of several big London bouts. Stretch came down to the ring at Olympia to the theme music from *Rocky*, which is normally so corny, but he pulled it off, it was very stirring. Nevertheless, that didn't bother me. What nearly did bother me was a big booming left hand he landed in the first seconds of the first round. I knew then I had to be on my guard. He did win some of the early rounds and even stood defiantly battling toe to toe with me, until I stopped him in the sixth. 27 and 0.

CHAPTER TEN
THE WARRIOR WITHIN

For our first encounter, Michael Watson was an eight. The lead-up to the bout was, perhaps not unusually, less than cordial. Watson said I had brought the business of boxing into the gutter, that I was working against the integrity of legends like Ali and Sugar Ray Leonard who had lifted the perception of the sport. This annoyed me very much, but I realise this was mainly due to the tabloid press goading us like fighting cocks. Watson was speaking in a colonial way to me. I felt slighted – I hadn't brought the sport into the gutter, this was about boxers getting misused and damaged. I was talking in his favour!

He also said that I was a 'phoney', but this was such a base comment it did nothing to rile me whatsoever. It was not offensive, it was just wrong. All I wanted to do after that was disprove my opponent. I had already shown I wasn't a phoney in the Benn fight and many others, but it was still for Watson, who was the Commonwealth champion, to recognise. After all, certain facts about both of us were indisputable – not least that we were the only two fighters to have beaten Nigel Benn. Watson was considered by many to be technically a very talented fighter and his sixth-round defeat of Benn in 1989 (despite being the underdog) was regarded as a definitive example of his calibre.

Watson said I had a good chin, but was 'much too brave for my own good'. The anti-Eubank media circus was in full flow for this fight against a man who was the newest People's Champion. One headline called me, 'Britain's Most Disliked World Champion Ever'. The boxing fraternity was still not giving me the credit I deserved. They knew I was good, but the people who have the power, namely the media, wouldn't give me any plaudits.

In many ways, I was not in prime condition for what was to be a £1 million showdown. I had a bruised sternum from a left hook I took off my sparring partner and former opponent, Simon Collins. I also had a cricked neck which restricted how much quality sleep I could get in the week before the fight. Most difficult of all, however, was that when Ronnie weighed me on the Tuesday before the fight, I was well over a stone above the weight limit. I had until Saturday to lose all that excess – in the event I lost 19lb in four days. That was through total abstinence of food and water and full, exhausting training at the same time. There is nothing harder than to train when you have nothing in your stomach – you retch, you feel faint, you are stretching yourself to the limit. When you dry out to that extreme, it is difficult even to blink, your eyes are so dehydrated. I had to periodically plunge my head into a sink of water to soothe the dryness. Four days without food or water makes you retch at your own breath. I used to even have the complementary fruit bowls removed from my hotel rooms, because just the smell of an apple or orange was torture. The evening before the fight, John Regan was with me in my room at The Coachhouse and I wanted to get a bag off the floor. I couldn't face picking it up, so I asked John to help me. Then I stood up and blacked out. I found out afterwards that this really scared John, that he went home and told his wife, Sylvia, 'Chris can't even pick up an empty carrier bag. Our lad's in trouble.' He couldn't sleep that night.

However, as I have said, it was training first, health second. Deal with the pain now, worry about your health another time. I needed to win here. I do not claim this was ideal – it was a method of preparing for a weigh-in that had worked for my 27 previous fights, but not this one. Even with intensive physiotherapy, the weight problems stopped me sparring four days before the fight, which was not my usual deadline either. There was always so much speculation about my weight. This time, there were also rumours that Watson had not reached the 11st 6lb weight limit too easily either.

I went into this fight in front of 11,000 people at Earls Court knowing that, once again, pretty much all of them were against me. I strutted up and did my usual vault, brimming with energy. John was in the front row, shaking his head, remembering how exhausted I had been the night before when I asked him to pick up that empty plastic bag. I wasn't worried. My exhaustion only ever set in after a fight, never before.

When Watson entered the ring, he was warned immediately for shadow boxing in my corner. None of this fazed me. Some observers had incorrectly stated that Watson would be too skilled for me, even making 'The Force', as he was called, the pre-fight favourite.

I stayed motionless for five seconds after the bell. Why? I don't know. Watson came as if to move forward and stopped, startled, unsure of what I was doing. The first six rounds were a breeze, all easy, beautiful. I won them unquestionably. He took some hard punishment in the fifth round, at the end of which he poked his tongue out at me. This was just ring antics; it didn't affect me at all. I never watched what my opponent was doing, I had to get them to think about what I was doing. Once I had them thinking about what I was doing, I had them beat. After the first six rounds, I'd done enough. I fought on the retreat, hitting and moving, something which large sections of the crowd did not like. However, I have always said I am in here to win the fight, to score more points than my opponent, and Watson was not a man to be trifled with.

At the end of the twelfth round, Watson actually jumped in the air in anticipation of triumph. However, if he had been given the decision, it would have been wrong. Two judges scored in favour of me and one gave a draw, so the decision was mine. Many people felt he had won the fight. I didn't agree with that and watching that fight now, you cannot give him the title. He did not do enough to take that belt from me. I was running on empty by the tenth round, but still he did not do enough. It was the right result but there was uproar. Watson's legion of vocal Arsenal fans were booing, in parts it seemed there was a near-riot. 'Scandal! He's been robbed!' they all shouted. 'Rematch!'

My immediate concern, however, was getting back to my dressing room in one piece. The tabloids reported that I had been harangued by an angry hate-mob and only narrowly escaped severe injury. This was not exaggerated, and it is true that for a few moments, with the coins, spit and verbal abuse flying, it was a little hair-raising. Nonetheless, I had again defended my crown. It was still a very bad time because I was regarded as the villian of villians.

No one wanted the anti-hero to win but I did. Ideally, I would have liked some rest, after all, this was my fourth title bout in only eight months. It was perhaps inevitable that a rematch was arranged as my very next fight, only three months later. In the press conferences and publicity for this second match, Watson took several angry verbal swipes at me. He said he was going to beat me and send me to the public. Where does something like that come from unless you have malice in your heart? Why say something like that? I suspect in private that Michael Watson knew I wasn't a phoney, he was only trying to get under my skin. Not a chance. I actually turned it around and said at one point that, unless he stopped insulting me, I would only fight him if I was ordered to (prompting Barry Hearn, when questioned about the forthcoming chance of a 'ring battle', to only half-heartedly say, 'It was a battle just to get the contracts signed'). I also said, 'I have a fabulous wife, two gorgeous kids, a big house with no mortgage and the world title. Do you still think I am a pretender?'

His comments were just uncalled for. The pre-fight atmosphere was one of strong mutual dislike and I actually stormed out of one press conference after first calling him 'a whinging child.' He seemed to moan about everything, even making fun of my habit for wearing sunglasses in a darkened room. We both made comments about each other that the BBBC frowned upon, although the media highlighted my statement that this was a 'kill or be killed' situation. I obviously had no such intent, it is just a boxing term describing the fierce competitive nature of the business. I also said Watson was, 'so low he could wear a top hat and still crawl under a snake,' which was just meant as a colourful jibe. Ironically, after six vitriolic weeks of bitter recriminations between us, the last press conference before the fight was remarkably subdued, even polite.

The fight was at the home of Tottenham Hotspur, White Hart Lane. The atmosphere was at fever pitch – hyped and mad. Watson came into the arena to the LL Cool J track, 'I'm Gonna Knock You Out', which didn't faze me, it just made me feel disrespected even more. As I was walking to the ring, a man in the crowd stopped my guards, looked me in the eye, and snarled a stream of obscenities at me before spitting in my face. I just recall thinking, *If this was in the street and I was a lesser man, I'd rip you apart.* The hatred vented towards me was quite shocking. I don't know if that could be attributed to Watson's strong Arsenal following, but the football hooligan element was very prevalent and threatening that night. I found out later that there were scores of plain-clothed police officers mingling with the crowd, looking for the known trouble-makers.

This second Watson fight was at the new weight of Super-Middleweight, a title which had been vacated by Thomas Hearns. The fight should have been made at 12st, but it was made at 11st 10, Watson's weight. I was actually lighter, weighing in at 11st 8. I don't know why this happened; the decision was made behind closed doors, but I didn't think to raise the issue with Barry at the time because I trusted him. It was also a matter of pride; I wanted to prove to everyone that I could fight and beat him at any weight.

Most bookies had us at even odds beforehand, but boxing insiders felt the weight would work to my advantage, not least by me not having to sap all my energy out for the weigh-in. Some people felt there should have been a longer gap before the rematch, and some felt Watson, after tough fights with Mike McCallum and myself, might have benefited from more rest.

However, from the first second of the opening round, Watson's pace was manical. To this day, the boxing fraternity says he kept up a pace of a lightweight, not a super-middleweight. Some even suggested that this is what cost Watson so dearly. He just did not stop. I hit him with everything, very hard shots, yet with every punch I landed he just kept on coming forward, hitting me hard, pressing forward, relentless, constant. I have never been beaten up as much as in that fight. I got absolutely battered.

By round four, I was in survival mode, even more so after he opened up a gash over my left eye. By round six, I was severely vulnerable, I was taking such a beating. At the end of that round, I slumped on my stool and said to Ronnie, 'He is so strong.' He was easily a 10+ on my scale. From then, I felt I knew he was unbeatable. The object was now just to stay on my feet. Subconsciously, I knew I could not win that fight from round six. People say to me, 'So why did you stay in the fight?' There is a very simple but extremely important answer: to take my beating. I was intent on taking my punishment, and from the sixth round to the eleventh round, I did. Why? Because that is the integrity of a fighter.

Deciding that I couldn't win the fight was a grim mistake to make however. I was getting pummelled, but to admit I couldn't win was a damaging error. I must advise every young boxer out there never, ever to make the same blunder. The reason for this is that as soon as you decide such a thing, the adrenaline in your body stops pumping, and suddenly the pain of the punches is no longer masked. That is why his shots were so painful, they hurt severely, excruciatingly. Even if you can't win, never give up or the pain will no longer be held at bay.

During the ninth round, I was taking a lot of punishment, multiple, hard combinations, it was so painful, especially these big right hands over the top. However, I would not quit, despite the continued barrage. I even managed to make him bleed from the nose. I remember thinking of Watson as a flame. I somehow pictured a candle in my mind's eye. I remember thinking, *If you so much as flicker, I will do my best to finish you.*

Crucially, he was now humiliating me. When you beat a man, just beat him, pick him off, move around, he will still come after you but he won't have enough venom to make any difference. If you humiliate him, then you effectively inject venom into his subconscious. Watson battered me into a sense of vindictiveness – he was beating me up with malice. It might not have looked like that on the TV, it might even have looked like I was holding my own, but I was being beaten dreadfully.

By round eleven, I was physically annihilated. In the final minute of the round, I threw everything into this last assault during which I spent the very last of my energy. I was flailing these punches at Watson, but by this point the exhaustion was so all-encompassing that there was absolutely nothing in them. He backed off onto the ropes, which slackened, and then he moved to the side, prompting me to fall onto the ropes myself, face first. I did not even have the strength to push myself back up off the ropes. Imagine if you can only do 50 press-ups, then imagine having to do 100 and then one more – that last press-up was how I felt.

Jim Watt was commentating and he made reference to this, saying, 'You can't fault Eubank's desire, but he seems to have used up a lot of effort.' Still Watson's pace never swayed, he just kept on coming. Watt said, 'He must be really demoralised, Eubank's given his best work . . .' at which point Reg Gutteridge came in and said, 'Here it is, can he have him over?' The end seemed to be near.

At that exact moment, my thought was this: I still wanted to do everything in my power to stay on my feet, to take the beating. If there was no power in my body, then I had to draw off every last ounce of what was left in my mind to stay standing. It was torturous. In such a state, I was barely able to punch. Yet, Watson, eleven rounds in, just kept coming in with blistering clusters of four- and five-punch combinations. Reg Gutteridge said, 'Eubank has so much courage,' and as he did so, Watson just stepped back from his onslaught, paused, then came in again with one last club. At that point, my senses had been impaired. Ordinarily that club would not have floored me, but before that, two right hooks had scored and concussed me, knocking my nervous system out. My body's muscle control had essentially gone when that club punch hit me on the back of the neck, so despite the gargantuan efforts of every exhausted sinew in my frame, I slumped down on my right knee.

I believe I know what knock-outs must be like, even though I've never been spark out. I have sensed this feeling, it is almost like those white lights and stars you see in cartoons. At that precise moment in time, I would not have had the strength to pick up a feather. Watson's punches had somehow stayed and rattled around in my head, which concussed me and fuelled the bright light.

People talk about the qualities needed to make a great fighter. There are many, but one of the essentials is constitution. That micro-second before my knee hit the canvas I was a spent force, battered, agonised and wrecked. Yet, the exact instant in time that my knee touched the canvas, I had recovered completely. It was almost as though a colossal pulse of negative energy, collected from this hideous beating I had taken, had immediately discharged itself. It felt like the canvas had earthed all the hurt.

When they have been knocked down, fighters are told to look to their corner if they are in trouble. The corner will gesture towards you to run and cover up, circle, dodge, evade, because they know the opponent is coming in for the finish.

I did not look to my corner. I knew my body had come back to me instantly. I stood up straight, breathed in and looked around the stadium. I sensed the crowd of 25,000 hovering for my demise. Their hysteria was tangible, 'Get rid of this man!' I could only really see the first few rows, but it felt like the whole stadium was salivating for my blood. Bear in mind, the only people in the arena who weren't baying for my dereliction were my immediate circle, perhaps about 50 people.

I spat and a globule of milky white phlegm hit the canvas – that morning at the Café Royal I had craved milk and had drunk four pints in one sitting. I am told that referee Roy Francis was so shocked by me going down, he forgot to give me an eight-count. He said afterwards that he was so surprised I had been knocked to the floor, because I was viewed as invincible.

I moved forward and threw just one shot, which had in it frustration, exhaustion, resolve and instinct. Watson's guard throughout the fight had been ready for one of my big right hands over the top, but in shielding against that, he left a three-inch gap between his fists and forearms that this near-perfect uppercut penetrated (some people said he was 'careless' – his defence was also near-perfect). His legs went backwards and the force lifted him off the ground. He got up and the bell rang for the end of the eleventh. I think the referee was about to stop the fight when the bell went. He was clearly dazed and his corner men had to pull him back to his stool. There was pandemonium in the auditorium mixed with silence and disbelief.

Watson had won eight of 11 rounds, all he had to do was stay on his feet to win the fight. With the twelfth round about to begin, I knew I had to knock him out to win, but he seemed too strong. *Would he recover?* I got up for the last three minutes not knowing if Watson would be able to carry on. We both stood up and the referee stood between us, but Watson wasn't coming to touch gloves, so I walked forward. As I moved towards him, the referee, Roy Francis, called out to Watson who muttered something and I read his lips. 'Just one minute . . .' *No, you get no minutes, this is my time now*, I said to myself. I fired off a flash of punches, very fast, and at one point I caught him flush. His rear leg wasn't moving, I wasn't sure, but I sensed he was in trouble. At this stage, even though you're in the final round, if you hit someone between 12 and 17 times unanswered and he's just covering up, the ref has a duty to stop the fight. We were only 29 seconds into the final round when Watson was stopped from continuing. Reg Gutteridge said in a tone of disbelief, 'Eubank has brought it out from nowhere!'

In the ring after the fight, Gary Newbon interviewed me and I said, 'I want him tested'. At that point, there was some kind of commotion in the ring but Newbon picked up on my words and said, 'What was that you were saying about drugs?' I said 'No!' but that was perceived by Watson's camp as defamatory (I had to settle out of court). I am not the type of person to accuse someone of taking drugs. If Watson had just been eating bananas, I would have wanted to know what was in his blood – he simply wasn't the same man as in the first fight. I never thought he was on drugs, not for one second. I just wanted to know where did his strength and drive come from?

Watson had to be stretchered out of the ring, but they couldn't get him out quick enough because it was pandemonium in the arena. I could see all my friends trying to get to me, other people were fighting and kicking ringside, security men were trying to keep people out of the ring. Utter chaos. At one point I thought the people trying to come into the ring were after me, but I later realised it was just acquaintances who wanted to congratulate me. That said, I did feel in danger, and on the tapes of the fight you can see I'm thinking: *Let's get the hell out of here*. Worse still, I was near to tears and dangerously exhausted, so much so that Ronnie had to help me get dressed. I borrowed a jacket of my cousin's to disguise myself, before heading back to the dressing room. Ronnie later said that in the ring, when he saw my severe fatigue, he was frightened for me.

In the light of the damage he suffered, some people have suggested Michael Watson should not have gone out for that last round. But if the ref had stopped the bout at the end of the eleventh which he should have, I was sure I would have been lynched and those in the crowd who were against me would have said, 'fix', especially in light of what was said after our first encounter – it felt like the British public didn't like me and the boxing fraternity liked me less. More appropriately, if there had been a clear path they would have got Watson out of the arena much more quickly. Then when he was clear of the crowds, they took him to the wrong hospital (since that fight, regulations stipulate there has to be a neurological hospital within ten minutes of the arena). By the time they got him where he needed to be, there was a blood clot on his brain and essentially the damage was done.

So the precise moment that the crowd thought I was finished, I was actually just beginning. This is what I call 'the killing time' (purely a term in boxing, nothing sinister is meant by my choice of words). When my right knee hit the floor, the killing time had been created, the finish of the fight was near. Whoever then had the conviction to go forward, without hesitation, would win. Watson created that moment, I took advantage of it. When the killing time arrives, either fighter can seize the moment. Watson could certainly have taken it, because I had absolutely nothing left in me but for that one punch. He created the moment for that punch. He had awakened the warrior within me, and that so rarely happens, only in the most extreme circumstances.

In the fight business, that degree of instinct can only be awakened in the most severe of situations, when you are already physically spent, when you have no more armoury other than your grit and resolve.

The warrior being awakened is never a conscious process. It all comes down to integrity. If you are not true within, the warrior will never be there for you. I had been comprehensively beaten in every round since the third, out-manoeuvred, out-punched, out-thought and out-fought. To stay in there and take my beating took immense integrity. When I was knocked to the floor with 30 seconds left of the penultimate round, when I knew all the judges' cards were against me, when I felt my opponent was still strong and still coming forward, why did I still get up? It was a fight I could not win – an impossible situation. I was only getting up to take yet more punishment. I wasn't thinking about winning, I was in there only to finish on my feet. Why? Because that is truth, that is integrity, that's what separates the men from the boys, the greats from the ordinary.

After the fight, journalist Harry Mullan wrote an article which said, 'Only the rarest kind of man can dig so deep into his soul . . . Eubank made the transition from strutting showman to a champion of genuine worth.' That is because I stayed the course. It was a unique fight, and you will not hear of another fight that boxing enthusiasts say ended like that. Benn 1, as desperate as it was, did not induce the warrior, there was no killing time. That fight was about unequivocal resolve. Watson 2 witnessed the killing time and that philosophy only ever happened to me once. The unparalleled circumstances opened up a conduit or channel that very, very few people know about and can tap into. Although Watson 2 was my hardest fight, both mentally and physically, it was also by far the most special fight of my career.

CHAPTER ELEVEN
GODSPEED
SHATTERED

In the dressing room after the Watson fight, I sat in the dark for a long time with John Regan. I was informed that Watson had been hurt, but it did not become apparent just how badly until the following morning. That, coupled with my total exhaustion, made me distressingly low. In the dressing room, I refused to go to hospital but could not actually stand up, so Barry insisted on putting me in a wheelchair. I was then indeed hospitalised myself, suffering from exhaustion and internal injuries. My body began to recover from the terrible beating, but unfortunately, Watson's injuries were far more severe.

After I had my treatment, I went to see him in hospital. I avoided using the front entrance, where all the cameras were waiting for the numerous celebrities with their excessively extravagant bouquets of flowers. Instead, I went at about 1.30am through the back entrance. Obviously, the media coverage had been understandably intense. Of paramount concern was Watson's health, which obviously overshadowed the fact that this had been one of the greatest contests ever seen in the history of boxing. Indeed, *The People* announced shortly after that I was their 'Boxer of the Year'. These are nice plaudits, of course, but at the time I don't think I was even aware of the accolade. This desperate situation was nothing to do with the front pages, I didn't need that kind of publicity. This was a man, a family man, in a terrible position, which I had been involved in. I went into his ward, my emotions were so mixed up. He was lying there in the bed, still in a coma, with a quarter of his skull missing. My very soul shuddered.

The extent of Michael Watson's injuries had a devastating impact on me. He was in a coma for a month and when he came out of that he needed incontinence underpants. Details like that shredded me. Other boxers had suffered very similar injuries – such as Rod Douglas – and fully recovered, but the signs did not appear good for Watson. I was very low, dejected, introspective. I didn't realise just how much it had affected me, until John Regan pointed out that I had hardly said a word for months. Mentally coming to terms with having done that to a person is not something that is easy to explain. Living with it was not good at all, a horrible experience. I was in touch with my human being and it could not have been more exposed, it was so raw.

At the risk of stating the obvious, I didn't mean to do it. This was a mother's son, there was a mother out there whose world had been turned upside down. That was very difficult for me to live with. Looking back, I see that I was probably severely traumatized. So many factors compounded my turmoil. Small things that you wouldn't think mattered. For example, Watson was one of the most handsome men I have ever seen. Now he was crippled. It was my punches that had done that. I had to live with that.

I did try to help on a practical level with Watson's predicament. I took part in an auction to raise funds, where I ended up buying most of the lots. I also sparred with Chris Pyatt to raise funds. I would like to take this opportunity to apologise to Chris. When we were sparring I hit him in the face when his hands were down. It was done in jest but in hindsight he was right, you should always treat another world champion with respect.

I noticed that although Watson was a People's Champion, there was no denying that many of those people did not come forward when he needed them most. I felt like saying, 'He was your champion. Help the man, now he is in a terrible position.' Oh, yes, they sent their condolences and commiserations, but that was not enough. They should have got together, raised some funds. It was all talk. I've seen talkers all my life. At least I did what I could to help.

I later said in a television interview, 'For anyone who is going to call this sport, go and have a look at Michael Watson. This is not sport, it is a blood business. Yes, it is brutal, yes, it is barbaric.' Surely my detractors who sniped at my 'mug's game' comments could no longer disagree with me?

Matters only got worse. I came back from a holiday and picked up the newspaper at the airport, an edition of the now defunct *Today*, and the front page quoted Watson talking about my visits to see him, with a banner headline saying, 'I never wanted him at my bedside.' I must admit, when I read that, my heart sank and I thought, 'I'm finished with him.' But that was a kneejerk reaction. One of my deepest wishes is for him to make a complete recovery.

I contemplated retiring after the second Watson fight. It was only natural, I suppose. I never wanted to be put in that position ever again. If I didn't fight, that would eliminate that possibility of it happening inside the ring. The buzz of boxing had gone. However, I didn't retire. Why? It was a simple equation, a matter of money. I couldn't quit because of money and I said this loud and clear to the press at the time. I needed to earn money for my family. My objective was still to raise my standard of living and my profile.

I was champion of the world, I had beaten fighters who no one believed I would, to many I was invincible. Prior to 1992, my will, my resolve and my conviction were so strong, I had what I called 'Godspeed'. This was a subconscious feeling that providence was on my side, a deep-rooted yet peripheral faith that things would work out for the best in both my life and my career. It was a subliminal aura I had.

When you keep on winning as much as I had, I felt it was my God-given right, no one was going to beat me. This was what got me through those early world championship fights with Benn and the fight with Logan. Of course, I knew that you had to train fanatically for each and every bout, but this was coupled with the sense that if I contested truthfully, I would be okay. One has to be willing to give his life in this sport. Another example is that sometimes, people hear me ranting and raving about something of which I am so sure, so absolutely cocksure that this is the only way. This is Godspeed.

I was heading along the A23 in my Range Rover towards Gatwick airport for a flight to Jamaica. Also in the car with me were my brothers Peter and Simon, plus a friend of mine. We were travelling within the speed limit, driving at 60 mph. At one point, I looked across to my left very briefly, but when I looked back ahead, the car just seemed to nudge itself to the right in a swerve. Obviously I reacted and tried to pull the car back straight, but in doing so the vehicle began to zigzag. The weave got wider and wider as the car began to career out of control. Instinctively, I put my foot on my brake pedal but nothing happened. The car was now out of control and I was still doing 60 mph, seemingly with no brakes.

I noticed some roadworks going on ahead by a bridge. I was swerving violently now and as we pulled level to the roadworks, the car dived off the road. The surface was coated in very slippery but light mud, so I couldn't control the direction and our speed did not decrease. There were piles of bricks arranged very neatly along these roadworks and directly behind one of the stacks was a lone workman. Even though I was desperately trying to steer the car to safety, we were badly out of control. Although it all happened so fast,

I could see this workman was looking directly at me, watching me veer towards him. He was just standing there, stock still, frozen to the spot with shock. I didn't even hit the horn. I hit the bricks absolutely in the centre of the pile, and as I did so he was looking me right in the eye. I was looking straight into his eyes too.

There was a massive thud when the car hit the pile which showered bricks everywhere. The car went into a roll and as it did, my door flew open and broke off against the ground. I was completely exposed in the door opening and not wearing a seatbelt. The force of the roll dumped me out of the vehicle which carried on rolling, leaving me behind on the ground. I watched the car, which seemed to be in very slow motion, roll once more before smashing into the bridge supports. Even then, when this awful event was unfolding, there was the possibility that my Godspeed was protecting me again. Yes, I'd had nose bleeds and cut eyes, but when a car rolls and the door opens, gently leaving you on the ground with not a scratch, you cannot but think that providence is playing its part.

However, at this point I had totally forgotten about the workman, I thought he had dived out of the way. I was just thinking *my brothers are still in the car*. It had smashed into the bridge with frightening force and I knew Peter wasn't wearing a belt either. I got up and – I know this sounds strange – I checked myself. You know that scene in the film, *Ghost*, where Patrick Swayze's character has been killed in the alleyway but his ghost doesn't realise? That was in the back of my mind. So I patted my body to see if I was okay, then ran over to the car. Simon had been wearing a seatbelt and he didn't have a scratch, so I helped him out. My friend was reasonably okay too. Although Peter had been in the back seat, the force of the crash had thrown him around the cabin and he was lodged between the headrests, with heavy bruising and a badly cut eye. We helped him out of the car and he limped to the side.

It was then the dreadful realisation hit me that the car had hit the workman. He was just lying there in the road. I ran over to him and said, 'Are you okay? Are you okay?' but he didn't move or say anything back. His eyes were just open and I could see flickers of life in them, but he wasn't moving. He was conscious but he couldn't even move his eyeballs. That shattered me, I was instantly torn to pieces. My cherished Godspeed was seemingly in tatters around me. Everything was not going to be okay. The devastation was absolute and sickening.

I ran out to the road to stop people in their cars and tried to get an ambulance. I was distraught, and as I ran around try-ing to get help, I was crying, moaning. There was a security fellow who was with me at the time and he was chasing me around the cars, saying, 'There's nothing you can do, he's gone.' I said, 'No, wait for the ambulance.' I couldn't believe his words, they were unacceptable to me, it couldn't be true.

At the scene, they breathalysed me and, obviously, it was completely uncontaminated. Remember, at this point, I was world champion and hadn't had a drink since I was a teenager. Now I've retired I may take a drink in my own company but when I was fighting I was religious about such abstinence. As I sat in the police station, my mind was raging with thoughts. The shuddering realisation came to me that I was not impregnable, I was not invincible, I could be pierced. Where was my Godspeed now?

I felt almost as if I was having an internal conversation with myself, questioning my infallibility. Suddenly, the foundations of my world view were very brittle. I could bleed, I can fall, I have fallen. The problem is that, once you start thinking this thought, it is like an insidious seed that grows relentlessly. That chink in my armour can never be closed. At that point in that police station, my Godspeed had been lost. Although it felt like it had gone forever, it hadn't, but to a degree, this accident took away some of my Godspeed permanently, and actually added to what people talked about after the Watson saga, that my finishing instinct also went with this.

I was quizzed for five hours and later investigations cleared me of any negligent wrong-doing, finding me guilty only of driving without due care and attention. Looking back, I could have completely exonerated myself at the time by not letting the police take my car. Had I kept the car in my possession I would have had it independently tested and the results would have shown brake failure. But I just didn't think of this, everything was happening too fast, it was so traumatic. Plus, there was another later incident when the brakes failed again, causing me to hit some bollards in the Kings Road, Brighton – I should have got out of the car and walked away, leaving it there.

The effects of this car crash on me were utterly devastating. The media were predictably scathing. However, their opinion was never something that was going to damage me deeply. It was my own thoughts, my own view that caused me so much pain. Many members of the public were similarly unsympathetic. Details began to emerge that compounded my despair and there was one aspect in particular I just couldn't get out of my head – the man who died had decided to stay and keep on working while his colleagues had gone for a break. His diligence had cost him his life. I found that profoundly distressing.

Initially, it was not something I could cope with. This was too heavy. I took a man's life by accident but what truly desolated me was that I took a mother's son. You see, a mother is accepting of all things when it comes to her son, 'whatever he is, he is still my son.' The father may be more objective but a mother's love is unconditional. I had taken a mother's son away. There were so many times when I wanted to approach his mother and give myself as a son, but I knew I could never do that. I just wanted to help in the way the son would have helped. I wanted so much to give, and still do, but there is no way I can approach her, it is not appropriate.

At the time, I was friendly with a middle-aged woman called Gay who had three kids, Tamara, Byron and Christabelle and all these dogs. My mother was living either in New York or Jamaica, so I found spending time with Gay very reassuring, she was a great comfort figure. No one knew that I used to visit her. I would go round to her house and just sit down, drink tea and chat. If I was in Brighton, I would be round there maybe four times a week, spending hours with her.

One particular night, about 18 months after the crash, I was driving along Western Road in Brighton, with my window down. This man was walking past and when he saw it was me, he leaned towards the open window and said, 'Murdering c**t.' In my life there have been two low points. The crash itself and that statement, those words levelled me. It was like a wrecking ball to my heart. Truly destructive. I went straight around to Gay's house but didn't tell her what had happened because I felt so low. She said to me, 'It looks like you are going to break down and burst out crying.' I said 'No,' and kept quiet all night.

When that complete stranger said those words, the effect on me was catastrophic. They were spoken with such malice, it was such a viciously unkind thing to say – this was an accident! To that man, it was probably no more derogatory than calling me a tosser or whatever, but those two words annihilated me. Said with such a swear word, it ripped me to shreds. I knew it had been an accident but I still had to live with what had happened. As I have said before, acceptance of any situation is the key, but it wasn't until maybe 1995 that I could accept this circumstance. I have heard those words since but they didn't have the same impact because I grew to be accepting of the accident, although I will never get over it.

Knowing that my whole motivation and chief desire is acceptance, you can understand how damaging this statement was. At that time, I still had this public persona where people were going along with what the media told them to think of me, that I was arrogant, gloated on all the trappings of success and all that rubbish. But no one understood that I was a human being, no one had embraced me except my wife, Ronnie and a few other very close friends. Remember, this was 1992, I had beaten Watson, I had beaten Benn, both people's champions. This increased my sense of isolation at a time when I craved acceptance.

It was an accident but I was shunned; acceptance could never have been further away. Furthermore, during that time the word 'murderer' was sprayed on the walls around my house four times. Each incident was very disturbing, it was very ugly and incredibly upsetting. That sort of abuse was calamitous for my mental well-being.

People say to me, 'What about when your father died, wasn't that a low point?' Well, of course, that was a terrible thing to happen, but I was immediately accepting of it. This is life; he was 71 years old and his heart failed. He was complaining of chest pain the night before, got up in the morning and made a cup of tea, went back to bed and died of heart complications. I am accepting of that because that is life. I couldn't be accepting of an accident. At the time I couldn't be accepting of being called those terrible things, because it was not my fault. I cried when I was 13 years old, I next cried when I was running around that dual carriageway trying to flag down cars to help me; I cried when Adonis Torres died in 1987 and also when my father died. But my father dying wasn't anything to be compared to those words that man said.

Time does heal but only if you are accepting and even then these sort of things are something you find hard to dwell on, because it is so indigestible. There are only losers in a situation like that, only hurt and remorse. I said at the time that because of what had first happened to Michael Watson and then to this workman, all my achievements in the ring were meaningless. Being involved in two such brutal tragedies stripped me of any positivity for a long, long time. Having been through that and boxed for a living, I can safely say that you don't know hardship until you've come through something as painful as that.

CHAPTER TWELVE

THIS SPARTAN LIFE

I was reasonably able to put all of these awful recent events out of my mind for the next fight, against Thulane 'Sugar Boy' Malinga in Birmingham. I had to put all my energy and concentration into training, I could not allow myself to be distracted. While I had considered retiring in the aftermath of the second Watson fight, the thought never crossed my mind after the crash, the two were totally different circumstances. One is an accident while your life is unfolding and the other is a business, there was never any comparison between the two. Boxing was my livelihood.

I trained at Brighton's Metropole Hotel and again opened up the sessions to make money for local children's charities. I wasn't scared of what might happen in the ring this time. The situation was helped by the pre-fight cordiality – I called him Mr Malinga and he was reciprocally polite. In the fight itself, I took things gingerly at first, but gradually built the momentum and dropped him in the fifth. He dragged himself back up and I didn't go on to stop him, causing sage heads ringside to murmur about my apparent apprehension. It didn't consciously feel like that.

Also, to be fair to Malinga, although I had only rated him a five, this actual Zulu showed his true willpower and launched a fierce attack towards the latter stages of the fight. I withstood the punishment and won the fight in 12 rounds on points (he later beat Benn for the WBC Super-middleweight belt). I was having plans drawn up for an extensive wall to be built around my home. When the Malinga decision was announced in my favour, I looked over to John Regan at ringside, went down on one knee and said, 'That's my wall paid for!'

Afterwards, we celebrated an excellent bout together at the post-fight party. However, although externally it seemed it was business as usual, there had indeed been a tidal wave of change in my career. Put simply, post-Watson I had lost the instinct to finish a fight. Gary Newbon found himself being criticised when he asked me if I had lost 'the killer instinct' after my fight against Watson. I felt this criticism was harsh; he was only using a phrase that is a boxing term. That said, I try not to use it because people do not seem able to see words as intended, namely 'going in for the finish, to win the fight'. (For a fighter who was criticised for not stopping opponents, it is worth noting that 24 of my 52 opponents did not last the distance.)

My goal was simply to win more points than my opponent. People always talk about two men bludgeoning each other – no! I hit you, I score a point, I don't have any malice towards you, even though it may seem that way because of the physical force used. If circumstances required a stoppage, my inner being would only want me to knock a man down for 10.0001 seconds. Then please get up and walk around and be absolutely fine. Any more than that length of time on the canvas was offensively unnecessary to me. Every man has a mother, a girlfriend, children maybe, those people would be hurting again because of me, just like Watson's family. I didn't want to put anybody in that situation. I wanted to defeat people, but never hurt them again. Ever. Mostly.

Understand this: boxing is a state of permanent social quarantine. People often ask me if the training for a fight is tough – I was always training, whether there was a fight booked or not. Training is winning. I had this approach even before I turned pro. Wanting to win isn't enough, are you willing to pay the price? There is a severe personal cost, namely obsessive training. If I train correctly and sacrifice myself, then the fight really should be easy because all I am doing in the fight is the same I do in training everyday, the only difference is, on fight night there is a decision.

Some people in the media used to insinuate I didn't train enough – absolute nonsense of course, I just chose not to make the extent of my regime particularly public, aside from the open training sessions. People within the business know the truth. Once you had a date for the bout, specific training usually began eight weeks before. From that moment, you focus not on the week of the fight, or the day, or even the hour. *Focus on the day the fight is announced.* This approach had to be paced with great delicacy: if your momentum was even one hour askew, you could get beaten. The key was this: the most important day of training is the day they announce the fight. If you do not start properly, you will not be able to catch up later.

Knowing that the fight starts on day one, the first phase would be conditioning. At this stage, you would not be sparring at all. Brighton was ideal for the early morning road work before the gym. I used to sometimes run up the very steep steps at the cliff tops which was pretty easy. Hill running, though, I didn't like at all. There is a place called Bear Road which was just the longest uphill slog you've ever seen! Usually I'd run, but sometimes cycle. Beach running sessions were also a real test. The large pebbles on Brighton Beach sucked the stamina out of your legs within 50 yards, you could almost instantly feel the lactic acid building up.

The late morning or early afternoon was gym time (often at Barry's Matchroom gym in Romford, latterly at my own gym at home). I would start by warming up, which consisted of 15 minutes of stretching, then 15 minutes of shadow boxing, but not just using my fists, using my feet and body to develop agility. Much of this would be done in front of mirrors, what I like to call the more fanciful boxing. Then, I'd do between three and six rounds (of three minutes each) on the heavy bag, moving around it, playing with it. Then three rounds on the pads – Ronnie rarely directed the pad work, I told him where I wanted him to place the pads, because I had certain shots in mind that I needed to perfect.

Box office!

Left: At a press conference with Don King in July 1993 to announce my rematch with Nigel Benn.

Below: With my long-time manager and promoter Barry Hearn – always smiling and stylish.

Above: It's not what people say at the start of your career when you are all the rage; it's not what they say during your career when you are being hailed by the critics for better or worse; it's what is said of you at the end of your career, how you are remembered, what matters.

Right: Simply The Best.

Above right: Early morning roadwork on Brighton seafront with my trainer and friend Ronnie Davies.

Right: 'Ronnie, get the fluff out of my hair...'

Far right: Having a shouting match with Benn in front of 43,000 spectators during the final round of our controversial bout at Old Trafford in 1993.

Right: English Gentlemen meets Harley-Davidson – capitalism at its best.

Above: I thoroughly enjoyed modelling Vivienne Westwood's 'Bird of Paradise' for her on the catwalk.

Right: Here I'm modelling another Westwood creation for her in Milan.

Left: Victorious in Berlin after beating Graciano Rocchigiani in his backyard. I regret not having had a Union Jack to hoist around my shoulders.

Above: Soaking up the bad feeling prior to beating challenger Henry Wharton in Manchester, December 1994.

Right: Although I beat Wharton with poetic efficiency, his heart and resolve were acutely disheartening.

Above: Nelson Mandela is an icon who I find deeply inspirational.

Left: Resilience.

Below: My 'brother' Rakardh.

Right: 'Take me to Manchester, I need to get my haircut.' Dougie Lawton cutting my hair perfectly.

Below: Training first, health second.

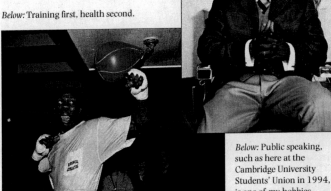

Below: Public speaking, such as here at the Cambridge University Students' Union in 1994, is one of my hobbies.

Left: I drive my original Peterbilt American truck – registration number 1K0 – to meetings, launches and even down to the shops for a pint of milk.

Above: Driving my Aston Martin was like falling in love every time you switched on the engine.

Soaking up the sun near Brighton pier.

Fighting fit.

The pads were great for target practice, accuracy and power. My need was to train for power, because I naturally had the accuracy. What I needed to achieve was landing a punch which would have a long-term effect, namely it would manifest itself three or four rounds later. If you keep on hitting someone with good shots to the body, maybe only twice a round, four rounds later it will catch up with them and break them down.

Then I would do six rounds of skipping, but without rest, I would skip straight through the four-minute clock on the wall. Then it was sit-ups. Although I cannot deny sit-ups are very important for the abdomen (compulsory in fact), I would only do 50 or 60 repetitions, twice a day. My experience taught me that there was nothing more effective than taking actual body shots. Just as I learned in New York, you would leave your body exposed and tell your sparring partner to work on it with full-blooded punches to really harden your stomach. It was not just about having hard abdominals, it was about immunity. You could do 1000 sit-ups a day, but if a fighter hits you correctly, you'd crumple. The only way to gain immunity was by taking hundreds of shots to the body.

This was where sparring came in. Throughout my career, I probably sparred more than any other fighter I know. I would start to spar about two weeks into the training schedule. The training would change slightly to half an hour of shadow boxing, between three and 12 rounds of sparring, then skipping, speedball and sit-ups. For a championship fight, I would spar usually 125 rounds. Nothing was more important than sparring. When you haven't sparred for a month or two, you go in there, the guy throws a punch and you instinctively squint. Within a week of intense sparring, he throws the same punch and you don't even blink, you stop flinching and move.

The first day of sparring was always very painful and I didn't enjoy it, because I used to take a lot of jabs on my forehead which would bruise for about two days. You can't wait for the bruising to subside – the point of the exercise was to work through that damage to develop immunity. Sparring was just fantastic when you were in the thick of it; you would come out of some real tear-ups with no bruises, no pain, at worst a slightly sore jawbone. If I took heavy punishment in sparring, then I knew I would be okay in the fight. When you are having it all your own way in sparring, then the championship fight will be in my experience a very very hard one.

I always picked my sparring partners. Depending on the fighter, I would say to Ronnie what was needed. It was a simple equation – find the closest fighter in style to the forthcoming opponent. Don't spar with a technically skilled man if you are about to fight a powerhouse. Another rule I had that was vehemently adhered to, was that my sparring sessions were an unconstrained free for all. When I first met a new sparring partner, I would always give them the same briefing, 'Protect yourself at all times and allow me no favours. Outside of the ring, I will shake hands, philosophise a little, offer you advice about this dogged business, but while we spar I will try and take you out, that is the objective.' Subsequently, about 80% of them would be sent home within three or four days, cut and bruised up. If the sparring partner was not good enough they would get a (unmerciful) beating, but if they were good then I would keep them and take the physical punishment for as long as I had to. Very intense, that was the only way I knew, that was the method Maximo showed me. 'Nothing personal, but if you're not good enough, sorry, you have to go.'

It is a well-known fact within the business that most brain injuries are an cumulative effect that often begins while sparring. The gloves in actual fights are lighter, so sparring is where you take the majority of the heavy pounding blows. It is rare that one 12-round match does the damage. I knew this, but my view was this – if you think about getting damaged by excessive sparring, you will get hurt. At the heart of my training was this single most cardinal requirement: *training first, health second*. That, for me, is the way it has to be. This is a golden rule.

Most trainers wouldn't agree, but that is what worked for me. The same theory applied to injuries. I said I never had any. Of course, I did suffer bodily damage (head, torso, knee, ankle and hand damage), but I never missed training and never cancelled a fight. That, for me, was being a temperamental fighter, whereas I was dedicated to being consistent.

I always preferred to finish sparring the day before the fight. This was a constant source of disagreement between myself and my camp, because Ronnie and Barry always worried about injuries. For me that missed the point, the goal was to constantly improve. Whatever level of fitness and immunity you had, it was not good enough. I had to get better. Very few fighters trained harder than me and that gave me confidence, or rather, a right to win. I had the right to beat you, because I ran one more mile than you, I trained one more day than you did. This was the intellect I had, the philosophy I used. This was my way of life.

That said, you do not need to train for ten hours a day to improve. Four highly productive hours is ideal. Doctor has a tenet he swears by, which is: 'Don't waste your perspiration', and this is something that I have come to comply with. There is no point doing seven sloppy rounds when three near perfect ones would be more efficient and practical. Anybody can work a sweat up.

There was always so much talk about diet and nourishment during training. I always ate whatever I wanted. When it was time to lose weight, the discipline would be there. If I could only eat vegetables, or I needed to consume more meat, then so be it. If it was no food at all for days, then that is what I would do. I needed to be reckless in order to succeed. I am not suggesting young boxers follow me, what worked for me may be poison to someone else. For me, to watch my weight for six weeks was far more painful than four days. I was an extreme character in an extreme sport. That was my view.

Abstinence was required from everything: contact with my wife, my children and the niceties of life. This is called purdah and was essential to success.

I hardly socialised at all and never during pre-fight training. Such a lifestyle was not an optional extra. Years later, I was at an Aids charity event for Blackliners, hosted by Scary Spice, Mel B. The young sprinter Darren Campbell was there with Linford Christie and I. Ten minutes after we arrived, I said to Darren, 'You shouldn't be here. I can be, Linford can too.' He said, 'Why?' and I explained. 'There are lots of attractive girls here, they smell of perfume, they have alcohol on their breath – you should go home and suffer. You want to make something of yourself? Go home and suffer. The longer the night goes on, the more uncomfortable you should feel. I have carved my name into the minds of the people, so has Linford. How much of a star are you going to be?' I don't know if he has a girlfriend or not but I said it anyway. He left about half an hour later. That shows he has potential!

On the day of the fight, I was as meticulous as during the build-up. For a start, I had to have complete harmony amongst my camp. If there were any arguments happening, I told everyone to make sure I didn't find out, or even sense it. If I did, they would be sent home. No one ever argued with me, when I gave a decision that was it, finished.

To this day, I have never watched an episode of *East-Enders*, *Coronation Street*, *Emmerdale* or any soap opera. Even when I am relaxing at home, I don't like to hear anything in the negative, it upsets my balance. I don't want the experience of seeing what goes on in these characters' lives, I've argued enough already in my life. It's no good for my balance, my wings. I'm a butterfly, I need to keep on fluttering.

If I watched TV soaps, it would clip my wings. On the day of a fight, this need for harmony was even more paramount.

Breakfast on the day would be lots of boiled eggs, toast and cornflakes. Hot water and lemon peel was my drink because caffeine raised your anxiety levels which was highly undesirable; you needed to remain calm. My temple was pure, I slept well, didn't use any substances and drank no alcohol; I didn't even think about such things.

While I was at the hotel before the fight, I would walk around, followed by all the security, and go to meet the public, sign autographs and chat. That boosted my spirits. I also always went shopping because that would lift my morale too. People used to worry about me being distracted but it was actually just the opposite, these routines kept me relaxed and buoyant. Besides, the alternative was clock watching in the hotel room and that could be stressful.

The precision of my preparation continued right up to the moment I stepped in the ring. It was not enough for the camp around me to be free of arguments. My room also had to be immaculate. By that I mean picture perfect. I did not allow anyone else to tidy up, not even the room maids. I would send everybody out and be left alone, when I would spend time making sure the quilt was devoid of even the slightest ripple, like a piece of slate. The curtains would be inch perfect, rigid as a marble pillar. I would check each drawer individually and on several occasions found some slightly opened or had dents, which meant that it was not exactly flush with the cupboard. I needed everything to be ordered; it would play on my mind if the smallest detail was incorrect. The same applied to my shorts, my laces, everything. I boxed in yellow shorts from the Malinga fight in 1992. I had fanatical routines for lacing the boots. People would lace them laboriously for me, but they never did it correctly.

The thinking behind such perfection was not superstition. If everything was in place in my hotel room, then everything was in place in my mind. I would think: *The room is done, it is correct, so everything is in a compartment and is clean and in order.* What I cannot afford is for my mind to be out of balance. If, during the entrance to the ring for a world title defence, I had realised I'd forgotten to push a drawer completely closed, I would have thought about turning around and going back to the hotel. Karron, my wife, has seen this from our first days together – even the bedsit I lived in when we first met was like a pristine show flat.

This need for order also applied to my relationships. I could not enter the arena, never mind the ring, if I had wronged somebody. On one occasion, an incident the night before a fight in Germany nearly cost me dear. There was a knock on the door and it was a fellow called Jess Harding, a heavyweight fighting for Barry Hearn. He had come all the way from England and had brought me a good luck card. The problem was, the humour between Ronnie and myself was so cutting, so hard, that outsiders sometimes found it difficult to stomach. Jess gave me this card and said, 'I've bought this from England for you from my son.' I said, 'Thanks,' and threw it in the bin. I didn't even open it.

I had intended this to be a biting joke, but Jess did not see the humour. He was devastated and tears welled up in his eyes. This was his son's card. He left the room without speaking, leaving me horrified. I ran out of the room but couldn't find him, so I spent half-an-hour scouring the hotel trying to track him down. When I did, I sat with him for two hours explaining that it was a joke and that I had meant no harm. Eventually he understood. I still have the card today.

In hindsight, this was a very good thing to happen to me the night before a fight. It made me perform better because I had upset a kind man. Otherwise, this would have plagued me. I had to right the wrong, apologise. I guess my performance that night in the ring was an apology to Jess too.

This obsession with correctness made us laugh sometimes too. Often, I would take a white towel, cut the traditional diamond out of the centre and place it over my head. The problem was, bits of fluff would catch on my splendidly trimmed hair and my head would look like it was covered in snowflakes! So, if you look closely in certain fights, after Ronnie has taken the towel off in the ring and I am in the process of giving it extra large with the pose in front of thousands of fight fans who were usally anti-Eubank, if you could read my lips I am saying, 'Ronnie, get the fluff out. Ron, have you got it all out?'

I never wore underpants, just the two cups to protect me. If I was really unlucky, when I vaulted into the ring the shorts would ride up into my crevice, for want of a better word! I'd be strutting inside the ropes, snarling at the crowd, puffing my chest out and giving it the full warrior routine, whilst secretly trying to pull the shorts out of my crevice. The difficulty was, by now I had gloves on, of course, so it was more of a nifty swipe round the buttocks, bouncing the gloves on my cheeks in the vain hope the shorts would slip down. I'd have thousands of people screaming at me, 'Look at him, strutting like a lion, who does he think he is?' when all the time I was thinking, *I wish these friggin' shorts would dislodge themselves from my arse.*

I am often asked what being in a boxing match is like. The best analogy I can suggest is that it is like chess, but speeded up to lightning-fast velocity and with physical contact. I was always very adept at reading a fight; it was almost as if I could see the bout mapped out before me. It's not that it was in slow motion, but I could observe the strategies and respond tactically in a very calculated manner.

It's all about reaction. The individual who thinks about catching a jab will get hit. You need to see the shoulders doubling to come forward then . . . *bang*! You catch it without even thinking. By the time you see it coming, it has hit you. It is a blend of instinct and training, a product of years of repetition and conditioning.

There is also an X-factor to boxing and that is the heart. Either you're born with it or you're not. I was. You see young boxers, analyse them, admire their fast moves, hand speed, foot movements and artistic edge, but there is one thing you can't see and that is the heart. That is only ever shown in the heat of the moment when it really gets tough.

It comes down to who is the hardest man, which is a combination of so many factors.

As an aside, my courage can be a strange thing. If it is myself on the line, I am a lion, I will never give up; there will be no surrender. However, if there is someone else on the line, I get scared for them. I once went to see Herbie Hide fight for the world championship. I liked Herbie because he had a certain naivety about him that, in a world of so much cynicism, was refreshing. We were only acquaintances. I had a ringside seat and took my place just before the fighters were due to enter the arena. I sat there waiting and became aware that the two women either side of me were staring at me with a puzzled look on their faces. I looked at my hands and they were shaking violently. It was only then that I noticed my body was pulsating, my heart was racing and I was in a cold sweat. Herbie was only an acquaintance, but I was worried sick for him, not because he was out of his league, but because I was very sensitive and fearful for the situation, for the unknown. That is the type of personality I have.

The attention to detail even continued after the fight when the job was done. Before the bout, I watched every tape available on the opponent – after all, this was a business plan. Afterwards, I would watch the fight in its entirety many times. Then I would watch it again this time just looking at my own moves. Then again for the opponent, the ref, the judges and even the crowd. I had to memorise everyone's reactions, contemplate every punch and every facial contortion of every person in the front rows. Perfectionism was the only way. The objective was to raise the fans in the positive or the negative, but I would try and get a reaction in the future.

CHAPTER THIRTEEN
THE SHOWMAN

I was world champion with five defences to my name and, of course, a substantial wealth starting to accumulate. I have always enjoyed the finer things in life and also find myself enthralled by exciting or interesting situations. So around this time, much started to be made of my supposed eccentricity. People began to say I was an oddball, but I have never agreed with this. Yes, I am a showman, but the episodes and items which seem to earn me this eccentric tag are just me having fun.

For example, in the spring of 1992 I was in Manchester for my next fight against John Jarvis, and I needed a haircut. So I went to this barber's shop owned by a fellow from Barbados. I said, 'Here's £20 to cut my hair the way I want you to cut it. I will give you another £20 when you've finished.' This barber said to me, 'Now listen, you are in my shop, this is my chair, I'm the boss here. I will cut your hair, I am a professional. You keep quiet and you will like what I do.' So I took the £20 back and said, 'Thank you very much. Are there any more barber shops around here?'

I was told there was another shop called Dougie's around the corner. I got Dougie's number from Directory Enquiries and called him up. This grumpy, old voice answered the phone. I said, 'Do you cut black hair?' and he said, 'We cut all types of hair here.' I said, 'Yes, but do you cut African hair? Do you have West Indian barbers there?' and he repeated the same answer, 'We cut all types of hair.' I asked him the same question again, he gave the same answer then put the phone down.

So I drove around in the Rolls Royce and stopped outside the shop, where I saw who I now know to be Dougie Lawton. He looked at me with an eyebrow raised in curiosity. I introduced myself, although he knew who I was, and asked why he spoke to me like that on the phone in a very heavy Jamaican-Mancunion accent before hanging up. He said, 'I have to say that because there is a lot of racism around here and I don't want a brick through my window. I didn't know who was asking the question.'

Dougie cut my hair perfectly, exactly the way I wanted. Ever since then I have been using him constantly and have never once had to tell him how to cut my hair again. He has been to many places with me; he still lives in Manchester so the airlines are the people who benefit the most, as it costs £200 most weeks to fly him to Gatwick, then drive him down to Brighton. Who else can I use? In 1993, he won 'Best Barber Of The Year' award, an astonishing accolade when you think how many Caucasians live in the UK compared to Africans and Jamaicans. That is very special so, of course, I still fly him down. People say that is over the top but women spend that kind of money on make-up, massages, hair, beauty treatments. I am an individual and my one hair cut a week isn't over the top.

I am a perfectionist and being in the public eye I have a responsibility to look good, correct and appropriate. My hair shouldn't be messed up, it should be well trimmed. Entertainment isn't just about talking, it is also the way you conduct yourself, the way you dress, the whole package. You've got to try and look brand new all the time. This is not a matter of being eccentric, it is just me being a total professional. One of the reasons I am where I am today is that all this rhetoric actually adds to my entertainment value. Don't look at this as a flaw in my character, if anything it is a positive, a good trait that I would like to pass on to other people. My cup is always half full, not half empty. My father told me as a boy, 'Always have a shirt and tie on and always be clean.' This is a very public way of doing just that, always making myself presentable. I think I should always be tip top, it is not done to show off, it's just what a showman does naturally.

My passion for presentation extends to all aspects of my look. I have a collection of very fine boots – at one point, I had an ex-Army man come in and bullshine them for £5 a time. Now I have fewer pairs of boots I do it myself, but I still polish any footwear I am wearing two or three times a day, because they pick up dust.

Of course, this all takes a lot of time, effort and money. The English gentleman look is a fine example. That started when I did a photoshoot for *Esquire* in May 1992, before then it was just smart suits. I was wearing my own trousers that looked like jodhpurs but actually weren't, so they worked with that and gave me a pair of riding boots as well. I really liked the look, so I got the proper jodhpurs, the English cut jacket with accentuated shoulders, tapered-in waist, big half-Windsor tie knot, the correct shirt, full cut-away collar. This progressed to the canes (of which I have several exquisite antique examples) and the monocle. If you understand tailoring, you will know they are all hand-sewn at Kilgour, French and Stanbury; this is not clothing you can buy off the peg. I tell them how to make my clothes. I know exactly how I want them. At first, it was trial and error, I didn't just fall into this, but now I've got it just right.

No matter how fine the clothes that you can afford look, no amount of money can buy you style. It is a matter of conditioning. I have been voted 'Best Dressed Man' on two occasions, in 1991 and 1993, by the Menswear Association of Britain. In 1993 and 1995 I was also voted 'Best Dressed Sportsman' by the *Daily Express* twice and have won a 'Tie Wearer of the Year' and 'Gold Tie Pin Award' from the Tie Wearers' Guild of Great Britain. True, I was also voted the fourteenth 'Worst Dressed Man' but that was just a media stunt which is simply not true.

The English country gentleman's look that I like is, simply put, the finest sartorial statement there is, for me that is. There is no look as impressive. This is not my opinion, it is merely a statement of fact. You take a man who wears a two or three-piece suit made of the finest cloth in the finest colours (namely subdued beige, tans, a little bit of contrasting colour). Have the suit made by the world's finest tailor. Then stand him next to me. All I will wear is jodhpurs, a pair of paddock boots, and a jacket. He will look good, but I will look good and charismatic as well. Charisma always stands out.

One thing I cannot agree with is that it is an unusual look. On the contrary, it is almost universally known. You may not see it too often, so it would be better to say it is not common, but this is a sophisticated style that has been known for many years. Maybe people think it looks unusual on me because I am black? The simple fact is, whatever age group or colour wears this look, it will always look very good and never go out of fashion. On this subject, my opinions happen to be factual.

You have to have courage to dress like that. Even those who do not give the credit that such magnificent attire deserves, have to acknowledge the bottle it takes to be such an individual. I was talking to Bob Geldof once at his house in Chelsea and I was saying how I know I am an African. He said to me, 'You're not an African.' I said, 'Okay, then I am a Jamaican,' and he said, 'No, no, no. There is no one more English than you.'

I am aware that such formal dress code can alienate people, or rather, I notice that when I am more casually dressed, people seem slightly more comfortable around me, they are more receptive. That is a simple example of how appearances can fool you – of course, I am no different whatever I am wearing. I am just a human being. Don't look at my dress code, this is just for show. Listen to my words and you will find out who I am. I have been in the public eye for a long time now, speaking the same way. Sometimes the gentleman's look gets people's attention and that is what I want – give me your attention for 15 seconds and then I've got you for an hour and a half. It is not the clothes that maketh the man, it is the mind. In time, they will see my look is just fashion. It may be unfashionable to some, but for them there is little hope.

Aside from the English gentleman's look, I like to have what is referred to as the 'in' and the 'not-so-in'. Brand snobbery? I'd rather not look at it like that, that is negative. I am not a brand snob, I am a brand stylist. That is probably a remnant of my days on the streets in south London where things such as designer labels carry great importance. You are always striving for the item that is 'in', regardless of cost. It has to be the right one.

My original American Peterbilt truck is one of my most well-known possessions. I wanted an awesome looking vehicle and was looking for over a year, but all the English trucks were flat-nosed and not outstanding enough. I wanted something Tonka Toyish, if you will. I went to Florida on holiday and on the off-chance visited a place called Palm Trucks. On the forecourt was this stunning truck and that was the one for me. The truck itself reminds me of the art deco period; there was nothing stylish about the trailer that was standard with the Peterbilt, so I didn't buy that. My truck is big, 12 feet high, 32 feet long, with ten wheels and 13 gears. The number plate is 1 KO, which I bought by purchasing the Rolls Royce it was on, just to get hold of the plate. I never even saw the Rolls, someone bought it for me, switched the registration, then sold the Rolls on.

Up until now, I'd only had a licence for automatic cars, so first I had to take my manual test in a Mini Metro. You obviously need an HGV licence to drive this size of truck. I failed my test three times and passed on the fourth attempt for a HGV rigid licence. I wanted to take the harder test just to get the certificate, although I have no intention of carrying a trailer which that level of certificate allows.

At 6am on the morning I took delivery of the truck, I called John Regan up and we drove up to the countryside above Brighton to test her out. There were no cars on the road and I was having some difficulty getting the clutch right. Consequently, I was weaving a little across the lane when suddenly I heard police sirens blaring! The officers who'd noticed this colossal vehicle driving gingerly along the road, pulled me over and were somewhat astonished to see who it was! After I had explained, they let me carry on. John said I shouldn't take it anywhere too congested until I had got used to driving it a little more. The next morning I went in to Brighton, down The Lanes.

If you think about it, you can hardly ever park the truck legally. I am willing to accept the parking tickets, but I don't like it when they clamp it, which has happened twice. Only Westminster Council seem to have clamps that fit the huge wheels, so when I park anywhere else, I am safe in the knowledge that the worst I will come back to is the flutter of tickets. If I get £100-worth of tickets each time I go out, it is worth every penny, because the truck lifts people, it inspires them. I always think, 'If I can make people feel how I did when I first saw it, then I'm doing what I do best.'

When I go to the grocery store for some milk, I often go in the truck. I pull up outside Cullens, hit the airbrakes, *whooosh*!! People literally stop in the street and stare! It's great fun, a good buzz. It never ceases to raise me and sometimes I sit down in the garage in awe of it. For the record, it is the best buy I've ever made.

Over the years, much has been made of my spending habits and material possessions. What these things cost is not relevant, I choose to stay away from the cost of things when I talk about them in public. The point is this: use your money, however much that may be, to enjoy it. As a child, I disliked Father Christmas immensely – he never came to our house. When I was very young, I didn't really understand. I was just confused, then as I grew up a little, I wondered why he discriminated against our family. Was it because we were black? Or was it because we lived on a council estate and were poor? Whatever his reason, I just knew he discriminated against us, so I always had a grudge against Father Christmas.

I don't mind him now. In fact, I think he's a very nice guy because he visits our house every year without fail. The only difference is this – my children know that Father Christmas may wear a red hat and red gown, but his nose is very broad, he's got a gap between his teeth and he looks exactly like me! I never had any presents, birthday or Christmas. The only gifts I ever received were a fire engine and trumpet toy from St Mark's Church in Dalston. So as an adult I am only having what I didn't have back then.

Take the Harley. That is a throwback for me to the Red Indian. It is a basic bike, with no leather saddle and excessive lights. People who are really into the Harley way of life might say the flames on the petrol tank are too fat, too cool, but that's me, 1340 cubic inches of Harley. I wanted that throwback, but with modern day quality, the fatboy.

Of course, the truck and my other vehicles all suit my showmanship perfectly. It is not about showing off, being flash, it is about being a showman. This level of showmanship is not easy. You need courage to get out of that truck in the middle of Oxford Street. At the heart of all this showmanship is my need for acceptance, not eccentricity. Some people are taught that if you keep quiet you are accepted. I learned that to get noticed you had to be a showman.

The relentless defence of my title continued with the aforementioned John Jarvis fight. For this, I was in fine posturing form, giving the spectators the 'full monty'. I was in fine form and knocked him out in the third round. I was pleased, not least because it meant I could go back home to Karron.

On 27 June 1992, I travelled to the resort of Quinta Do Lago in Portugal to fight the American tactician, Ron Essett, in an open-air bout. We stayed at the ultra-luxurious Quinto Do Lago Country Club for my training. The night of the fight was hot and very tiring, so the 12-round unanimous points win for me was extremely demanding. There was a near mishap when they realised they hadn't called me correctly – Essett was in the ring and I was still on my way to the arena.

Back in Hove, we had just moved into a large house which we had bought the previous winter but spent months renovating. Eighteen months later, we bought the house next door and joined the two gardens, so we now have a one and a half acre residence. One house is used as my office (during my career it contained my gymnasium), the other house is my private residence and there is space for the children to play.

A fight is always a mental battle before the actual bout. One of the most unsettling pre-fight situations I have ever come across was when I fought Tony Thornton in Glasgow. He was a good American fighter, with a sound pedigree, strong chin, big punch and had been in there with some top names – many insiders likened him to Marvin Hagler. He was given a seven by me beforehand. However, what really bugged me and had me flustered and unsettled for some weeks beforehand was this fact: he was a postman. Benn's ferocity and venom I could accept. Watson's derogatory remarks I could live with . . . but this was a postman. This was singularly the most annoying mental obstacle for me to overcome in my entire career. Why? Because he was still a postman at the time, despite challenging me for the world title. He was going to be persistent, methodical, relentless. His job demanded he behave in this manner. This thought really stayed in my head and upset my equilibrium for a long time because persistence like that can break your spirit.

Whatever unsettles you as a boxer, unless you come to be accepting of it, nine times out of ten you are likely to lose the fight. As in life, you must accept your position. I was normally very good at accepting my situation, but the fact he was a postman troubled me immensely for six weeks. This hurdle proved very, very hard for me to overcome.

He exacerbated my unease when he came into town by admitting that he had suffered injury worries with one hand, before going on to say on national television, 'If the hand is going to go, it may as well break on Eubank's jaw.' I was the world champion – where's your respect? I was particularly annoyed and concerned with his attitude, so I knew then that I had a fight on my hands. When you have a fighter who respects you, you inherently have him under control, because he will respect you in the ring. What I needed was for the opponent to respect me for three minutes and I'd got him. With Thornton, I didn't get that.

People have said to me that Benn didn't respect me and I beat him. Yes, but the difference there was that Benn was being plain unreasonable and had no regard for the will of the other man. Tony Thornton on the other hand seemed to me to be a perfectly reasonable man and, unlike Benn, he wasn't totally terrifying. His deportment was considerate to his public when he was talking and he seemed very together. The whole situation really spooked me and what bugs you, can beat you. Neither Benn nor Watson spooked me because they were just great fighters. They weren't postmen.

Fortunately, I finally came into acceptance of him being a postman about a week before the fight. Once I overcame that obstacle I was okay. That said, on the night of the fight I didn't have my usual yellow shorts which I always wore, I only had a red pair. This could have unsettled me, but I practised the philosophy of putting the positive before the negative, something that is absolutely quintessential to my entire life. I told myself that there is no luck involved here, this is about technique, work, persistence, being dogged, training, expertise, the art I had been learning for years, and my resolve; this was not about the colour of my shorts. Ultimately, the hardest man wins a fight. Thornton tried to go one better and turned up in a kilt, which wasn't very well received by the Scottish locals. Boxing for me has never been about gimmicks, its about fighting ability and resolve.

In the actual fight, I used hit-and-run tactics in as much as he was all pressure, exactly what I expected (I upgraded him, though, from a seven to an eight). I used my boxing ability and skill along with side-to-side foot movement and by round ten, I had the fight won. For the last two rounds, I just stayed away from him, circled the ring, running from danger. The crowd don't like that, but as I said after that fight, 'I may have had to run for those last two rounds, but the objective is to win. The aim is not to show that I am a hard man and knock him out at the risk of my victory.' People call you names, but the idea is to win. After all, I was a fighter by trade, the hardest profession on the planet. It didn't make sense. I simply had my eye on the objective which was to win. If that meant beating him for the first ten rounds then running for two, then so be it. That's what I did with Tony Thornton and despite all my earlier reservations and concerns, I won. 33 and 0.

My next fight, in November, was against Paraguayan Juan Carlos Giménez, at Manchester's G-Mex – my fifth opponent in under ten months. Gimenez was a capable boxer with a strong 35–5–3 record. He'd had Roberto Duran off his feet in an early knockdown, so I knew I could not take him for granted. Having said that, when I got in there, he punched so lightly I was never going to get hurt. My jab was constantly in his face, one of my best ever use of that vital punch. He was probably in his twilight years and I was a strong champion, so I won the fight on points, but was again criticised for not finishing my opponent in more style. Personally, I thought that bout was most notable for my extravagant showmanship, the vault, the music, the prowling around the ropes, whipping the crowd into a frenzy. They were standing on top of their chairs, craning their necks to catch a glimpse of the fighters.

Despite my recent difficulties, my detractors kept accusing me of taking easy fights. My next opponent, Lindell Holmes (a former IBF world champion), told the UK's press he had come 'to take the title back to America.' He didn't, of course, although it took me the full 12 rounds to beat him on points. He was a mature, experienced boxer and naturally gifted.

I still had to beat the man they put in front of me; this was not the walkover they made out it was going to be. I had trained very hard again, this time opening the doors to my gym in my childhood stomping ground of Peckham, just two miles from the Dulwich hospital where I was born.

Less than three months later, I took on Ray Close in Glasgow at the Scottish Exhibition Centre. Beforehand, I was walking with Ronnie along Brighton seafront one day, when I saw this crane that was set up for bungee jumping. As I walked past, I could almost hear the crane saying to me, 'You haven't got the bottle to do me, have you?' I continued walking, but this voice kept coming at me, 'You haven't got the bottle.' So I turned around, paid my money, went up and jumped off head first, arms outstretched. Sometimes things grab me like that, if I feel it is a challenge to face, I have to take it on. Ronnie said I was mad and thought it was unprofessional to do it.

I caused much consternation when I booked myself into Nuffield private hospital for a circumcision only two weeks before the Ray Close fight. People told me that after such an operation, you should avoid contact sports for some time. I wasn't interested. Over the years I had studied many philosophies on the subject and had decided long ago to have the operation. It was simply a matter of hygiene. When I was in the operating theatre, I insisted on no anaesthetic as I wanted to be fully aware of what they were doing down there, to make sure everything was as it should be. I even got them to place a mirror near my waist, so I could see and observe. Ronnie was with me and, at one point, it was so fascinating that I said, 'Hey, Ronnie, check this out!' He didn't seem too keen to look!

Shortly after, we were in my office and I was still extremely sore from the operation. They had given me this cream to soothe the post-op tenderness, so I got the old man out and applied the cream. John was there and said, 'Remind me not to ask you for help next time my lips are chaffed.' For the Close fight, I just put two cups on and everything was fine, no problem.

Ray Close had a solid record and was known for his diligence in the ring. This proved to be the case on the night – he had such a workmanlike attitude it annoyed you. His actual punches (like I would later discover with Steve Collins) were like being hit by a kid, he never hurt me. In fact, each time he punched, he made this really loud, rasping grunt, which to be honest caused me more irritation than his actual shots. Ray's ability to keep a very high work rate was exceptional, but unfortunatly for him, he was a light puncher.

It was never about work rate after Watson 2. My aim was to hit the man two or three times a round with big shots, proper jabs and so on, then they would catch up with them in the later rounds. I concentrated on every shot being hard, not just throwing hundreds of punches for the sake of it. Although I won a lot of fights on points, I didn't build my score through a sheer volume of shots.

Nonetheless, by the end of the twelfth, the decision was given as a draw. Some said he would have won but for an uppercut which poleaxed him in the penultimate round. His legs and eyes were gone, he was in trouble. However, he stayed the course and it was called as a draw. I didn't agree, but the judges had a job to do and they did it. I was immediately accepting of that, despite this being the first draw of my career. People thought I would be gutted afterwards – why? He had not taken my belt, he had not done enough to win and I was still champion of the world.

People often complained when they felt an opponent had won but didn't get the decision. However, the point is this: the challenger must take the belt from a champion. It is also a matter of who is good for the championship – the judges unavoidably take into account charisma as well as points. It shouldn't be like this, but it is. Of course, there is a mathematical procedure but charisma is vital. That is why if I had ever lost a round 10–8, I wouldn't trudge back to my stool and sit down, I would strut around the ring, bait the crowd, put a show on. I always portrayed total confidence, even when the chips were down. Then the judges might think: *That big shot he took in there clearly hasn't hurt him, he looks like he's loving this.* Charisma is an intangible part of the equation that decides fights. You should look haughty, confident, arrogant, brave, superior, all these things can put the judges on your side.

This only backfired for me when the tabloid press took this persona to be my character outside of the ring. I always made it clear I was something of a Jekyll and Hyde character. Hyde was the strutting showman who always won in the ring, the man people loved to hate at times. In my personal life I was Dr Jekyll, a much softer, emotionally intelligent, likeable and liked person. That misunderstanding was a constant frustration which only started to dissipate when I retired the Hyde character from the ring. But I don't think I truely shrugged off that persona until I went into the *celebrity Big Brother house*.

I spent ten years trying to tell the public who I am. I showed them in 36 hours on Channel 4's *Celebrity Big Brother* and with my series *At Home with the Eubanks*. More of that later.

CHAPTER FOURTEEN

DESTROYING THE
DESTROYER . . .
FINALLY

With the first Benn fight, I had to accept that lower purse just to finally get him into the ring. For the rematch, the magnanimity I showed in offering him a second bout paid off too, but in a different way. It was the fight everyone wanted; the media, the public all wanted to see a rematch. Benn had fought back from his defeat and gone on to win the WBC belt, so this was the first time that two British world champions had fought each other. The global interest was staggering. I found out later that the fight was screened in 60 countries and watched by over 1 billion; a combined audience of over 30 million people saw the fight in the UK alone, immediately after the ITV *News At Ten*. Simply put, it was one of the biggest fights of all time.

In the preparations for the rematch, I was overconfident, I had this man beat. Despite what the public and fight business assumed from my persona, this was probably the only fight where I was actually overconfident. John Regan has since said he was worried when he saw how relaxed I was in the hotel room before the fight. I was so confident, in fact, I had 'WBO and WBC Champion' sewn into my shorts and robe beforehand, even though I was trying to win Benn's WBC belt. The contest still has to happen and you have to allow for the passion of the man, which in Benn's case was fierce, combined with his ability. By being so presumptuous, I was playing a very dangerous game indeed.

Looking back, it is easy to see why Benn was so motivated. Apart from our mutual history, someone else said the specific circumstances leading up to the fight wound him up still more. At one American press conference, I psychologically slapped him around, all the middleweights and super-middleweights champions were at this press conference. This was at a time when the awesome Gerald McClellan was saying he was the 'baddest motherf***er' on the planet. Benn was getting beaten up in this conference and he eventually got so angry, he stood up and said, 'I'm going back to England and I'm going to train for this f***er.' He was so fused, I had got to him.

Walking out to an audience of 43,000 people at Old Trafford was absolutely overwhelming, it was just a seething mass of faces – they had all come to watch me and Benn. This took my focus away, probably the only time in my career that I really didn't have my focus intact. Normally I was totally tunnel-visioned, but for this fight my heart wasn't pounding, I was distracted by the sheer volume of spectators. Also, as champion in my own right, I knew I was more emotionally intelligent than Benn, but what I couldn't have known was just how fused he was. He was wired.

This focus within Benn made him much more calculating and that made him even more dangerous. That had always been his weakness before, his brutality exploded without prior thought. Now he was combining this venom with forethought. It was a potent formula.

Benn 2 was an occasion more than a fight. I felt victory was a foregone conclusion and that explains why I just wasn't as focused as I might have been. Benn was up for the bout but I just didn't have the focus I had during our previous contest. For that first fight, it was my chance to honour myself, this was the acid test. For Benn 2, I was already champion of the world, I had proven myself. It takes both men being completely psyched up to produce a legendary fight like Benn 1 or Watson 2.

The fight itself was a maul, nowhere near as explosive or memorable as our first encounter. Reg Gutteridge said as I entered the ring, 'The ego has landed!' (they still couldn't see that this was only my ring persona). The only highlight of note was perhaps that this is the only fight you will ever see where one fighter kicks the other man in the head and does not get disqualified! (I slipped and as I went over caught him on the head with the back of my heel.)

Even so, when the decision was announced as a draw, no one could quite believe it, except myself. However, my view appeared to be in a clear minority. Although the media made much of the supposed public dissatisfaction with that decision, especially in the actual arena, when I talk to people in the streets, half think I lost and the other half say I won. Personally I think that, with two world title belts at stake, neither fighter did enough to prise the other's title away. For that, there needed to be a clear victor. There was a lot of talk about the points deducted for Benn's low blows. This discussion is a non-starter for me – you have to abide by the rules and regulations of the game and if you don't, as I had found out to my cost against Dan Sherry, you will have points deducted. Bear in mind, a low blow can really damage your groin area and leave you very unsettled. If you are then finished off in the immediate aftermath, the opponent will have gained an unfair advantage by that illegal punch. I'm not saying Benn intended to throw this particular shot, I don't think he did, but in general fighters can learn to throw in a few tricks. Benn had to have that point deducted. If that pulled the scorecards back to a draw, then so be it – you make the wrong move, you pay the price.

Unbeknown to the public, a draw was actually a tremendous result for me. Better than a win, in many ways. Why? Simply because my contract with boxing promoter Don King did not allow for a draw and therefore I was freed of any legally binding association. If I had won or lost, the paths were mapped out for me, but no one had conceived of a draw. Barry Hearn took some stick from Don King who said, 'Yes, a draw, but you knew what we meant,' to which Barry said, 'There was no clause regarding the draw, we have no obligations.' I said to Barry after the fight, 'What does a draw mean?' and he said, 'It means you are not tied down to anyone and you've got to do it all over again.' That's typical Barry Hearn – always with a smile.

The last thing I wanted in my career was to be tied to Don King. Although he can take you very far and get you the opportunities you crave, at the same time he is taking away too much control, your career may well end with him. I don't know whether it was my mother praying or providence intervening that we scored a draw, but it was a blessed result.

When I arrived home after the Benn 2 fight, Karron revealed that on the morning of the bout, she had received a death threat against me. A poison pen letter had been left in our letter box, saying, 'Your husband will die in the ring tonight.' She has since explained to me that this was a quite awful experience, as she decided not to let me know, but obviously had to involve Special Branch and the authorities. Barry Hearn was intimately involved with the operation and it sounds as though it was quite a big deal. I knew absolutely nothing about this until after the event. The only slight oddity I noticed was when we were walking to the ring. I was behind Ronnie and saw a lot of huge men, maybe 20 or 30, around my entourage, all with ear pieces and wire microphones. Even Barry had one. I just assumed at the time that it was all part of the razzmatazz, the showmanship, so I thought nothing more of it. Karron watched that fight at home on the television in the kitchen and was worried sick, waiting for me to suddenly fall over in the ring from sniper fire.

Had I known about that death threat, I may still have fought, because I had all that organised protection. No matter what you would have put in front of me, at that time I probably would have taken on the situation.

At the start of February 1994, I travelled to Germany to fight Graciano Rocchigiani, who was unbeaten in 35 fights. He was not the mandatory challenger – that was Ray Close, whom I would fight again shortly. However, the WBO agreed to this bout first. Earlier in my career, as I have said, I had jested that there was a formula for getting on in boxing – never fight a southpaw, or anyone over six foot or face an unbeaten record. Rocchigiani was all three, a very big man and fighting in his own backyard. The media in England said this would be my burial ground, highlighting his impeccable record, size, style and the fact I'd had back-to-back world title draws. He was something of a local folk hero too, notorious for his bar-brawler reputation and a recent prison sentence. Even though this was my thirteenth defence, many observers felt it could be a step too far. I felt I might not be able to knock him out, but I knew I could win. He said that when he had beaten me, he would get married to his girlfriend.

We went to Berlin and were asked to do a photoshoot at the Brandenburg Gate. The showman in me was absolutely delighted. I wore my riding boots, jodhpurs, English jacket and carried an umbrella. When it came to taking photographs, I was very theatrical I was standing there in my English gentleman's clothes, pointing in the direction of Hitler's bunker with the peacock strut in full flow.

I knew the friction between Germany and England and how that had added an extra *frisson* of tension in so many sporting contests over the years. Giving it so large in Germany meant much more to me because of that genuine animosity. Let's not forget, this wasn't just their German boy against the Englishman. It was a black Englishman, who dressed like an aristocrat. Can you imagine what they must have thought?!

Just like that bout against Cronin and so many of my other fights, my view was this: the more you dislike me, the cheekier I am going to be beforehand and the more poetically stylish I will be with my moves. By the time of the fight itself, I was so primed and ready. When I came to the ring, all 10,000 Germans in the Deutschland Halle seemed to be hissing and sneering, abusing me and threatening me. Bear in mind, there were only eight of us in my camp, plus a handful of British soldiers, who were stationed in Germany. The only respite from the abuse was when the Germans were shouting, 'Rocky! Rocky!', their nickname for Rocchigiani. There was a heavy Hell's Angel presence too and they were certainly forthcoming with their opinions! I don't understand a word of German but I didn't need to – this was such a torrent of bile, it was as if they had researched the most depraved and despicable words in their language just to hurl at me. To say they were baying for my blood is a substantial understatement. I took my time getting in the ring such that, at one point, Barry was worried for my personal safety as I was strutting around the ring apron. He said, 'What on earth are you doing,

Chris?' and I explained, 'Barry, I am soaking up the hate.'

My actual performance in the ring was of sterling pro-portions. I never dropped him and won on points. I used a combination of light punches to the head and accurate hard body-shots, coupled with a lot of ring movement and eccentricity. I spoiled his wedding plans for sure. Still, he should have kept his word to his girlfriend.

One of the reasons I was able to be so comprehensively in charge was due to the genuine dislike his fans poured towards me. However, to my regret, after the victory I didn't have a Union Jack to furl around me in the ring. Rocchigiani had dyed the Italian and German flags into his hair, and I had viewed the entire event as a highly nationalistic affair. Not having the Union Jack to hold aloft is one of my two biggest regrets of my professional career. The other is more serious, namely what happened to Michael Watson.

A few weeks after this fight in Germany, I had tickets to see Barbra Streisand at Wembley Arena. Everyone was sup-posed to be seated at 7.30pm and Ms Streisand was due on at 8pm. We were at a hotel nearby but Karron was still breastfeeding Emily, so time slipped by and we found our-selves getting later and later. We got there at 7.58pm. As I walked in, several rows of people started whispering, 'It's Eubank.' Now, keep in mind that our seats were next to Barry and Susan Hearn in the very centre of the front row. (George Michael was six rows back.)

Ours were the only two seats left in the house. We had to walk all the way down to the first line of seats, right by the stage. An usher took us down and as I got towards the front,

I noticed people starting to stand up – I looked up and saw a huge block of people were giving me a standing ovation! I was so genuinely moved that I welled up and physically shivered. Someone said I walked tall across to my seat, a splendid sight at the stage's edge, but I felt like I was walking with my head bowed because their acceptance humbled me. Remember, I had been vilified in the media and by certain sections of the public for so many years as an aloof man and an arrogant man. However, for that 30 seconds, I had acceptance. I had been champion of the world for nearly four years at that time but this was genuine acceptance. My emotions seared through me; I put that wave of affection and respect down to the friction between the English and the Germans.

There is a story that Barry Hearn tells loud and clear (I don't remember this) about that night. He says that when I completed what he describes as a 'full strut' to my seat, I turned to the usher and said, 'You can tell Ms Streisand she can come out now.'

The second Ray Close fight was in Belfast's King's Hall. Close had been at the Rocchigiani bout and claimed he saw nothing to be scared of. In the reception after that fight in Germany, I found Close and told him this time I would defeat him. Ray was a nice enough man, a Mormon in fact, so there was no great animosity between us, compared to earlier fights. Perhaps this explained why both my fights against him were much lower profile than the Watson or Benn contests. I did, however, place a £1000 bet with Ray's manager that I would knock his man out in one round.

I didn't arrive in Belfast until just before the weigh-in for which I was criticized, suggesting I wasn't helping to promote the fight. After the death threat at Benn 2, for the second Ray Close bout I made an extreme, albeit mis-informed, decision. I knew of the troubles and general atmosphere of violence, guns and bombs in Northern Ire-land. At this time in the UK, the vitriol against me in the English media was acidic. Assuming the Irish people would be equally odious, and in light of the environment of firearms, I felt very vulnerable. I had two plain-clothed RUC officers with me as security – this was not particularly unusual to have personal security. What was unusual was this – when I walked to the ring wearing a big white towel with the usual hole cut through the centre for my head, no one knew that underneath I was wearing a regulation bullet-proof vest.

The day of the fight, a soldier was killed as the troubles flared again. That afternoon, while the press were outside assuming I was resting or contemplating the forthcoming bout, myself, Ronnie and John Regan were stitching the bullet-proof vest onto this towel. When it came to removing the towel and vest, Ronnie swiped them both off me in one movement, so that no one noticed.

At the time, this made perfect sense to me. I had been unsettled by the death threat at Benn 2, so I thought it was perfectly reasonable to wear this protection. I was wrong.

This merely highlighted my ignorance of the Irish people. Their attitude towards me at this point in my career was diametrically opposed to the standpoint at home. In the UK, you could taste the venom, whether it was being showered with spit as you walked to the ring or vilified on an almost daily basis in the press. I was the arch villain and people poured their scorn and hatred on me. In Ireland, however, their opinions were the polar opposite. Yes, they wanted Ray Close to win, of course, but they recognised me for what I was – a character.

On the night, the Belfast King's Hall was packed with 8,000 fans and the atmosphere was excellent. Matters were delayed somewhat by a bizarre occurrence when, of all things, a very small man dressed as a leprechaun threw glitter over me. Even though I had been wearing my bullet-proof vest, I figured that this was unlikely to be some covert assassination attempt! The glitter fell all over the canvas and took a while to sweep up. It also took some time to wipe it off me. Lots of it had got stuck on me because of the oil I had on my body. Only in Ireland.

Ray had the heart of a lion in both our fights. He took big shots in the tenth round this time, but kept in there. I even needed some butterfly stitches to my own eye afterwards. I enjoyed that crowd very much. This time, in another tough fight, I performed sufficiently well to win the judges over. After I took the decision his team were very, very angry but I thought it was a fair decision. To the credit of the Irish, as I now know, they are very warm hearted people so, although there were some who felt the decision was wrong, there was no violence, no aggression towards me and no fracas in the arena.

Of course, the media were not so understanding, talking me down again, pointing out this was my eighth 12-rounder in a row (since Watson, I had only stopped one man, John Jarvis, within the distance). Yet, still I was champion, 39 and 0. Don King was even less pleased and besieged the organisers with a flurry of immediate post-fight complaints. Afterwards, I said I would be happy to fight Ray again, but this time I wanted the bout in London.

I was very upset when my brother Simon sold a story to the *Sunday Mirror* in July 1994. He had been asking for some money, but his preconception of what wealth I had at that time was way beyond the reality. People from the street often think that because your name is in the newspapers that you have millions of pounds lying around gathering dust. At this point, I had already allocated much of what I had earned to developing the new house and various other interests. I was working very hard for my money and trying to secure my family's future.

One day, Simon came around and we had a heated discussion about money. He left and I also went out for a while. Then Simon came back and Karron answered the door. She had seen the way my brothers have been with me over all these years and she was cross with Simon, so she said, 'Go away! Leave us alone!' That was why Simon went to the newspapers, he later told me.

I had said to Karron not to get involved with this, because we were blood brothers and it was not wise to interfere, sometimes the third party gets pushed away and the blood remains strong. Simon has a simple way of thinking. I was very upset when I saw that story – bear in mind, all these years, I have been fighting against media misconceptions of me, misinformation and such like, yet here I am having fuel thrown on the fire by my own family! It was very hurtful.

When my father released a story to the newspapers, saying words to the effect of, 'My son has found a pot of gold and left me in the gutter,' I was easily able to forgive him. My father was illiterate, an uneducated man. He had wisdom of years but he was easily wound up. People would say, 'Mr Eubank owns the Bank of England.' They put that in his head. I could forgive him for that, I understood the way my father was.

CHAPTER FIFTEEN
TYSON

Before that second Ray Close fight, unbeknown to Ronnie, I had flown out to America to visit Mike Tyson, who had recently started a five-year jail sentence for a rape conviction. Mike and I did share a degree of mutual history. I didn't train at the same gym in New York, but I do recall seeing him on several occasions at fights. At one of my first amateur bouts, I remember this young man just sitting there on a table, very quiet, just a great presence of a man. Of course, back then he was just an amateur too, but I remember him being quiet and very gentle but still a powerful presence. Later, in 1989, when he was the heavyweight champion of the world, I was in Versace on 67th Street and Madison Avenue when someone informed me that Mike was also in the store. I took my son Christopher over and we spoke, but he barely talked to me, he just played with Christopher.

The hardship involved in the life of a fighter is why I still respect Tyson, to be at the top takes a rare person, and I acknowledge that. This is not football or rugby, this is a very tough, demanding profession.

I have sympathy for his predicament, but I also don't think he had too much time for me really, which is sad. So why should I speak about him here? I do so because he is a human being and we all need love, some more than others.

He served his time for the crime he was convicted of, but if I did not feel any sympathy for him, I would not have had his name mentioned in this book; I would have boycotted him years ago.

I will always look at the positives in any situation: he applied himself to his trade, he ran, he trained hard, he boxed, he learned the art, he kept his schedule, listened and applied what he heard. As he is a short man for a heavyweight, only 5'11", he often fought much bigger men, but he was persistent. All of these elements of Mike Tyson are key ingredients of success – his failings will always be in terms of his conduct.

As a boxer, his approach in the ring was ferocious, vicious, intimidating, a pure knock-out artist with a 'kill or be killed' attitude. It was almost as if he was saying, 'You know what I am going to do, but try and stop me.' But also more than that he was a learned man with regards to the four-cornered circle and the art of war. He had his own niche and his body, weight and size, suited this to such a degree that he developed into an exceptionally brilliant fighting technician. He was one of the greats, of course. They will still be talking about Muhammad Ali in 1000 years and they will also be talking about Mike Tyson, maybe for different reasons, although the foundation, the common denominator, will be boxing.

Tyson got himself into so much trouble because of his poor conduct outside the ring. In throwing caution to the wind as regards to personal behaviour, he has nullified all his remarkable accomplishments within the ring, in that people will highlight the bad things rather than the historical achievements. So, in a sense, that is a fantastic example for my children, emphasising the pivotal importance of conduct. People often say 'Why did he do this or that?' The point is, he has a naturally short fuse. He is impulsive and I understand this. I sympathise with him and his situation because he is an intelligent man but his fuse is short and he refuses to control it. This is not uncommon. There is no question he is intelligent – for example, he is renowned for his encyclopaedic knowledge of boxing history. Where I studied the philosophy of the art, he knows the history. So this is an intelligent man with regards to his boxing knowledge.

The problem is that people do take liberties with you in life, it happens all the time, but when someone disrespects Mike, he instantly retaliates. You shouldn't do that. Your first action should never be your reaction. The key is to use your intellect to override the animal instinct or impulse. When you retaliate and disrespect someone, you drop down to their level. I stay where I am. *I am not coming down there with you to that level*. Some people don't learn. Many never learn this or learn it very late, although late is better than never.

The hardest thing to do in boxing is to keep yourself calm

and controlled. Once you lose control, it's unlikely you will win. Take the ear-biting incident when Mike fought Evander Holyfield. I can relate to that personally. The fact is this – there are rules and regulations in a fight and you absolutely must abide by these, but it is still a fight. It is still aggressive, vicious and desperate. But you must stay in control, that is paramount. Inevitably, in some fights a person breaks the rules, they hit low, or they hold on too much or wrestle, it's all a matter of frustration. The only thing to do, and yet the hardest thing to do, is to keep yourself controlled. When I was fighting, I was the calmest person in the entire arena. Opponents would see this and say, 'Who does he think he is?' They would think I was showboating with them, they would get angry and then try to showboat themselves or hit me harder – a mistake. I would take them out because they were not in control. My well-documented tapping of the gloves, one on top of the other, was my nervous twitch. But it was a nervous twitch with style. Eyebrow always raised. Some boxers get in the ring and they are frantic, moving around, grunting. I didn't do that. I always tried to show that I was calm even though my heart was racing, always in control.

When you lose control you are likely to break the rules. Tyson told me, as he had said in the media at the time, that Holyfield was headbutting him and the referee would not intervene and warn him, so he just did what came into his mind. It was impulsive. That was his explanation and I understand that, not only because I am on the inside of the business but also because unfortunately I experienced this circumstance in my own amateur career. In the semi-final of the Golden Gloves, I felt I could not beat my opponent – he had me in his zone. We got into a clinch on the ropes and I bit him. I was so ashamed. I bit him on the shoulder. I had a gumshield on the top teeth but not on the bottom row, so they did actually make an impression on his skin. All that did was bring shame on myself. No one spotted it except the fighter and his trainer, but the point is this – I knew I'd done it and I was ashamed. I had got frustrated. You don't do that. I was ashamed of my conduct.

There is a referee who is now retired called Roy Francis and he was once asked, 'Who stands out in your mind as the most exciting fighter you ever refereed?' He said, 'By far, Chris Eubank, and he *never* pulled any strokes.' I could have fought dirty, I know how to look where the referee is and hit the opponent low on the blind side. Use a three-punch combination to the head, two to the body, one to the groin, then a left hook to the head when the ref's on your blind side, I know how to cover it up, but you mustn't. It was never my way.

So what I say to amateurs now is this: observe all the mistakes you make in the amateurs and don't make them in the pros. I did make a similar error of judgement against Dan Sherry in the first defence of the title with that back headbutt. I would never have bitten him though.

I visited Mike 12 times in prison at the Indiana State Correction Center. I contacted Don King through Barry Hearn and asked for a visitor's pass – being world champion means you can command privileges like that. I would fly from Heathrow to New York on Concorde on the Friday, see some family in the Bronx, then on the Sunday fly to Indiana on a 737 to see Mike, then get back to England on the Monday morning.

Mike was just a normal inmate, I didn't see any special treatment at all. You'd wait in the reception area, then, when your name was called to go in, you had to put all your belongings into a locker. You then had more checks before walking down a long corridor, through a metal detector, get checked again, then at the bottom of that walkway there was another locked door. Here there was an ultraviolet machine to check that you had the appropriate security stamps and after that you were led into the visiting room. Everybody would sit down and wait and then they would lead all the inmates out at once, including Mike. You could either go outside into a garden area where all these tables were locked down or, if it was too cold, you would stay inside. Twice I was unable to see him, once because it had not been sanctioned by the warden and once because he had family waiting to see him. I gave them my slot and returned home.

We would meet for two hours each time. On the very first visit, I said to him, 'Give me the story, short and sharp, about this Desiree Washington.' He said, 'She gave me the pussy then she put me in prison.' Then he just kind of laughed. He was always very subdued when I met him, but always extremely affable as well. We had lots of conversations but never about material goods. The discussions were always about intangibles, philosophy. He said to me,

'I didn't want any of this, I didn't want all this fame and money. What I wanted was for the other guys in the gymnasium who trained next to me to say, "Hey, that's a good fighter."' He didn't expect the infamy, the rhetoric, all he ever wanted to be known as was a good fighter. I had a better understanding of Mike Tyson the moment he first said to me, 'I only ever did this for a pat on the back in the gym.' What do you say to that? It knocks you back! It was such a noble aspiration.

We would have these lengthy conversations in a room full of other inmates and visitors, but I didn't notice anyone looking over. Yes, this was two champion boxers sitting together in a prison room, but I never saw it like that. For me, I was in the presence of a great fighter, I wasn't remotely conscious of my championship stature. I think of myself just as you think of yourself, it is all relative. So as I am sitting there in that jail, I'm just an ordinary person, sitting opposite Mike Tyson, the youngest undisputed heavyweight champion ever.

I said, 'Mike, you do understand that your position makes you a role model?' I continued, 'Mike, whatever you do, make sure it is positive, because if it is negative it will be reported enormously, so be a role model in the positive. Whatever you do it will be reported. If you step in mud, the headlines will read "Mike Tyson, convicted rapist, steps in mud."' He said to me, 'As far as being a role model is concerned, I don't want the job, I will take a rain check, I just want to live my life.' For that, I was disappointed because he has the potential to influence a lot of people, both young and old. I said, 'Whether you like it or not, you are a role model, you cannot back out now.' He wasn't interested.

During the rape trial, Tyson's defense raised questions about why Desiree Washington did not report the crime for a week after the alleged incident, and also why she was in that hotel room at 3am. To a degree, I can sympathise with those observations. It is all about Tyson's angle on it at the time and no one outside of that room will ever know what really happened. Apparently, it was reported that he wouldn't walk her home either; he just said to her, 'Go'. If that was so, then it was just plain inconsiderate; you are obviously going to put someone's back up by saying that. But in no way do I think he expected to go to prison for three years.

Nevertheless, he is a convicted rapist by the law of the land. People ask me why I like Mike Tyson. It's because I know his fuse is short and the media and other opportunists take advantage of that short fuse to make some easy money.

I was due to visit Mike two days before his Friday prison release. *The Sun* newspaper contacted me and offered £100,000 for the last interview with Tyson in prison. I mentioned this to two fellows called John Wischhusen and Andy Ayling, who worked for Barry Hearn and sorted out my media work around boxing. They knew me for who I was, they knew me correctly. John just looked at me and smiled, wondering whether I was going to do the story or not. We both knew there were people who would take that money, but we also both knew it was never an option for me. I went to visit Mike and told him about the rejected tabloid proposal immediately, saying, 'If I want money, I will fight, I will earn it. I don't want that type of money, that would be dirty money to me.' It would have been a complete betrayal of Mike.

So, yes, I do have an empathy and respect for Mike Tyson. In the same way he only ever wanted to get that pat on the back, I only ever wanted acceptance. There is a camaraderie between most boxers, because they know the uniquely spartan life, the extreme lifestyle that the public have no accurate perception of. That creates a deep respect for what we do, as modern-day gladiators.

There was a lot of press talk that Mike Tyson had converted me to Islam. This was not so. All he said was that if you are a good Christian, then you are a good Muslim, because you don't harm your fellow man. The Muslim faith appealed to me for a time and still does, but since then I have developed and have become a person of understanding. When that happens you accept all faiths as well as all non-faiths. I understand and accept the Sikh, the Buddhist, the Christian, the Muslim and the Jew, but I also accept and understand the atheist. Be considerate towards your fellow man, no matter what his religion or non-religion. If you are a good person you will go to heaven whether you believe in a God or not.

Talking of good people, I would like to say a bit about the magnanimous and great champion Lennox Lewis. The reason I've said so much about Tyson and not Lennie is that Mike has issues and problems, while Lennie handles himself perfectly well. Whenever Lennie has fought genuinely dangerous fighters he usually knocks them out in a few rounds, it's when he takes a fighter lightly that he gets into trouble.

Anyone who has been good, even great he beats emphatically – Razor Ruddock, Holyfield, Tyson, and it must be said that after Tyson everyone else will be a step backwards for him. He will not have a better performance than that and to Tyson's credit he showed what a great fighter he was by allowing Lewis a clean kill.

I am glad I visited Mike Tyson in prison and I have gained a considerable amount of experience and wisdom from meeting him. I have a photograph of Mike that to me shows his true self, away from all the media hype, the column inches, the frenzy and speculation. When I first had this picture developed, I gave it to my mother and said, 'Mom, pray for this man.'

It is so unfortunate: you have here an ordinary guy with an extraordinary past, an extraordinary career and extraordinary media coverage. I know that, like me, he is just a man.

PART FOUR

ACHIEVE THE FAME

CHAPTER SIXTEEN

THE SKY'S THE LIMIT

There was a lot of talk about a Eubank–Benn 3 match at Wembley Stadium with figures of £5 million being thrown around, but this never happened. Besides, Barry and myself had been busy. For many months now, we had been negotiating an unprecedented television deal with Sky Television. The satellite channel were keen to sell dishes and win subscribers and they saw me as the ideal vehicle to do that – after the vital Ray Close win, my position was only strengthened. Remember, at the time the ratings for my fights were repeatedly record-breaking. They bought into my character, my ring persona, my style, the clothes, the English gentleman look. They knew I would win viewers.

Much was made of my slogan, 'Simply The Best.' I had originally used this phrase in reply to a Nigel Benn headline taunt of, 'I'm going to get you,' but it was Barry Hearn's wife, Susan, who thought of making this my public byline. Every fighter has a gimmick, but I wanted no such fanfare, I was for truth and integrity, not gimmicks. However, Barry explained this could be of benefit, so I just thought: *Do whatever it takes, I am not the PR man. If this helps, let's go with it.* That phrase obviously became synonymous with myself, but one thing that was always misunderstood was that I was not using it with reference to the fight business. I have never talked about 'Simply The Best' as a boxer but, as a person, I was simply the best. That was my take on it. As for the Tina Turner song, I made an unannounced entrance on stage with that performer at one year's MOBO awards – she was rather surprised!

The Sky deal was about big money, £10 million for eight fights effectively, the richest ever contract in European boxing. There were many high powered meetings, which for me was all part of my job, facilitating my earning capacity. One such meeting was arranged with all the very top executives of Sky and all the various financial parties involved. I turned up in the full English gear with a riding case. This was actually meant for polo gear, but I carried my picture cards and various other personal possessions in it.

We sat down for the meeting and I could tell all eyes were on me. The most senior executive present said, 'Would you like some tea or coffee, Mr Eubank?' I said, 'Yes, please. May I partake of a coffee, double espresso with hot cream, please? If you don't have any cream, would you mind sending someone out to get it?' I thought it would be a good way of breaking the ice. Although they offered no hint of their feelings, it was all very poker faced and proper, I could tell they were bemused.

When the drinks arrived, the same gentleman said,

'Would you like some biscuits, Mr Eubank?' I said, 'No, thank you, I have my own.' At that moment, I pulled out a delicate silver tin containing a selection of scrumptious biscuits. I said, 'Gentlemen, here are some of the finest biscuits known to man. These are the type of culinary delight that you cannot but eat all in one sitting.' I meticulously removed the ornate lid and, offering them to the stunned faces in front of me, said, 'Would any of you gentlemen care for a biscuit? They are truly delicious, in fact, they are simply the best.' Shortly after, we signed the deal. He didn't know I often carried a tin of biscuits. You never know when you might need them.

We announced the deal at the Royal Geographical Society in Greenwich, watched over by portraits of some of the great explorers (Barry later told me he felt like we 'had the keys to the sweet factory.'). Although five of the eight fights were scheduled to take place in the UK, the bouts were touted as a globe-trotting campaign. Barry said it was 'a mission to spread the gospel of Eubankism.' As part of the deal, I made a fun video where I was transformed into a panther by an amazing £100,000 worth of special effects. It was a long day's work, but it was fun. The only disappointment was when the animal's trainer would not allow me to climb into the cage to get acquainted before we worked together.

The eight fights would take place over roughly one calendar year, between July 1994 and June 1995. In the process, I would become the highest paid fighter in the world, outside of the heavyweight division. Indeed, it was said some Sky executives who signed me rather than Lennox Lewis got into a lot of trouble! In purely boxing terms, many observers considered this schedule a ludicrous proposition. Someone called me insane to which I jokingly replied, 'I never said I was sane.' Many insiders felt taking on a world title fight roughly every six weeks wouldn't allow me sufficient time to recover between fights, even for cuts to heal. The British Medical Association stated that they felt such a workload at such a high level could have a detrimental effect on my permanent state of health, but I had Godspeed and this was my business. This was the sort of opportunity I had been working for all those years in the gym.

One day in 1994, I came back to my house in Hove at a time when we were having a lot of building work done on it. Near the kitchen, there was this man coming down my stairs from the bedrooms and I said 'Hey, how are you?' A very strange conversation followed.

'Hello,' he replied.

'Who are you working with?' I asked him. 'John Regan?'

'No, I'm not working with anyone. I've just come to see you.'

I was walking into the kitchen and I said, 'What do you mean, you've just come to see me? Who are you?'

'My name is Russell. Russell Bennett.'

'What are you doing here? You've just come from upstairs.'

'I've come to see you. I was just having a look around.'

By now, I was beginning to realise that I had a bit of a situation on my hands. He was walking around my private quarters, calm as you like, and when he spoke to me he was perfectly casual. He was carrying a bag on his shoulder and I could see there was nothing in there but I asked anyway (I would prefer to say I trusted this complete stranger and didn't ask to see inside his bag, but I did!). He showed me inside and it was indeed empty.

Slightly concerned now, I said, 'What are you doing here?'

He said, as calm as can be, 'The reason you have done everything you've done is because of the love I've been sending out to you and the prayers I've been saying for you.'

I stood there listening to this total stranger telling me we are going to save the world together, because we are 'two people who have love in us.' I kept direct eye contact with him at all times, and if I had sensed a hint of nervousness I would have restrained him there and then. He was, after all, in my house, nobody else was home. But there wasn't a hint of nervousness in his demeanour.

I asked him, 'Where are you living?' and he said, 'I'm not, I'm looking for a place.' So I called a fellow who was working for me, gave him £20 and said, 'Will you take this gentleman to the council office and see if they can get him a place.' We took Russell's details and shortly after, we managed to get in touch with his mother. She told us that he had escaped from a mental institution. When I called her up, she said, 'I thought that would be the first place he would go.' Apparently he had been obsessed with me for some time. He was only 24. That was that, or so I thought.

Two months later I was in London when I received a call to say there was a man in the garage who'd locked himself in my truck. They said he wouldn't talk at all, other than to say his name was Russell. I instructed them to put the phone they were calling me on through the truck window, where-upon I said, 'Listen, Russell, you can't keep doing this, this is what they call stalking. This is against the law.' He quietly said, 'Okay I'll go,' promptly jumped down out of the truck and left.

A couple of weeks later, Russell broke into the house while we were out but a neighbour saw him and alerted the police. They found him hiding in the gables where the truck garage meets the house roof. After this third instance, Karron went to the courts and took out a restraining order on him which banned him from coming within a mile or so of the house.

Two months after that I was in Dubai on business. Last thing at night, I was on the phone to Karron, just catching up on the day's events back home. As we were talking, I heard a siren in the background. Karron was very tired and she said, 'Damn, the alarm's gone off in the other house.' She said she was going to check because sometimes a spider will make a web in front of the sensors and trigger the alarm. In light of the recent events, I wasn't comfortable with this at all but she went across to the other house and pushed the front door open. She couldn't see anything, so she started to walk into the living room. As she did so, she heard footsteps upstairs. She told me she screamed, 'Who the f**k is in the house!?' then ran out and locked the door behind her, and then called the police. She handled it perfectly. Meanwhile, I am in Dubai on business wondering what the commotion was, and yes, I was very uncomfortable. I called my brother who got there about the same time as the police. They sent sniffer dogs into the house and found Russell in the attic room, crouched up in the galleried beams of my gymnasium. He was wearing a pair of my boxing shorts and had a workman's hammer in his hand.

It was a very disturbing series of events, very unsettling especially for my wife and children. As I was frequently away on business at that time, this exacerbated the nervousness. I said to the police, 'What can I do to protect my family?' but they said, 'Basically, you can't do anything because he hasn't harmed anyone.' I said, 'The fellow who killed John Lennon hadn't harmed anyone before that day either.'

We haven't heard from Russell since. It was a troubling time but this is life, this is the way your cookie crumbles and you have to accept it. There is no point getting frantic about it, it's just one of those things.

I always enjoy going into communities at grassroots level and involving myself in any particular situation where I feel I may be able to help. Back in early 1993, a 14-year-old boy called Benji Stanley was shot dead in a case of mistaken identity amongst Moss Side's drug gangs. At the time, that area of Manchester was being called 'the Beirut of Britain' and 'the British Bronx'. Benji's young age and unfortunate demise hit the community hard and caused an uprising of sentiment against the omnipresent gun culture and drug dealing in that town.

I really wanted to help and so travelled up to Moss Side. On the first day, I marched with local parents in protest at the drug wars; on the second day, I visited various schools to talk to the youngsters; and on the final day, I was interviewed by numerous radio stations, including many pirate outfits, where I played some reggae music and talked in my mother tongue, Jamaican, espousing the need for empathy and consideration. I was in training for the Lindell Holmes fight at the time, so I later set up camp in Moss Side Leisure Centre, opened the doors and people flooded in to see me work out, chat and entertain.

The press coverage of my activities up there was deeply misleading and bitterly disappointing. Their spin was that I had used the shocked community's plight to garner some personal publicity. They even claimed that I had barged into the schools without permission and disrupted classes. All completely untrue of course. One local black community newspaper said I was unwelcome because, as a boxer, I was setting a bad example to the youngsters. Barely a mention was made of the actual purpose of my visits, no thought was given to how they could benefit the Moss Side community, no one acknowledged that I was a parent too. It was all negativity aimed squarely in my direction, questioning my motives. Good news does not sell newspapers, so if it is only good news, twist it into something bad. After my visit, I was informed by key community figures that a gunshot was not fired in that particular area for a long time.

It disheartened me but my spirit will not be broken. It is a good fight I am fighting here, I like my fight. My view is this: there are few good people out there who are willing to put themselves on the line – here's one of them. If you care about the younger generation, I can be a useful tool, I want to give advice and help.

I put this to Tony Blair one of the times I met him, in this instance at the 'Pride of Britain Awards' at the Hilton. Whenever he sees me, he has a bemused and playfully warm look in his eye. I was with my friend, Terry Johnson. I spoke to Tony and said I would like him to meet Terry, so Tony walked over with me and met my friend. I spoke at length to the Prime Minister about my desire to contribute even more to society. I said, 'You do realise, there are very few role models who teach by example. I happen to be one of them. Not only that, but I can hold the respect and attention of these youngsters, I can hold an audience. Let me go into the schools, with the authorisation of the government, to talk to the youngsters.' Mr Blair obviously liked what he was hearing and replied, 'I am going to give you more work than you can handle.' I said, 'Please, task me.' No one has been in touch yet. Nothing. It's a shame he didn't folllow through like he did with the unjust war in Iraq. Going against the UN and Mandela was not wise; history will not forgive you.

I also saw him at the Labour Conference in Brighton when Nelson Mandela was in attendance. After Mandela's speech, I made my way to the back door to say hello. I wrote a note for Mr Mandela saying, 'Please call me on this number,' but I couldn't persuade the security guards to let me through.

They knew who I was and that I was obviously not a threat, but they had their job to do. I couldn't get through to Nelson but then Tony Blair noticed me and said, 'Hi, Chris!' He came over, shook my hand and asked the guards to let me through. He then escorted me over to Nelson Mandela. I spoke briefly to Mandela and was delighted by both that and the fact that Mr Blair showed me a great deal of respect by helping me through the cordon.

If you're reading this book, Tony, I am still here, waiting.

CHAPTER SEVENTEEN

MAX

In the early summer of 1994, after I had been champion nearly four years, I met a fellow called Max Newton. I had been staying at the Grosvenor House Hotel and as I walked out of the entrance one day, I saw this vagrant standing nearby. He had his little trolley with all his life in it, complete with a picture of Princess Diana and Prince Charles. He approached me, and in an exquisitely sophisticated voice, said, 'Excuse me sir, do you know you can get a cup of tea for 5p down at the Embankment, sir?' I wasn't sure if he knew who I was, even though I had been champion for some time, and I was more than a little surprised at how delightfully he spoke. I politely said, 'Really? Okay, thank you. That's very good of you to tell me that. What's your name?' He said, 'Spencer, sir.' I replied, 'Hello, Spencer, my name is Chris.' Now at this moment I was waiting for him to ask me for some money but he never did. He simply turned around and went on his way.

This was around the same time as the Sky deal was

beginning, so I had much on my mind to think about. However, for two months after meeting this gentleman, I would find myself thinking about him, maybe two or three times a week. He had been such a strange fellow. He reminded me very much of Terry-Thomas, of whom I am very fond and admire greatly. This vagrant had those exact same elegant mannerisms, that same delicate articulation and most poignantly, *he never asked me for money*. I was captivated.

At this time I had bought an Aston Martin Volante and it was due for delivery on 1 August. It was an incredible machine which I'd had customised from the standard 5.3 litre engine at a cost of £60,000 in addition to the purchase price of £140,000. I was savouring the day of delivery. That same morning, I was due to fly to New York for a press conference with Don King, Nigel Benn, Gerald McClellan and some other fighters, so I arranged for the car to be delivered to the Dorchester Hotel where I would be staying. My intention was to take the car out for a drive at one second past midnight, then retire to my bed to catch a few hours sleep, before the transatlantic flight. I went to bed eagerly looking forward to my midnight excursion in this gleaming new car, which I had registered with the plate M1 AMV. However, next thing I know, I have woken with a start and it is 5am. Somewhat confused, I tried to recall what I was supposed to do in the night – the Aston Martin! I quickly got dressed, knowing there would be just enough time to take it out for a spin before heading off to the airport. I raced down to the garage, jumped in the car and gingerly threaded this very wide, brand new Aston Martin up the narrow, spiral ramp on to the street. By now it was 5.30am and Park Lane was basking in brilliant dawn sunshine.

I lowered the hood and started off down Park Lane, up through the Queen Mother's Gate, past the army barracks before turning around. I was completely in awe of this beautiful monstrosity. The mighty engine made a truly magnificent, roaring sound, it was like falling in love every time you switched the engine on (I later discovered just driving it through The Lanes in Brighton set off every car alarm). It was vermilion red with flared wheel arches, upholstered in the most luxurious cream parchment leather, you couldn't hope for a finer cream. The rich red carpets flooded around the seats. Then there was the music system! It was Alpine, four mid-range and two ten-inch woofers which were specially built into the chassis to make the entire car act like a speaker. Not that I was playing any CDs at 5.30am on that morning. Just listening to that engine was music to my ears. The performance was astounding – 0–60 in just over three seconds, do you mind! Aaah, never a chore! What an awesome vehicle, a genuine piece of art-work. As a stylist, the Aston Martin appealed to me as English to the last. I also like Austin Healys like the one driven by Terry-Thomas in *School for Scoundrels*.

On maybe the third circuit around Park Lane, I was just cruising at 20 mph, listening to the engine purring like a giant cat. All of a sudden, I see this same vagrant again, who I thought at the time was called Spencer. He was sitting on a park bench near a few other commuters at a bus stop.

I drove just past the bus shelter and pulled over, left the engine running and got out of the car. I called out 'Spencer!' and he looked at me and said, 'No, sir, that's not my name.' I said, 'That's what you told me your name was, do you remember me?' to which he politely replied, 'Yes, I do remember you, sir, but my name is Max.'

At this point, out of the corner of my eye, I notice that there are people in the bus queue who recognise me. I was, after all, the current Super-Middleweight champion of the World. Undeterred, I said to Max, 'I have just taken delivery of my brand new Aston Martin. Beautiful car, isn't it?' Max, in that sumptuous voice of his, said, 'Yes, marvellous, sir.' I said, 'Would you like to go for a ride in it with me?' 'Oh, love to sir, love to,' came the reply.

So I took all his bedraggled belongings, walked to the nearside door and put them on the back seat. I then held the door open for Max. As I did I noticed his shoes, an encrusted pair of old plimsolls, both of which were completely worn through at the front, exposing his leathery toes. I think by this stage the people at the bus stop were somewhat surprised by the scene unfolding before them; indeed, I recall one of them was actually standing with his mouth wide open. The media had continued to fuel this perception of me as a quirky character, so I guess they might have expected as much.

Max walked to the open car door but paused, apparently uncertain. I said, 'Please, Max, get in.' He replied, 'Oh, no sir, I couldn't get in there sir, I'm filthy, sir, filthy.' 'Don't worry, Max,' I said, 'it's no big deal, don't worry.' So he sat down on the cream leather seat and I asked him if he was comfortable. 'Oh, yes, marvellous sir.' He put the seatbelt on, I walked round to the driver's door and off we drove, leaving the bemused line of commuters at the bus stop.

We drove around the Park Lane area several times, then after a while I said, 'How do you like it, Max?' to which he replied 'Oh, marvellous, sir, marvellous.' We headed back to the Dorchester and parked the car at the front. I told Max to leave his possessions in the back and then asked the doorman to take great care to watch the gear with an ironic look on my face. We walked into the hotel and, as I started towards the reception, I said, 'Max, just wait here a moment.' I went to the front desk and asked the lady if she had any available rooms. She knew who I was but glanced over my shoulder in Max's direction and said, 'No, sorry sir, we are fully booked.' So I took Max up to my own suite.

'Would you like a cup of tea, Max?'

'Oh, I'd love a cup of tea, sir.' he replied with a chuckle.

'Would you like a bath?'

'Oh, that would be marvellous, sir. I haven't had a bath for five years, sir.'

I started running the bath for him and shortly afterwards the tea arrived. We sat together drinking tea and chatting, during which time I found out that he was actually a very well-educated man who had even been to Naval School. This was such a refined gentleman, with a regal poise, he even drank his tea in a refined manner. All this time, I was thinking back to that first day we had met, *Excuse me sir, do you know you can get a cup of tea for 5p down at the*

Embankment, sir? He never hit me for money. He was a tramp of class, of great dignity, of tact, characteristics that certain people from his era possess.

We finished our pot of tea and I told Max to help himself to a dressing gown and take a bath. As he was going to the bathroom I said, 'Would you like some breakfast, perhaps a full English?' He said, 'Marvellous, sir, marvellous.' His face was pure bliss. At this point, let me explain that this was essentially a selfish thing for me but I also felt sorry for him.

He went and had his bath and then came out with his hair all slicked back, although it was still pretty bedraggled and matted. However, this had exposed his face and it was a vision of character: drawn, worn, but deeply interesting. I noticed his heels were absolutely embedded in grime – the dirt seemed to somehow be under the skin, rather than on top of it, that shows how long he had gone without bathing. I said to him, 'Max, you're going to have to go back in the shower,' which he did with great calm. He was still dirty, even after the second shower.

After Max had eaten his breakfast, I had this man who was working for me at the time go with the concierge to Marks & Spencer. I instructed them to buy two ties, two suits, two pairs of shoes, two pairs of socks, two shirts, every-thing in twos. They had measured Max up and came back with all these clothes. It was 9.30am by now and I had to leave to drive to Heathrow for the Concorde over to New York. Before I left, I arranged for Max to be driven down to Brighton and given a double room at the Ramada Hotel for the four days I was away.

On my return from America, I found a little one-bedroom apartment for Max to stay in. Two weeks into his stay, I introduced him to my wife and children. While he was waiting to meet them, he sat down in my office on this antique walnut chair, which is about 200 years old, gnarled and flawlessly upholstered. As he sat there, blood began to trickle out of his rectal orifice. He was excruciatingly embarrassed but I was at pains to ease his concerns, saying 'Don't worry, Max, let's make sure you are alright first. Forget the chair, it's no big deal, we'll just get it cleaned.' At first, I asked him if he would care to be my valet ('Marvellous, sir') but I gave up on that idea after he spent three days polishing one toe cap of a boot.

Keep in mind that although I was world champion, I've always been a loner, in that I get on best with myself. So many people have agendas and I can't really get on with that, so I find I prefer my own company. However, during the next three months, Max became my close companion. We went everywhere together and both had a splendid time. I would take my Aston Martin out, go and pick up Max from his apartment, and we would drive into the country and have a nice day. Often we would drive to Devil's Dyke, deep into the country and find a little village where we would sit and take afternoon tea in a local shop. He was both very witty and highly intelligent and we had some wonderful times. During this period, with all the distractions and issues that go with being world champion, Max was my companion and I was very fond of him.

He went everywhere with me. One day I had a very high

level meeting with some advertising executives from this agency working with Levi's. Max was with me as I started to tell them a story about Prince Naseem. Keep in mind that Max is standing there with his hands in his pockets listening intently . . .

I was explaining to these executives why I wasn't speaking to Naz at this time. I had seen him on ITV saying, 'Chris Eubank stole all my moves.' Bearing in mind that I am eight years older than Naz, this seemed strange enough. Naz was this cheeky little chap whom I had always offered advice to, I always gave him my time, he had my mobile phone number if he ever needed me, and he regularly used to call me up for advice. He was even at my wedding. He was such a cheeky little character and I always liked him for that. So when I heard this statement on television, I was very upset. It was such a snide thing to do. For a start, they *were* my moves, but it was knowing how considerate I had been towards him that pained me.

Shortly after this, I was at the Royal Lancaster Hotel in London for a charity boxing event. Naz had come to a changing room and we were talking. I said to him, 'Naz, how could you do that? Me? I don't mind, but how can you lie to the people?' I tried to pass over to him the philosophy that your boxing career is not just about how good a fighter you are, you have to be a good person too. Apologising to me didn't cut it – the apology needed to be to the ITV viewers, the great masses. He listened and then said to me, 'I don't think you want me to apologise for me, I think you want me to do it for you.'

I said, 'This isn't about me, it's about you, you lied. You need to tell people your truth, explain to them that maybe you were cajoled into it, explain to them that your trainer Brendan Ingle made you say it, like you've told me. Tell them the truth. I can't accept you lying to the public at large because you will hurt yourself, can't you see that?'

I was very adamant about this, so I went on to give him example after example of the same principle, basically trying to show him that what he had done was underhanded and backstabbing and that things will not work out well if you live your life that way.

'In life, if you cheat,' I told him, 'you will be found out. You can't be imitation, imitation is suicide. Be yourself, you're talented enough, you don't have to put me down or stamp on my name to climb the ladder. You have to work. It's about substance, it's not about making me look bad.' Then I quoted him a small extract from the poem, 'Desiderata', which was believed by some to have been found in a churchyard in Baltimore (author unknown). One of the stanzas goes like this:

'*If you compare yourself with others you may become vain and bitter, for always there will be greater and lesser persons than yourself.*'

I also quoted from a pop song that was out at the time, called 'Everybody's free (wear sunscreen)', whose lyrics listed a litany of guidance, one of which was, '*Don't waste your time on jealousy, sometimes you're ahead and sometimes you're behind, the race is long and in the end it is only with your-self.'* I was trying to pass on these real nuggets of advice to Naz but he couldn't take it on and I became quite frustrated. In the end, I spoke to him thus, 'If you don't understand or perhaps won't accept what I am saying, especially that you should apologise to the ITV viewers, then remember this. I expect you'll make champion, and I expect you'll win all the honours. I expect you'll make your name and fame. When you do and they make you King for a day, as they will, you understand this: when you walk by me, when you see me anywhere near you, walk on by like the little runt that you are.'

Now, remember, I was telling this story in the hotel to all these advertising executives and Max had been listening quietly, fascinated all along. He was standing bolt upright just like an old English gentleman by the end of the table. As I said, 'Naz, you bow your head and walk on like the little so-and-so that you are', Max burst out loud, saying, 'Oh, marvellous story, sir! Marvellous!'

After myself and Max had been friends for three months, I went to his apartment as usual one morning to see how he was. I knocked on the door and there was no answer. I went back later that day, and again that night, but still no answer. He had simply gone. Soon after, I started getting nonsensical postcards and letters from him about pirates, ships, the Royal Albert Hall, telling me how everything is connected by water under the desert near the pyramids, all very peculiar. They were postmarked Portsmouth, a place where he had spent much time in his earlier years. Then, a year later, I saw him in Oxford Street back on the streets. Back with his trolley full of all his possessions, back with his worn shoes and back with his pictures of Princess Diana and Prince Charles.

A small postscript to this story came in late 2000. I took a call from a mental hospital saying there was an old male patient who insisted he knew me very well and had been for day trips with me to tea shops. They said they were very sorry to trouble me but sometimes had to go through the motions just to placate the distressed patient. When I turned up at the hospital and proceeded to have an enjoyable time catching up with Max, I think it is safe to say some of the nurses thought they had gone crazy themselves!

The first fight of the much-vaunted Sky deal was against Mauricio Amaral at Olympia, west London, on 9 July 1994. Amaral was a very tough Brazilian, the Latin American champion, ranked sixth by the WBO and fourth by the WBA, a competent opponent who had won 14 of his 16 pro fights. After Ray Close, I did not have to meet another mandatory challenger for a year, so the Sky deal came at a good time. Much was made during the Sky fights of the supposed disparity of pay between my purse and the challenger's. For example, with this bout I received £750,000 while Amaral got £25,000. I always justified this by pointing out that these men were getting a title shot and still bigger purses than they had ever earned in their career. The idea is to get the championship, then you make the money. That is what *I* had to do.

Amaral was robust enough and actually cut my eye in the seventh, leaving me fighting with a stream of blood obscuring my vision. I won on points but once again incurred the full wrath of a hard-to-please press corps. There were inevitably some critics who thought I had lost, but Amaral was not as inferior as they made out, he put up a good fight and some even suggested he might have won!

On 27 August, I took on Irishman Sam Storey at Cardiff Arms Park. This fight saw me stop my opponent for the first time in 30 months, when his corner threw in the towel in the seventh. He had gone down in an earlier round and hurt his ankle but I think psychologically he had too much fear to fight me. I went in the ring, we were both being cagey then I jolted towards him and he reeled in horror – I knew then that his game was up. I was much stronger than him, so I just powered him out of there. I did sustain a cut on my eye though, which was never welcome. That said, the butterfly stitches they gave me always looked good – I always liked that, it was a battle scar and made me look tough!

The Storey fight contained my 300th professional three-minute round. Despite such a lengthy record, I was still phenomenally fit and motivated. The next fight after Storey was against American Dan Schommer in South Africa's Sun City. I flew in and stayed at the King suite in the Sun City Palace hotel complex. The man who developed Sun City, Sol Kerzner, regularly used this room himself. It was magnificent, with a baby grand piano, a sauna, jacuzzi, dining room, two sitting rooms and incredible views. I stayed there for the three weeks I was in the country, but when I returned home I was taken aback somewhat by the £30,000 bill! I felt I had brought media attention and value to Sun City and perhaps should not have paid that much, but then you learn by your mistakes.

While I was staying at this luxury suite, I was told that Sting wanted the room and could I move out? Needless to say, I didn't. I thought: *You're Sting, I'm Chris Eubank, you don't have any rights over me!* Sting did not take offence at all, he was just asking. Indeed, I was later invited to his birthday party at this game reserve. I took him a present of these really splendid army trainers that were very 'in' at the time.

Although I had ample time to hit the weight limit, at one point I was 21lb over the allowed mark. I worked very hard to get down, training with little or no food. John told me my skin had turned grey from the drying out. For that fight, I had an acute craving for pineapples. The morning of the bout, I actually sat in that suite and juiced 25 – it made me nauseous. I was okay though, no harm done. That said, this was the first time Ronnie publicly aired his reservations about my weight loss routines. It never troubled me though, despite what people thought.

On the actual night, John Regan took his seat as usual near the ring while I prepared in the dressing room. This cathedral-like venue within Sun City had several tiers and John has since told me that for one of the fighters on the undercard, namely the flyweight Baby Jake Matlala, the upper levels were filled with Zulus, chanting tribal mantra and stamping the floor in orchestrated unison.

Dan Schommer was a very tough fight. I got him totally wrong beforehand; I had him as only a three. He is the only person who, in my opinion, beat me despite the decision going my way. I was the aggressor, which is always welcomed by the judges, but I was being picked off. His boxing ability allowed him to do that. He was always just out of range, so when I struck I missed and he would always counter. He hit hard too, and broke one of my teeth in the early rounds, just like Johnny Melfah had back in 1989. The tooth was half-hanging out and causing me great annoyance, so during the next round, I sucked it out of its hole in my gum and spat it onto the canvas. That's not painful, bear in mind I am being hit with severe venom by a very strong and capable boxer, so a loose tooth is the least of my worries. By this time, I had a lot of regard for Schommer, because I knew he was a technically very able and skilled fighter. He had successfully disarmed me before the fight and I had not expected such a test. The reason I was disarmed was because he looked like a pizza chef.

We had walked into this press conference a week or so earlier, and I was looking around the room for my opponent. Normally, one fighter knows another boxer without even asking, because there is a certain look in their eyes, pools of isolation and hardship, it gives them a certain fix, something you come to recognise. I looked around this room – nothing, no one. I looked again. I turned to Barry and said, 'Is he here, Barry? Where is he?' Barry said, 'Yes, he's over there,' and pointed at this pizza chef-looking character. I couldn't believe my eyes. He was podgy, he had no boxer's poise and he had no aura. He was just like some mild-mannered man in the street. There was no fix, no focus. There was not one ounce of threat in his persona. I said, 'This is going to be embarrassing.'

This assumption very nearly cost me dear. My preconception had disarmed me when, in fact, this was a hard, skilful puncher-boxer. All the boxers who strutted in looking tough, that was old news. I knew who they were; I had their number. In my entire career, I've never ever seen this in any other fighter. He was the only one who looked like he flipped pizzas. When he got in there, he still didn't look dangerous but that's why he picked me off left, right and upwards. By the end of round 12, I thought I had lost the fight. In the end I got the decision and put this down to my aggression. However, I believe a technically accomplished fighter should always be given the benefit of the doubt over a boxer who relies on aggression. I considered myself very fortunate on this occasion.

CHAPTER EIGHTEEN

COMMUNITY SPIRIT

Apart from my hectic schedule of fights for the Sky deal, 1994 also saw a project very close to my heart in Brighton. The plight of the homeless has always troubled me. This was not really because I was without a roof over my head myself when I was a teenager, although that experience meant I knew what was involved. When I was homeless, as I have said, I lived like a king. I was young, fast, courageous and had a quick-witted sleight of hand. The problem is, what about the elderly homeless, those who should really be looked after in mental institutions, or very young kids who have no real street sense and are abandoned to the elements and the vultures who prey on those sleeping rough? How will they fare? Who will step in when they are at their wits' end?

When I left London in 1982, I don't remember seeing homeless people on the streets. When I came back to Brighton in 1988 they seemed to be everywhere. London was worse, of course – doorways, alleys, the Embankment, all over. When I used to get up at dawn for road work, I would run past the shelters near Brighton beach or the side streets protected from the elements and see these people, huddled up and without hope. It was like an invisible population, just lying there. Almost always, when I went back later in the day, these people had gone, like a vision of dejection passing through.

I resolved to do something to contribute towards helping this improve. As world champion, you simply cannot take on the troubles of the world and sort them all out, it is impossible. It is hard enough replying to all the thousands of letters you receive, many of them openly begging. I try to siphon out the worthy causes, and help where I can. However, these homeless people I saw in the mornings had played on my mind. I decided to buy a derelict building and convert it into a hostel with flats for the homeless.

I thought that if I made this bold, positive statement from the private sector, it would be a flame that was championed by other like-minded individuals and soon a string of privately funded projects would spring up. It would serve the dual purpose of highlighting to the government that progress can be made in the long term, whilst simultaneously treating the problem in the immediate future. I was convinced we could make a difference.

John Regan was an invaluable help as always with these sort of projects. He told me there was an auction coming up which had an ideal plot of land available. He also instructed me that this piece of ground was worth no more than £250,000, because the derelict and burnt out structure on site would have to be pulled down before any work could commence. He told me that as soon as the bidding reached £250,000, I was to withdraw from offering, explaining to me that there would be so-called 'mirrors' in the auction room inflating the price. The day of the auction came and I was very excited about the possibility of starting this project. The piece of land we wanted was chased by several other bidders and quickly reached John's £250,000 limit, then went on to £260,000 then £270,000. There seemed to be no more bids, so the auctioneer said, 'Anyone for £275,000? £275,000 anybody?' I shouted, 'Yo! £275,000!' I had got it! John went away with a frown on his face but I had my piece of land.

The name of the project was St Anne's Court, Buckingham Place, near Brighton train station. The council said it would fail and become ghettoised, frequented by drug abusers and the like. I could not listen to such negativity and had to press on. The builders started the building and refurbishment programme in 1994 and finished two years later. We had a few inevitable problems, mainly with people living there and not treating it with respect, but after these teething troubles, it settled down nicely. People began to live there together and a real community developed, it became a quality halfway house for homeless as well as working single people in a transitional phase of their lives. It definitely helped to get local homeless people off the streets.

Just after it was completed and filled to capacity, I put a tent in the yard and had a meeting with the residents. I said, 'Understand that this building is your home. If someone sprays graffiti on my house wall, I have it removed because it is my home. I don't leave garbage in the yard, because I don't want to see trash everywhere, I put it in the bin. Treat this as your home, it is not mine, you must understand that this is your property.' That simple edict was abided by. Over the years I only ever saw two or three examples of graffiti and they were cleaned off within days.

I had gone to great lengths to make these flats welcoming and practical. We had studied various similar buildings in London and found that the units were tiny, cramped and usually had a small communal bathroom. We endeavoured to make these flats as large as possible and each one had its own bathroom facilities. There were over 70 studios in a space which might have seen 150 units in London. I knew this more expensive version was always going to lose me substantial amounts of money.

The Prince of Wales came down to Brighton one day to look at the homeless situation and we had a meeting at the West Pier. He was interested in getting the homeless off the streets too, but his thinking was to put them into buildings that were of architectural character. I told Prince Charles all about my project, so he sent down a fellow called Dominic Richards, who was his Architectural Assistant. He came and looked at the project and reported back to the Prince of Wales, who then wrote to say what a fantastic residence we'd created. He asked me if we'd like to get involved in a homeless project in London and, of course, I gladly agreed. There was a building that was to be converted in Camden, based on a classic structure in New York's Times Square, but to my great annoyance, that proposal fizzled out.

By the time I sold up, the whole St Anne's project had cost

me an awful lot of money. The point was, I had tried to achieve something positive. However, perhaps the most damning fact to come out of this project was the reaction it garnered. The media impact was almost nothing. Now, when I had said boxing was a 'mug's game', there was absolute media frenzy. I could show you folders full of argument, coverage, criticism and rhetoric, at the time of, and since, that statement. For my homeless project? Two sheets of ink coverage, maximum. They never wanted to report on me doing good deeds, being a warm human being. All they wanted was the controversy, the caricature. I found that very sad, a great shame. Equally disappointing was the fact that, to my knowledge, I was the sole person in the UK to try such a project. All this frustrated me but that's life, accept it, that's just the way it is.

Another property project I became involved with around this time was the majestic old West Pier in Brighton, with which I have long had a fascination. Even derelict, it was stunning. It is a Grade 1 listed structure of immense architectural importance. Originally, I wanted to live in it. If you had the money to restore it and then live there – what a house! I wanted to fill it with the most exquisite Regency period furniture and transform it into a living museum that people would come to visit from afar. The master bedroom would have been truly stunning. I had earmarked this unbelievable chandelier, which would have hung above a 20 foot square bed. It would have been a treasure trove of the finest antique furniture money could buy, the cost was no object. When I say the furnishings would have been rich,

I mean plush, full of class. You can only buy furniture like that if you think about it in an almost child-like way – if it looks right, that's it, the money cannot be the issue. A similar but unrelated example is my authentic Indian jeep. This is like a mini version of my truck. This jeep is true old school, absolutely splendid. It cost me £1800, but I have so far spent far more refurbishing it. The first renovation came to £12,000, but then I gave it to Doctor. He said he really liked it, so I said, 'It's yours.' However, he didn't look after it the same way as I did, so I had it refurbished exactly the same way again. Such things need to be right.

Coming back to the West Pier, yes, it would have been my home but I would have allowed the public access to it as often as possible. The pier means so much to so many people, it should have been treated like an important stately home. However, when I put in a request for this usage, it came back rejected.

It is still a project I am very passionate about. Unfortunately, since the fires in early 2003 the pier's future is somewhat in doubt. All I ever wanted was to find that one perfect day when the sun is shining, the breeze is very light, there is a great buzz in the town of Brighton and Hove. I would walk along the beach and soak up the whole experience. Marvellous!

The press were all saying my next opponent, Henry Wharton, was a highly talented and capable fighter. His record seemed good enough, 20 wins, 1 draw and a single loss to Nigel Benn (he put Benn on the canvas), but I was more than happy to take him on. I jokingly called him 'easy lolly' but I knew that anyone who had put Nigel Benn on the canvas had to be useful. The fight before me, Wharton knocked his opponent spark out, completely cold, so it was clear he knew his business and packed a punch.

Before the Henry Wharton contest, promoter Mickey Duff referred to me as 'scum' at the pre-fight press conference. His insult gave me the opportunity to show my dignity in as much as I got up to leave the room. It was defamation of character, pure and simple. I know I am not scum and, what's more, the public at large know that too, so I read that slur simply as a shallow attempt to antagonise me before the fight. Over the years, people stooped to all kinds of levels to try to beat me psychologically before the fight, but my opponents only succeeded once (which I will tell you about shortly). Calling me scum? I am a bit more refined and intelligent than that. Was that the best he could think of? That said, in fairness, it did flame the fires of the fight and fuel ticket sales.

Boxing is renowned for its Machiavellian tactics outside of the ring. Over the years, I have had to deal with people who, to put it politely, have 'unusual' ways of doing business. Promoters are a mixed bunch, for example. As I have said, Barry Hearn always did everything with style and charm. Most promoters are not like that. When I was looking for a promoter to get me the fights I wanted, I went to see most of the big name men and was often treated with complete disregard.

When I first met Mickey Duff, he acted as though I should be privileged to even be in his company, talking about all the champions he had worked with, telling me I should be on a winning team. As I told the media at the time, that meant nothing to me. What he had done in the past was irrelevant, this was not about him, it was about me. Another promoter owes me £800 from 1989, over a television rights deal. This is the nature of the business.

Barry Hearn had been very concerned, as indeed were the local police, about the potential for crowd violence at the Wharton fight. A great deal of money was spent on extra policemen and security, with 150 riot officers being posted outside alone. On the night itself there was also a bomb scare, but I was not to be distracted. I entered the arena on a raised platform with fireworks whistling behind me into the air (Barry felt this defused the tension and made for something of a celebratory atmosphere). I was in great shape, and although the BBBC had asked to be allowed unofficial weight checks in the weeks leading up to the bout, I was in great condition. I had prepared for a hard night's work. Wharton's loyal traveller contingent made their dislike for me quite vocal! It was a packed venue – apparently even Ryan Giggs couldn't get a ticket.

However, I was in fine form and disposed of an impressive Wharton with poetic efficiency, albeit in an incredibly tough fight. I jabbed relentlessly and closed his eye, which swelled up like a balloon. When they cut his eye open to release the build-up of blood and fluids, a female reporter at ringside fainted. He brought the fight to me, to his immense credit, he used his great strength and persisted, persisted, persisted. However, with the benefit of hindsight, Wharton came in there with almost too much heart, because I worked around that and used my technical skills to defeat him. If he had pulled back a little, reviewed the terrain, strategized perhaps, he may have had the beating of me. If you come to get me with such tunnel vision, I am ready for you.

Some have said that it was a sterling display. Afterwards, Ronnie, at times my harshest critic, told me that, in his opinion, this was one of my three greatest fights. However, even knowing I had excelled, that contest was so hard, that it almost broke my spirit. After the fight, there was a press conference in which I sighed deeply, saying, 'I can't do this anymore.' This was my 43rd fight.

The reason I felt so jaded was the effect on me of Wharton's resolve, his heart. Yes, I had won the fight and it was a spectacular performance. However, when you hit a guy so heavily and repeatedly but he just keeps on coming, it eventually breaks your morale. I couldn't stop Wharton, he was like a choo-choo train, huffing and puffing, he just wouldn't stop coming forward. Before the fight, I had given him a six for technical ability which was accurate, but he was easily a ten for persistence. His spirit was unstoppable.

He had nearly broken my spirit with his persistence because I had expected to stop someone like that. I'd hit him with some heavy shots but he just wouldn't stop. That's what people want in a fighter, the skills are secondary. The question is: 'Where's your heart?' Henry Wharton had great heart.

Although I have always said the boxing business is my living, which is true, I also believe that before the money comes the spirit, resolve, conviction and grit. I will fight as hard for pennies as I will for a billion pounds. Ultimately, the heart is the measure of the man. Money is the objective of boxing, but the heart is the essence.

CHAPTER NINETEEN
PSYCHOLOGICALLY CHALLENGED

After Wharton, there was some talk of fighting Roy Jones, who had recently disposed of the abrasive American James Toney. For me, however, the Sky deal was now very much back on track. I had won much acclaim with that performance against a very capable Henry Wharton, arguably my best display since the Benn, Watson, and Rocchigiani bouts. I was ready to take on my next challenger. This particular man I had met before – he was given a four. His name? Steve Collins.

At the second Ray Close fight in Belfast, Collins had come into my dressing room and congratulated me on my performance. As he was leaving, I looked at John Regan and said, 'Easy money.' He was a six, maximum. Isn't it funny how things work out?

The first fight against the so-called 'Celtic Warrior', Steve Collins, was at a tiny village in County Cork, at Millstreet.

Collins had fought 31 times, 20 of which were in America, so he was obviously going to be of strong resolve – that much I knew from my days in New York. However, I felt he was a very ordinary fighter, who'd been around for years but achieved nothing spectacular. Ronnie, as with Michael Watson, warned me about underestimating him. There was an initial postponement before the date was set for 18 March 1995.

In short, Steve Collins made me dislike him. His psychological mind game before our first encounter was the only instance in my entire career that I effectively lost a fight before I got in the ring. However, it was not, as is widely believed, Collins' talk of supposedly being under hypnosis that unnerved me. The words that most unsettled me were at a pre-fight press conference in Dublin. He turned up $1^1/_2$ hours late, which was an insignificant and old trick to play. He spoke in Gaelic which was also transparent and weak. However, then he turned to me and said words to the effect of, 'You dress like a Brit, speak like a Brit, I've helped the Irish, what have you ever done for your race, the Africans?'

That could be taken as a good observation by an uneducated or emotionally unaware person, but it was such a preposterous, ridiculous statement.

However, it did make me hate him intensely, which is the gravest mistake to make as a boxer. If a man can anger you, he can conquer you.

At the moment that question first registered in my mind, Steve Collins had got the better of me. The reason he had done this was because I instantly disliked him immensely. Once you dislike someone to that degree, you will find it very difficult to beat that person, because your judgement is clouded and all you want to do is hurt them. You have allowed yourself to become too subjective. If you anger someone you will conquer them. He achieved his goal.

My wife gave me a quotation from a book she had been reading called *Memoirs of a Geisha* which read thus: 'I never seek to defeat the man I am fighting. I seek to defeat his confidence. A mind troubled by doubt cannot focus on the course to victory. Two men are equals – *true* equals – only when they both have equal confidence.' Steve Collins and myself did not have equal confidence; if we had, I would have beaten him. I let him get into my head.

The famous hypnosis story was secondary to these comments about my ancestors, but also made me uneasy. The night before the fight, the journalist John Rawling took me to one side and said, 'Chris, I think you'd better listen to this.' He played me a radio interview where Collins' hypnotist was saying how his fighter would not get hurt, how he would not bleed, how he would be constant, that he would not feel pain because he is under hypnosis. That spooked me. When I'd fought Watson for the second time, he was three times the man he was when I fought him a few months earlier. The thought actually crossed my mind back then that perhaps he was under hypnosis. After what had happened on that night, I was not prepared to go in with another fighter who might not have the capability of protecting his own well-being.

I wasn't ready for that type of fight, I was prepared for an ordinary boxer. So, psychologically, Collins had broken into my refuge. I said to Barry the night before the fight, 'I want to go home. I am not prepared for another Watson 2.' Barry said to me, 'If you leave you lose all your credibility.' So I took the fight. That was a mistake.

A few months later, I said that if Collins was to lose his life in the ring with me, then I could not be held responsible. This seemed a fair observation to me. The British Boxing Board of Control fined me £5000 for saying that, but it made perfect sense and still does. My theory was this – it is a medical fact that hypnosis can negate physical pain. Therefore, it followed that if Collins was under hypnosis, he would feel no pain and would be reckless towards his own physical well-being. I maintain that I was completely in order, but the Board of Control fined me for stating a fact. Your body suffers pain and, eventually, if you insist on carrying on, the brain shuts down – Collins had apparently removed that safety valve. This was not even a medical issue, it was common sense.

He has since stated that he was faking the whole scenario, but the fact is he was playing on what had happened to Michael Watson to unnerve me. The final insult came when he offered to cover all losing bets from people who might back me. This raises a very key point about boxing, sport in particular and also life in general. Collins said he faked it and that he would do it again if it meant he would get the decision. To him it was win by any means necessary. I could not win like that. What he did may not be against the rules, but it was also not noble.

On the Tuesday before the fight, I was in bed with influenza. At one point, Ronnie thought we should consider pulling out of the fight. I couldn't do that, it was not an option. On the actual fight night, I entered the arena on my Harley Davidson, raised on a crane with fireworks spraying out into a sea of laser lights, possibly my most outrageous entrance ever! I was told afterwards that some people saw Collins enter the ring with tears streaming down his face. When I got into the ring, he was just sitting still in his corner, eyes closed, listening to the theme tune from *Rocky* on his personal stereo. I don't know if this was a ploy to make me think he was indeed hypnotised or not. In a sense, the damage to my equilibrium had already been done.

The huge build-up continued when there were head-counts of 4000 people at the weigh-in! After so much hyperbole, though, the fight itself was not a pretty affair, more of a mauling really. A decisive moment came in the tenth, when I hit him with a straight right hand and poleaxed him. He got up . . . and I didn't go forward. I knew at the time you must always go forward to finish the job, but I just stood there. I didn't want what became of Watson to happen again, so I froze. It was never tangibly conscious but that was the source of the hesitation. I have since learned if you want to acquire greatness, you cannot suffer from mental anguish when you are going to strike with extreme power.

If I had gone forward at that moment, I would most definitely have stopped him. It has been said that one more right would have finished the fight. There was talk of a long count, possibly 14 seconds. Whatever, I had not moved forward when I needed to. Ronnie slapped me hard at the end of that round, saying, 'Finish him off.' That mistake cost me my cherished title.

Many people thought I should have got the decision, but I lost. Ronnie felt I had thrown the fight away for not ending it in that decisive tenth round. In the dressing room afterwards, I was very melancholy, turned to John and said, 'Well, it's been a good journey.'

However, I had won 43 fights in a row, 19 of them world title fights. I had a private plane waiting to take me back home, but I kept that waiting at not inconsiderable expense so that I could face the world's media with the dignity a former world champion should have. I had no intention of dodging their questions. I did not complain. To those who suggested I should have got the decision, I said, 'There were decisions in the past that could have gone against me but didn't, so now the rub is against me, so be it. The judges had a job to do and they did it.'

The proposition that the Sky deal was just too much to achieve carries only a little weight, I took that on in good faith and gave it my very best effort. It was my way of life, this was how I lived. The problems only started when Collins got inside my head. No excuses.

Looking back on that night, I should have pulled out of the fight. I had my reasons and they were sound ones. I should have gone home and not fought him, I wasn't prepared for that type of fight. However, I did fight him, I did lose the decision and I am accepting of that outcome.

One of the aspects of life I enjoy acutely is helping people. I don't say that in any self-righteous way, in fact, it is almost as though I am being selfish when I do these things. Simply put, it makes me feel good. I am almost child-like in this way, I am helpful, I am trusting and ultimately I am the one getting gratification – if it helps the other person then fantastic. Unfortunately, people do not always reciprocate my good intentions.

On one occasion I was in London for a week or so on business and I'd packed my little Louis Vitton case that I carry around all the time with jewellery worth about £100,000. I was on one of these old-fashioned rolling stock trains which had individual box compartments. I went into this one compartment and sat next to this fellow who was wearing a business suit, aged about 27. He didn't say much, he might have mumbled 'hello'. I was champion at this point.

Then this young lady came into the compartment and started gesturing to me inaudibly. It appeared she couldn't talk properly and I struggled to understand what she was trying to say. She was gesticulating quite frantically now, and I thought she asked me if I had a pen, to which

I answered, 'no'. She went out of the compartment, then I suddenly heard her start to moan more animatedly. Within seconds, someone put their head into my compartment and said, 'There's a girl who has collapsed out here.'

I asked the young businessman to watch my bag and went out into the corridor. This lady was on the floor. I asked if anyone had a mobile telephone and told them to call for an ambulance to meet us at the next station Clapham Junction. Before this girl had collapsed she had managed to scribble something down on a scrap of paper. It said, 'Insulin, I need sugar.' She was half-conscious, so I went and got some bubblegum, it was all I had. She said, 'No, no, coca, cola,' then she went into a convulsion.

Her eyes rolled up into the back of her head and the convulsions became maniacal. I picked her up to try and help her regain consciousness, but it wasn't working. Then the convulsions stopped but she seemed to have slipped into some kind of diabetic stupor, she was just motionless. I slapped her face but got no reaction and by now was really concerned for her. I put her in the recovery position and put my finger in her mouth to stop her swallowing her tongue. I waited with her until the next station, Clapham Junction, where paramedics had fortunately arrived in time to take her away.

I went back to my compartment and sat down next to the besuited fellow. He said, 'That was scary,' and I replied, 'Well, yes, these things happen, so if you can help you've got to help.' Out of three other people around, no one had gone to help this distressed young girl. I arrived home late that evening and went straight to bed without unpacking my bags. The next morning, I opened my bag and my jewellery pouch had gone.

I got in touch with the insurance company and explained everything that had happened. They reimbursed me fully for my losses. For me, however, it was an ideal opportunity to put one of my opinions over to the public. I was booked to do a morning television show and explained that I did not essentially object to the theft, they had used sleight of hand. What's more, it was only material goods, they can usually be replaced (although some antique jewellery could not be replaced like for like). I did, however, use the opportunity to point out this – if you hurt someone, just like all those years ago when that thief had barged into that old lady in The Lanes, you must be stopped. Of course, the newspapers had their own angle on things. They said I had been duped, the victim of a sting on the train. I simply saw a situation and went to help without hesitation.

A similar incident occurred when I was driving my truck home from four weeks staying at the Dorchester on business in London. I noticed a red car had broken down on the motorway hard shoulder, so I pulled the truck up to see if I could help. The motorist and his girlfriend were in their mid-20s and both recognised me immediately. They had run out of petrol. So I offered to take them to the service station, they agreed and jumped up into my truck for a lift down to Pease Pottage Services. I also called the AA on my mobile, gave them my credit card details and asked them to come out to help. Once we had the petrol, I drove them back up the motorway, over the flyover and back down to their stranded car.

In the back compartment of the truck, I fortunately had two wardrobes full of clothes, because I'd just done many various functions and events and I must always be appropriately dressed. It was a cold day and the young man had no coat, so I said, 'Take a coat out of the back. How about this?' and I picked out the first one I saw, a brand new elegant blue three-quarter-length coat, with paisley lining, worth about £800. I said, 'You know who I am, just drop it back to me when you're going by.' I didn't take any names. I had allowed these two people, who had probably read many misconceptions about me in the media, to glimpse who I really was and that made me feel good. However, I never saw them again.

These sort of incidents don't reflect badly on me. Maybe it doesn't reflect badly on them. Maybe I'd rather take the positive view about this latter couple and believe they needed a coat (he seemed like a nice enough fellow). If he had sent me a letter saying 'Sorry, I didn't bring the coat back because I needed one actually, can I have the coat?', then fine, that would have been okay. The only material possessions I guard are my photographs. They cannot be replaced, I am sentimental about them, they are your history. This was only a coat, just a piece of material.

If people take advantage of my good nature, the fault lies with them, not me. It is not about me being gullible, it is about them taking from someone who was helping them. I will lose part of my essence if I stop trying to help, because that's what makes me happy. That's why a child is happy because they know no boundaries, they don't know bitterness, they don't know cynicism. I will not let anyone get me down. Karron tells me I shouldn't always be so forthcoming and helpful, but that is my grain and I can't change – nor do I want to.

I feel very strongly that people should help each other more. One day I was driving up and down the seafront and I saw these three guys standing beside a drunk who was lying on a bench in a shelter with his dog next to him. They picked his head up, pulled his pillow out from beneath him and seemed to be searching through his belongings.

'Hey, leave him alone!' I shouted out.

One of them walked over to me. 'He's my mate, Chris,' he said in a Liverpudlian accent. 'Wake him up, you'll see.'

'Well, if he's your mate, you shouldn't be going through his personal property.'

They woke him up and the drunk said, 'It's okay, Chris, it's okay.'

Then one of the three men turned to me.

'F**king Eubank,' he snarled. 'You've always got to play the hero.'

That surprised me – and I liked it! 'I can't help who I am,' I said. 'You should think that if it was you in that position, you would want someone telling them to leave your gear alone.'

They asked me for £4 to get them back to Eastbourne, then when they had walked away the drunk fellow said, 'Thanks a lot, Chris. I don't like them, I don't trust them.'

Another day, I was in Portland Place, central London, I saw this woman stumble and fall over right next to this very big man in a grey pin-stripe suit, standing still using his mobile phone. He never even moved to help her. I ran across the road, but by the time I got there the lady had got up and walked off. This man recognised me and perhaps was a little startled. I said to him, 'Excuse me, you probably don't want to hear this, but why didn't you help that lady?' He said, 'I was going to finish my call and then I was going to help her.' I said to him, 'In life, you get very few opportunities to be a human being, never ask, never think, just react. You have let a very good opportunity go by.' Then you will be a hero, if even only to yourself.

The Sky contract allowed me to have two ten-round non-title fights before being put forward for a fresh title challenge. I was lined up against Bruno Godoy on 27 May in Belfast, and I took him out in one round. I comprehensively outclassed him and the referee stopped the fight. My purse was halved for this and the next fight, so I was bringing in about £350,000 for those ten-rounders.

Next up was José Barruetabena in Whitley Bay, and he lasted only 55 seconds before I caught him and switched his lights out. When I knocked him out you almost see it ripple and course through his body, as it wreaked havoc with his nervous system. Within six months of my first loss, I was scheduled to meet Collins again to try to win the title back. In fact, the Barruetabena fight was far more notable for a trip I paid to Durham prison the day after. Sir John Hall of Newcastle United football club offered his Rolls Royce to escort me around for the day, a kind gesture which I gladly accepted.

Bold as ever I went to speak to the inmates of Durham prison after I had been invited by the authorities. I wore my boxing boots, shorts, white T-shirt and an orange cap. I was walking through towards the hall where I was going to talk, when I saw a section for isolation prisoners, those who were being punished with a 23-hour lock-down for violent and unruly behaviour. This one inmate was especially rowdy, banging the doors and shouting abuse at the warders. The warder I was with said, 'Listen, I've got Chris Eubank here, so pipe down,' and this inmate said, 'F**k off, you've got Chris Eubank, no way, you're winding me up, f**k off.' The warder said, 'Will you behave yourself if I have?', to which this prisoner replied, 'Too f***ing right I will, you're a wind-up merchant.' So he opened the door and I was standing there with a big smile on my face. You should have heard the stream of obscenities coming out of this inmate's mouth! In disbelief I said, 'Calm down, be cool,' and we talked. He told me before I left that it had made his time inside the isolation area most enjoyable!

I then asked to be introduced to the most dangerous prisoners in the jail, and although they said this was not a good idea for me, I insisted. They were in an area where they couldn't mix with other inmates because they were considered too dangerous to socialise with. I went and spoke to six men who were lifers, none of them older than 24.

There was no advice I could give them really, because they will never have children, they will never go on holiday, travel outside England or maybe even venture outside the prison walls. So it was simply a matter of playing pool with them, telling them about particular fights, explaining the essence of the business, the intimidation of the game, all the inside track. I wanted to see everybody, it was good for the morale.

Then I made my way to the main hall for the scheduled talk with the bulk of the prisoners. John Regan had suggested it might not go down too well if I philosophised too much. Most of these inmates were in for three to five years. I thoroughly enjoyed our discussions. I explained about common sense and the philosophy of getting on in life. I said, 'Understand that you are not here because you got caught, you are here because you broke the law. Do not break the law and you will not end up in here. Nothing is worth being away from a woman. Also, understand this: there is an institution in this country called Her Majesty's police force, namely "the long arm of the law." They are a business and they are more clever then you are, so don't compete with them. Their job is to study people like you, apprehend them and put them away. Ultimately, no one escapes, it is only a matter of time which often comes around very quickly. When it does happen, it's too late and then you are banged up.' There was total silence.

I continued, 'You think you are hard? Do you want to know hard?' At this point, I puffed my chest out and gave it the full strut. 'I am hard, truly hard.' There were a few perplexed faces, but I strutted around a little more and they laughed. I continued, 'Let me explain to you what hard is. The person who goes out there and puts a shotgun to someone's throat and takes their money is not hard. The man who sticks you with a knife and robs you, he's not hard. He's stupid. People like that are an insult to people like me. Why? Because I will not take anything that does not belong to me. If someone is nasty to me, I will not retaliate or beat them up, either intellectually or physically. Being truly hard is practising restraint.' At that moment, this tiny little fellow, who had been absolutely captivated throughout, jumped up from his seat, pointed at one of the meanest, most menacing guys in there and shouted, 'Yeah, that's right, d'you hear that!'

We chatted lots more and afterwards they all told me how much they enjoyed the afternoon and expressed their respect for me. They were very receptive to what I had to say. They know how I earn my living and they respected that, so my words made sense to many of them too.

We left the prison and got back into the Rolls Royce. By now, the chauffeur was very edgy, saying he was anxious to get the car back to Newcastle for Sir John. I knew his boss had given me the vehicle for the day, so I said to the driver, 'Would you mind if I just made one more journey?' He seemed very perturbed, but politely asked, 'Where to, sir?' 'Manchester, please,' I said, 'I need to get my hair cut.'

CHAPTER TWENTY
LUCK OF THE IRISH

The inmates at Durham Prison were a very respectful, interested and interesting group. I have talked at many universities and colleges over the years and always thoroughly enjoyed myself. I know that some people say I am verbose. I do listen to every word people say and often pick them up on something if it seems strange or incorrect. For example, if someone wishes me luck, I will always say, 'What sort of luck do you mean? Good or bad?' I will ask questions, that are refreshing and entertaining. That is why I find talking at Union Debating clubs so rewarding.

Ordinarily, the crowds are attentive and delightful to be in front of. The very first such talk I attended was with 12 doctors of philosophy at Sussex University. That was daunting, these people were renowned academics! I had this attitude that I was this emotionally intelligent boxer. I was explaining my method of living and how I've done things. Halfway through the seminar, I found I was the only one who was talking and so I kept on philosophising. These people were spellbound! Afterwards, one of them told me that everything I'd said concerned things they had only read about in books.

Since then I've spoken at Eton, Cambridge (five times), London School of Economics, London University, University of Exeter, Trinity (twice) and Oxford (twice). Ironically, the prisoners at Durham jail were far more accommodating and respectful than the crowd I talked to at the London School of Economics. Although I can hold any crowd, at LSE I was so surprised by their rowdy behaviour that at one point I said, 'This is LSE isn't it? Is this the institution that teaches the people who are supposed to be running our future?' The lady organising the evening said, 'Don't worry about those people, they're just being lads.'

I have a passion for speaking. I do bring boxing into the talks because that is where people know me from but, most importantly, the fight business is the best metaphor for life, especially in regards to application. Boxing was my way of making money, and I did love it, along with poetry, the spoken word and philosophy. I tell them, 'You can have fun taking drugs, drinking, being rude to people, cutting class, not studying and so forth, but your life is going to be very difficult later on and the only person to blame is yourself. When it comes to conduct, there is a serious course to take, it is going to be very hard, and if you pay nothing in, you will get nothing out, simple. No one owes you anything.' You reap what you sow.

I also explain that, 'I am here to entertain, but I am also here to talk about method. If you use method, it allows you to be more at peace with yourself. For example, here are three words that will make you happy if you apply them: Integrity, Reason, Forgiveness, in that order. Those three virtues are tough to apply but, if you can, you will stand out. The best thing you can do is practise integrity, but that is so cruel for me to actually advise you to, it's cruel because it's just so hard because the people who surround you are usually void of it.'

The youngsters and students often ask me what it is like to be famous. It can be very demanding, testing, you need to remain in control and behave with good conduct at all times. Bad people will sometimes try and provoke you. One story I often tell is about the time I went to a night-club with Doctor. We were walking through this club and there were bottles and debris all over the floor. As I walked through, I kicked a bottle but thought nothing of it, as there was so much mess all over the place. This hand suddenly grabbed my arm. These two men were standing there and one of them said, 'You kicked my bottle over.' I said, 'Surely you understand if you leave them on the floor, they will get kicked over?' Unmoved, he said, 'Pick it up.'

I was trying to say to him, 'Do you see who I am? Please, don't be silly?' Remember also, I was standing next to Doctor, a 6' 4" martial arts trainer. This fellow knew who I was and repeated his demand, 'Pick it up.' Doctor said, 'No, Chris,' and went to pick it up for me. I stopped him and said, 'No, it's okay, Doctor' and I picked the bottle up. I handed it to the man and said, 'If you live your life this way, you will end up getting killed.' This is experience.

It would have taken me five to six seconds to drop them both, but that was totally the wrong thing to do. This fellow will no doubt have gone around telling his friends how he had fronted out Chris Eubank. For me, there was no other response, indeed, it gave me a perfect opportunity to show what I have learned by being a boxer and being in the public eye. If I had hit that man or verbally provoked him to hit me, it would have been all over the newspapers the next day. The only person who would have been affected negatively was myself, not least because I would have set a bad example. In that sense, the policemen in my life are the media. But more importantly it would have shown to the emotionally intelligent person that I'm weak, because it takes strength of character to walk away.

I also enjoy going to talks. Perhaps the most notable was the night I went to Oxford to see OJ Simpson give his account of the murder trial and case. I was invited upstairs to speak to OJ and PR guru Max Clifford beforehand in private. When it was time to take my seat, I made my way down to the debating hall and as I walked in the applause was absolutely deafening, rapturous and warm. I was taken aback. This puts me in mind of the time I was at Madison Square Garden in Manhattan for the first Lewis–Holyfield bout. When I walked into the arena, the clapping filled that cavernous hall. It has been said by John Beckworth, who was there, that I received even more applause than stars like Jack Nicholson and Lenny Kravitz. In my opinion, Jack

Nicholson got the biggest round of applause, then Keith Richards, then me.

So back to the Oxford Union and OJ. I took my seat at the front and quietly listened to what he had to say. All these questions were being fired at him and I was a little disappointed to note that they were essentially queries that had already arisen in the trial. So OJ was very comfortable answering them each in turn.

I could see several girls were unsuccessfully trying to get their questions in, and one young lady in particular was getting quite distressed about it, even tearful, so I put my hand up.

'Yes, Mr Eubank?'

'There's a young lady over there who has been waiting patiently to ask a question. Let the lady take a question.'

So she did, but unfortunately, it was only another rather impotent trial inquiry. About three or four questions later I put my hand up again.

'Yes, Mr Eubank? Do you have a question?'

'Yes.'

'What is your question?'

'My question is this: when you look into the eyes of your children, what do you see?'

I knew that if he was evasive to such a thrust that would seem to point to his guilt. If he answered the question without hesitation, then he was surely innocent. To me, that was not a deep question. Does he see fear? Acceptance? Resignation? He must see something in the children's eyes. His answer was calculated. He suggested that his children were too young to offer him a perception of their feelings from their eyes. This was not true for my children. At that time I had three kids and I knew exactly what was going on, even in the two-year-old's eyes: joy, when they see you after you've been away, sometimes cheekiness, love, acceptance, lots of emotions. He was evasive and that speaks volumes to me.

When I dress as an English aristocrat and go in to talk to a hall crammed full of students. I recognise some of them keep me at arm's length, but that changes if you show them empathy and when they discover that the language is never a show they listen.

I regularly go to schools, secondary schools and colleges and universities as well. I always begin by saying, 'What I am going to tell you, you already know. I'm just going to jog your memory.' It is just common sense. I enjoy most of all the reciting of pieces of knowledge about conduct to receptive 15–18 year olds. When I do, it doesn't tend to make the headlines, because as I have said, good news is no news. That is frustrating but there is nothing you can do about it, all you can do is keep on banging the same drum. I've come to realise that common sense is so uncommon.

Of course, just because I enjoy offering advice does not mean I have all the answers and know how to react to every single circumstance. For example, in one of my guises of helping youngsters, I am a supporter of the Prince's Trust. I first met Prince Charles at Sussex University at a Trust event in the autumn of 1994, but I made several serious errors when introduced to His Royal Highness. We had to line up to meet him and at first I didn't want to do this. Then I realised the only way I was going to be able to meet him was by blowing this protocol, I really wanted to meet this man. I had always thought that Prince Charles had integrity, which is evident in the way he deports himself. He obviously cannot be bought – his recent stance on GM foods is very strong and highly admirable. I like a man who will take that type of stand. A role model who teaches by example, I aspire to be like that. So I had to talk to him.

When he walked level with me, he said, 'Hello' and shook my hand. I went to shake his hand very firmly, as I always do. First mistake. I said, 'Mr Windsor.' Second mistake. He said, 'Thank you for coming,' to which I said, 'I understand you like Aston Martins. Would you like to come and try out my 6.3 Volante? I only live down the road.' Third mistake. Then I said, 'If you ever become king and the press keep giving you a hard time, you can always abdicate.' Fourth mistake. He said, 'It is not as simple as that,' and by now his people were desperately trying to get him on his way. He went to move on to the next person and I said, 'Okay, if you have to go now, I understand, Bye.' Fifth mistake. Between 1994 and 1998, I was never invited to any further Prince's Trust events. What a shame. But it is because of these immature mistakes I can say to youngsters, I wish I had someone to tell me the things I'm telling you. *(Footnote on the Aston Martin: I was travelling back from London one day and the Aston was making some very strange sounds. I struggled home and had an engineer check it the next day – the engine had fallen off its mountings about thirty miles outside of Brighton!)*

This is a great example which I tell the youngsters of how sometimes you need to be taught how to behave. I admire Prince Charles and his conduct, so I wanted to talk to him, but I went about it completely inappropriately.

In 1999, there was an event for Breakthrough Breast Cancer, an excellent charity which I had launched in 1991 on GMTV. Prince Charles had become a patron, so all the other patrons were invited to hear a speech by him on the charity. As he came over to me this time, I shook his hand very lightly and because, I assume, he felt the warmth and respect, he held his hand there for a fraction longer. I said, 'Good afternoon, sir,' and he smiled and returned the greeting. He asked me about my connection with the charity and I politely and briefly told him. I then said, 'I know I was rude the last time we spoke, but please understand that no one taught me protocol, so I spoke in a too familiar way, but I know now I was very rude.' He said, 'No, really, it was fine.' It couldn't have been because I wasn't invited to those events for four years. I had been too forward and too full of myself with him that first time.

I gave him a letter where I had put my feelings in writing and I also gave him two of my 'Ultimate Gladiator' postcards (which I give to people who ask for autographs) for Princes Harry and William. On the back of one card I had written, 'If and when you would like to understand the philosophy of this boxing way of life, I will give you an in-depth view anytime.'

The television presenter Vanessa Feltz was standing next to me, and Prince Charles had started to speak with her, but then paused, came back to me and said, 'I can't believe how much you've mellowed.' The next day, I was at a Royal film premiere which Prince Charles was attending. As he walked past me, I bowed my head slightly and he nodded in recognition and approval.

How had I learned the correct way to behave? By reading quotations and proverbs. One of the most succinct and tellingly appropriate was this one from Winston Churchill, who wrote that, 'On being invited to a party hosted by the Prince of Wales, I knew I had to be on my best behaviour, punctual, reserved and subdued, qualities of which I was least endowed.'

Although my relationship with Barry Hearn had been very enjoyable and mutually beneficial, after the Collins fight I decided I could no longer work with him. Essentially, the reason for our disagreement was this: for the Sky deal, he said the £6 million basic package could be supplemented by additional gate receipts. I said, 'This Sky deal is so good that you should take 25%.' He said he would be very happy with just 12.5% but I insisted, I felt that strongly about it.

By the fourth fight of the deal (against Wharton) I thought that the gate receipts should have been greater so I suggested Barry should take a 12.5% cut rather than the 25% I had initially insisted upon.

But Barry said, 'These fights are not making enough money, there is no extra to be made yet.' If you watch the

Collins fight, you can sense that I am having problems with Barry, I was hardly looking at him. You could see from that fight interview that we were finished.

I made my decision and told Barry, saying 'I can't work with you unless you go back to 12.5% now because the additional receipts are not coming in as expected.' He said, 'I can't do that, I have this company to run and I have people to look after.' I replied, 'Sorry, Barry, then we can't work together anymore.' We shook hands and parted as friends.

This was a shame, because before that fallout our relationship was made in heaven, it really was. Barry has said some very warm and graceful things about me, for instance, 'Eubank certainly changed the whole face of boxing as we know it. I don't think there is anyone straighter – you may not have agreed with him, but he was his own man throughout and the respect I have for him has never diminished to this day. I enjoyed my time with him and wouldn't swap a moment.' I am still extremely fond of Barry – he has class and he always smiles even though I felt he took money from me.

Before the second Collins fight, I trained exceptionally hard. The arena in Cork for the bout was open-air, which was a little strange, as it was during a very wet spell. During the evening it was raining hard, so much so that I saw John Regan putting carrier bags over his shoes to keep the water out as he went to take his seat.

In that second fight, Steve Collins had a resolve the like of which I had never seen. It was pure desire. He had seemed tense, perhaps even uncertain in the press conferences beforehand, but in the ring that aura was nowhere to be seen. His motivation was so immense I was taken aback, I didn't think he had that type of resolve.

In the seventh round, I cut his eye but this just seemed to spur him on, especially when the referee took a look at the gash. His resolve was maniacal and, despite my best intentions and meticulous preparations, I could not wrestle the crown back from him. This time, unlike the underhand first victory over me, Collins beat me fairly and squarely. Barry later told me he watched this fight on television with tears in his eyes. Ironically, in the dressing room after this second defeat, I was surprisingly philosophical. This time I was not even as disappointed as after the first fight. I was understanding of the events of life. It was due to happen after so many victories, so many title defences, having been a professional boxer for 11 years. Winning and losing is just part of life – I just lost.

After the Collins rematch, I announced my retirement. It was essentially a knee-jerk reaction to not prising the title back. At the time, I fully believed my decision was final. I called a press conference at my Hove home and invited members of the media down. Before I started to speak, we held a one minute's silence in memory of Jim Murray, the Scottish bantamweight who had unfortunately died the week before, aged only 25. I had to make some gesture for him and to further highlight the plight of boxers, but what is a minute's silence when a man has lost his life?

As I said, I genuinely believed my time was done. However, as time went by, it became apparent to me that I still had things to achieve in the business. Analysing my career, I could see various landmarks that feature in what I felt would be the 'perfect' career. The first thing you do is learn the art, then you apply the philosophy, which is consideration, so then you make the money. With the money and the victories comes fame. Then, if you've shown yourself to be a warrior of integrity through all of these steps, you earn respect.

I knew the art and philosophy intimately. I had earned my money and I had fame, I had even been in some of the most revered fights in the history of boxing. However, I still did not have the respect I wanted. That is so elusive because this was a business that is made out to be a thug's game. It obviously isn't and I'm proof of that. The odd and confusing thing about earning respect in this business is the fact that to have ability and talent amounts to only 33% of what it takes to acquire respect; another 33% is about being able to take and accept a severe beating when a fight is going against you; and 34% is about being dignified. This equation isn't a rule, just an observation. Despite everything I had said and done outside of the ring, so many people still saw me as an oddball or provocative, which I wasn't trying to be. The truth is that standards are low and anything which is dignified goes well over the head of some of the media.

People would walk up to me in the street and say, 'How can you do that for a living?' This was usually a person who worked for someone else for 50 years only to be told,

'Goodbye.' So my thoughts were always, *How can you do THAT for a living!* I gradually realised I had to attain this respect before I retired, otherwise there would always be a sense of unfinished business. I started to become anxious and contemplate winning a title again. Basically, it was the wrong time for me to retire.

CHAPTER TWENTY-ONE
STYLE ON THE NILE

People thought I was just being quirky when I bought the title, Lord of the Manor of Brighton for £45,000 in 1996. But one could say that it went well with the English Gentlemen dress code. However, the historical background alone is fascinating. Brighton used to be known as Brighthelmstone, originally separated into three estates, one of which belonged to Earl Godwin, the father of King Harold who suffered an eye injury of his own in 1066! William the Conqueror held the Lordship at the date of the Domesday Survey in 1086. Five hundred years later, Thomas Cromwell, later Earl of Essex, was the Lord before being executed by Henry VIII in 1540, who then bestowed the title on Anne of Cleves. On her death, it passed to Queen Mary I, then Elizabeth I. The Virgin Queen awarded it to the Sackville family, who became the Earls and Dukes of Dorset. They held the title until 1988. In 1996, the Lordship of the Manor came to me, Chris Eubank.

There were two levels to acquiring this, one which was quaint and one which was much deeper. Some people say the money I spent was a waste. No, it was a quixotical move and these are the reasons why. Firstly, there are people who linger long in the memory after they have departed this mortal coil. For example, I have read about slaves in the southern American states who escaped to the north and created railroads and underground conduits to smuggle people up to a more relaxed way of life. These people are heroes. They are talked about centuries later in revered tones. Or take Jack Johnson, the Edwardian-era African–American heavyweight who was always berated for going out with white women, despised by many, but always came into the ring with a dignified smile before going on to demolish his opponent. He was a brilliant fighter, yet was kept away from a title shot until 1908, when he was 30 years old, because of his colour. After he beat Jim Jeffries there were race riots and 19 deaths, such was the passion that surrounded this man. When he died in one of his own fast cars in 1948, he was already a legend whose name still burns brightly. For me, with my dress code and being the Lord of the Manor of Brighton, hopefully in 300 years they will speak about me in the same way as they speak of other trailblazers – people who don't accept the standard, but instead set standards.

The second reason is very profound for me. According to the historical documents, 1000 years ago the Lord was entitled to anyone's livestock within his manor, including several herds of cow, 4000 herrings and such like. More poignantly, he was also due from his subjects one slave. Slaves at that time were not black men, they were Englishmen, but they were still slaves. So in taking the Lordship, I felt that, had I been Lord of the Manor 1000 years ago, I would have freed that slave. In so doing, I would have freed myself being decended from slaves.

Another point of note is this. When the Queen bestows the name Lord on someone, she does so because it is deemed that this person has contributed to the system or country – for example, Lord Sainsbury. Well, I have contributed, it's just not recognised. *I* recognise it, that's another reason why I made myself the Lord of the Manor.

The press said this was more evidence that I am eccentric. They talk about this English gentleman look as a gimmick. Maybe if my ancestral line were English, I wouldn't care at all about this, but I love to make a real effort to actually be the quintessential English gentleman. This is no gimmick, when in Rome . . .

The vehicle for me to plunge back into the gladiatorial life came when I was approached by businessmen from the Middle East with a proposal to stage the first ever professional bout in Egypt.

The fight, which I promoted myself and dubbed 'The Lord of the Manor Presents Style on the Nile', was against a reasonably competent fighter named Luis Barrera. The press made much of him being of a poor standard, but the British Boxing Board of Control was fully involved, it was not as if

I drove into Cairo and picked anybody off a street corner. Obviously, this was no Nigel Benn, but neither was it a foregone conclusion. He was of a certain calibre.

Training for the fight in Egypt was a very hard but interesting experience. Generally, I was treated with first-class hospitality. I was considered a kidnap risk, so everywhere I went I was shadowed by these enormous bodyguards with what seemed like enough armoury for a small Middle Eastern country each. This one particular bodyguard was a man mountain and seemed to have absolutely no sense of humour or light-heartedness whatsoever – he was hard work! He was a national basketball player, about seven feet tall and incredibly surly. He had this bruise on his head and when I asked him how he got it, he said it was where they bowed in prayer. At one press conference, I pointed out all these pictures of various dignitaries on the wall and he just looked displeased and said, 'I kill them.' When we took a trip to the pyramids, he took me to one side just before I took this camel ride and said, 'Any trouble, I kill them,' and pulled up his trouser leg to reveal an enormous machete.

One day we went to the gym in no particular emergency, but I was given a full lights-flashing, sirens-blaring, three-car cavalcade through town. At one point, there was some overtaking on the wrong side of the road as we went, causing one old car to crash into a fruit stall. I used to drive to gyms in the UK in a Rolls Royce sometimes, but even that had been upstaged.

The work involved in promoting these fights myself, training as usual, acclimatising, avoiding illness and so on was exhausting. We had an enjoyable time though, away from the workload. We were told never to drink the water, but I made the mistake of having a salad which, of course, had been washed with local water. I got up the next morning and met the two bodyguards who went everywhere with me (even doing road work) so they could escort me to a car. We drove out of town and began the morning's run, flanked by the men and followed by a two-car motorcade. I started jogging in the searing heat, but after only two miles I had a sudden uncomfortable rumble in my bowels. My left eyebrow raised as I realised what might happen next. Another seismic rumble and my right eyebrow raised. Now we had a situation. I grabbed my stomach and dived into the back of this car and shouted, 'Hotel! Hotel!'

We flew through the town, blaring our way past ancient markets, flying past donkey-driven carts and screeched up to the hotel reception. I was really struggling by now, so I jumped out of the car and sprinted through the foyer, but the lift was on the top floor. I couldn't afford to wait, so I dashed up the staircase, fumbled for my keys, stomach resounding like a pained hippo, pushed the door open, and ran to the bathroom.

The fight itself was in a very big local stadium, which had originally been built for the African Games. By the time I entered the arena, there were 16,000 people waiting. The UK press said it was all army personnel, but as the army had been helping so much with the organisation (I trained at some nearby barracks), there were troops watching, yes. Ringside seats were £1000 and they were these plush armchairs! These were, perhaps not surprisingly, filled by extremely rich looking men in traditional robes. Richard Furlong did the compèring and had learned an introduction in Arabic, which was very well received. The bout itself was a relatively comfortable win – I disposed of Barrera in five rounds.

After the fight, the cynical UK press said I had proved nothing. I had worked so hard to push that bout through, promoting ceaselessly as well as training, but they totally dismissed it. The fact is, this was the first-ever professional bout in that country, I had introduced top-level boxing to the Middle East and for that I am very proud.

I was in the Thistle Hotel on Brighton seafront on New Year's Eve 1995 with my family. We were having a nice evening, looking out at the sea and enjoying ourselves. Nearby, there was a little boy who looked miserable, really down in the dumps. I went over to him, crouched down and said, 'Hey, it's New Year's Eve, cheer up.' He just said, 'Yeah, well, you know,' and continued to look depressed. I thought I would give him something to smile about, but he just shrugged his shoulders. I felt sorry for him so I said, 'Listen, in about half an hour, you look out of that window and you will see a sensational fireworks display.'

I told Karron and the kids that I was going to get some fireworks and tipped them off to keep an eye out too. I had a substantial stockade of fireworks at home in the garage, because throughout the year I always felt like celebrating something. Even if I wasn't celebrating anything in particular, I would get bored, go down to the seafront and let a few fireworks off. I liked them. It was for my enjoyment only, I still didn't really frequent with anybody despite my high profile status. There was only really Max who had been my companion.

I drove home and loaded up the Range Rover with about £4000 worth of fireworks – big, professional stuff. I had to put the seats down to get them all in. I drove excitedly back to the seafront and, with the four-wheel drive on, mounted the pebbles and guided the car about 60 feet away from the promenade, which was itself another 30 or 40 feet from the main road. I unloaded the fireworks and then reversed the car back to the tarmac area, before walking back down to the stash which was only about 15 feet from the water's edge. I really wanted to create a great family night out and help to brighten this kid's evening too.

I had some spectacular fireworks in there. There were about five bin bags filled to capacity with what are called '50,000 Bangs'. These are a roll of substantially large bangers, each roll being quite a fantastic thing to see. However, I started by setting off these huge four-inch mortar bombs into the air, which was intended to let people know there was going to be a display. *Bang*! The explosions were massive. Next, I took some Roman Candles which were bound in packs of five, then I taped up bundles of five packs each. I stuck these into the gravel and lit them. Unfortunately, what I had forgotten to do was take the bulk of unlit fireworks far enough away from where these were going off. They were maybe five yards away but the fireworks exploded in such a vast spray of light and sparks that this was simply not far enough away.

The whole incident seemed to happen in slow motion. Each firework was lasting about 90 seconds. However, 30 seconds into one explosion, this gentle breeze started to drift the sparks towards the bin bags full of fireworks. I was frozen to the spot, looking up at the sparks in the wind, looking down at the debris landing closer and closer to the bags. I started mumbling, 'No, no, oh no . . .' but before I could even move, the first bag of three '50,000 Bangs' exploded.

What occurred next felt like World War III. The first bag had ignited every other bag and so now we had these thousands of pounds worth of industrial fireworks going off at random, without any control whatsoever. By now, I was running away from the heart of the inferno, there was no way I could stop it. I was 100 yards away down the beach and still sprinting but still had to duck and dodge fireworks as they whistled past my head. I found out afterwards that even people who were above the promenade, looking over from the main road, were running in front of cars to evade the fireworks, such was the distance the sparks were travelling. It was hellish. The noise was immense. There was an almighty bang as the twelve-inch mortar bombs exploded into a shower of pebbles. If anyone had been watching this from afar in safety, it would no doubt have been the single most awesome firework display ever. It was so spectacular but I had messed up, it was supposed to go up in a considered and controlled manner, not all at once. The whole eruption lasted about two minutes.

The havoc started to calm down, but I couldn't see anything because the smoke was so thick and acrid. I ran back to the promenade area to see what was going on, shouting, 'Is everybody okay? Is anyone hurt?' I heard a faint female voice say, 'I'm hurt.' I looked over at these two ladies and the first thing I saw was that the skin was hanging off their hands and face. My heart sank. This display had clearly been a mistake and now it was a tragedy. I had hurt somebody and that appalled me. To hurt others in such a fashion goes against every sinew in my body, I was so upset.

To add to this, as a public personality, I knew the story would be all over the papers and there would also be legal repercussions. That said, the priority was to get these girls (Amanda Marsden and Anita Wyness) to hospital, so I got hold of an ambulance which came to pick them up within about ten minutes. We were putting cold water on them while they waited. They were walking but their hair was singed, their necks were peeling, it must have been very painful. They weren't crying because they were so shocked. I insisted I went with them in the ambulance to the hospital. They knew it was an accident, but they didn't really say much to me, even though I tried to comfort them. It may sound strange to some, but for me it was worse that they were women. If it had been a man, it would have somehow been more digestible, but this was two young ladies. I was only trying to cheer that kid up and give my family a nice night out and that's what had happened.

So the legal process went into action at Lewes Crown Court and I finally pleaded guilty to the charge of grievous bodily harm in April 1997. I was ordered to pay costs of £1140 and to do 200 hours of community service by the court. I was told the judge had considered a custodial sentence but recognised the substantial work I did in society and felt I could do much more good with community service. We also settled a figure with the two girls in a civil action.

For the community service, I worked first at Hamilton Lodge, a school for deaf kids between 14 and 20, where I learned sign language. For some of these sessions, I had to fly back from my training camp in Abu Dhabi, where I was training for my second Middle Eastern bout in Dubai. After a month or so at Hamilton Lodge, I went to Westdene Primary School where I had to help five-year-olds to read and write. That was less purposeful I felt. My feeling was that I was more than happy to help the community, but that I should have been asked to do so in a way that was more constructive, which had been the case at the secondary school. Plus, it is worth bearing in mind that what I was being told to do as a result of this court case was only what I did all the time anyway.

I invited the media down to my first day of community service. I had no problem with doing it. After all, the law of the land had to prevail and being in the public eye I fully accepted that I should be made an example of. I understood and accept that. That said, since that day I haven't looked at or even thought about fireworks.

As I have mentioned, the next stop on my Middle Eastern jaunt was Dubai, in the United Arab Emirates, a part of the world I like and travel to often. I was scheduled to fight Camillo Alarcon on 27 March 1997. In London before the fight, some of the people involved in the promotion were in a bar with me and I was buying people drinks. I offered to buy John a £148 per glass brandy from 1847, and after much persuasion he graciously accepted. I didn't notice, but he later told me that one of the Middle Eastern entourage was knocking back these brandies, which I was paying for, like it was orange juice.

While I was out in Dubai, I bought one of those enormous Hummer trucks in which I wanted to make my grand, Hollywood-style entrance to the fight. However, it was so big that when we got to the stadium, it wouldn't fit through the gates of the Dubai Tennis Club! The fight against Alarcon was over by round four, but what Dubai was most notable for was a major conflict with Ronnie Davies that was to test our professional relationship of ten years standing.

While we were preparing in Dubai, a situation had erupted with Ronnie that left me feeling bitterly disappointed. The initial impetus for this was a disagreement we had over training but there were also other underlying issues. I was adamant but he argued with me and, for me, that was that. You see, I run my business. I always did. He worked for me, whether he liked that or not, but Ronnie has the old style manager's approach of saying to a fighter, 'You stay with me, you'll be all right.' I used to think: *No, you should make sure you are okay with me. You work for me, you follow the rules and directions I give you. This is my business, not yours.*

So the relationship came to a stop. I was very disappointed with him at the time but the disagreement we had was in part due to the risk I was taking in having no contracts with Sheik Hamdan who had appointed Merser Al Fayegh to help coordinate the promotion. In my opinion Al Fayegh in fact did very little to help me promote the show and Ronnie, who knew we were promoting in the dark, had reservations about the whole affair.

Anyway, I fixed my focus on training and promoting this boxing match, paid for all the fighters to come and fight which included flights for fighters and trainers, doctors, matchmakers, British Boxing Board of Control officials, hotels, purses for the fighters, food etc; I took care of everything to achieve the objective.

The promotion took place at the Dubai Tennis Stadium and was a complete success, if not financially for me. I have received nothing for my endeavours and I am still waiting patiently for this issue to be resolved.

With hindsight Ronnie was right. I've had the best times of my life with this man, he guarded me; advised me; worried for me; nursed me, even sang for me, I know he has been a blessing in my life. I can truly say that I love this man and truly regret the time I have lost not being in his company. Money can be replaced but the two years that lapsed in our relationship cannot, and for that I blame the events that occured in Dubai.

PART FIVE

EARN THE RESPECT

CHAPTER TWENTY-TWO
WINNING THE LOTTERY

In September 1997, I announced a new package of fights with Frank Warren in Piccadilly Circus, with my truck in tow. They tried to clamp the truck but the device didn't fit, so I just got a ticket for my trouble! Although Warren and I had had our differences in the past, I needed to get the fights I wanted and he was a promoter who could do that.

I had a new, more relaxed attitude and made it clear I was going to enjoy myself. 'Last time I didn't stop to smell the flowers,' I told the intrigued British public. On reflection, the only reason I might have ever said I hated boxing was because I was doing too much of it. It becomes pretty extreme when you are getting a torrent of criticism for doing a very hard job, no one seems to understand you or like you, and the media misrepresent and ridicule you. How could I like that? All I was doing was getting material trappings but no acceptance, no credit at all. I didn't hate it, I had a fantastic time, I was just too immersed in the events to enjoy myself. Plus, I shouldn't have used the word 'hate', that was just my exasperation at how much negativity was coming towards me from the media and the way they pigeon-holed me with this stereotype. I distanced myself from it, but if you really understand the nobility of it, then I would tell you the truth: I loved it and was in love with boxing.

Describing what it was like dealing with many people in the business puts me in mind of one of my all-time favourite movies, the classic Western, *The Good, The Bad and The Ugly*. Tuco (the 'ugly') is actually a very likeable guy, he is dangerous and you have to watch him, but even knowing that you can't help but find him endearing. The loveable rogue. That is Barry Hearn. Clint Eastwood (Blondie, the 'good') was myself, the good guy who takes from people with precision and humour, his every move coated in style. He beats people with brains as well as his sharp shooting. Lee Van Cleef (Angel Eyes, the 'bad') was like many other people I had to deal with. Such films as this, and the aforementioned *Once Upon A Time In The West* are comfort movies for me. It is relaxing for me to see characters I can dream of being. I apply these characteristics but in everyday life, not in a make-believe world.

There were many reports in the media at the time about my supposed difficulties with American Express and the taxman. I found all this to be hugely invasive. What happened was a combination of (as I saw it) bad advice and recklessness on my part. I had advisers from whom I don't think I received the best counsel – I was a fighter, I didn't have time to look after financial matters myself. There is only one thing worse than being skint – being famous and skint. I am not laughing when I say that. The public sometimes even gloat, because they always want you to be the fallen hero. The media fuelled these rumours about me, which fortunately were not at all true. Let's just say that financially I am in no difficulties.

There is an exceptionally skilled fighter called Joe Calzaghe, whom I took a bout against at 11 days' notice after his proposed fight with Steve Collins fell through. Despite Calzaghe's impressive reputation, I was prepared to enter the ring with him with less preparation than would be ideal for such a contest.

I had been training for a fight against undefeated Londoner, Mark Prince, for the WBO Inter-Continental Light-Heavyweight belt. Consequently, I had been using sparring partners that matched his style and bigger size but that did not deter me from accepting the Calzaghe match. This was a good opportunity to regain the WBO Super-Middleweight title so I was keen to accept the gauntlet that had been thrown my way – indeed, I said at the time it was like 'winning the lottery' just to get the shot. I looked at his record, unbeaten in 22 fights with ten first-round knockouts and 21 early finishes in all. He was also the three-times amateur national schoolboy champion and a triple ABA champion. He could obviously box and punch, but I wondered if he had fought anyone of pedigree yet. After all, I had been in 21 world-title fights. Even though I was always in superb condition, to accept the bout was nonetheless a brave decision but one Ronnie probably would have advised against if he had still been with me at the time. I did acknowledge that I was 'worried' about certain aspects of the fight, probably the first time in my career I used that word. That said, I was much more relaxed around the boxing business now, I even told the press I was having fun!

That choice was brave, my next decision was unwise. I had been having knee problems and using the Versaclimber, as I couldn't run on the road. Although road work is the ideal stamina conditioner, the Versaclimber was helpful. Nonetheless, I was concerned the knee would play up on the night, especially if you recall the emphasis my style placed on multi-directional foot movements. Half an hour before the Calzaghe fight, I got permission from the doctor to have an injection to assist my knee joints. The morning after the contest, I couldn't walk because my knees had seized up. The Harley Street doctor said I had just masked the pain and worn down the ligaments in the knee. I gave myself a future physical problem right there.

My pre-fight work continued to be somewhat beleaguered when my helicopter to the Sheffield press conference was stranded at Gatwick because of high winds. Fortunately, my weight-loss programme was carefully overseen by Karron, who put me on a liquidized fruit and vegetable diet that worked miracles. I weighed in four ounces inside the

12 stone limit, although I had to take my two pairs of thick socks and a T-shirt off to finally nail the weight!

The fight was at the Sheffield Arena and Naseem Hamed was on the same bill, so there was some fanning of the flames of animosity that people felt existed between us – the take here was the old master upstaging the new champion in his hometown. I wasn't interested in all this really, it was just publicity talk. Sky moved my fight until after Naz's bout so I guess they must have felt it was a bigger attraction.

I came out of my corner for round one smiling. I was moving around and sizing up the terrain, when *Boom!* Calzaghe hit me with a huge shot that literally came out of nowhere and knocked me down. I simply did not see that punch coming. A first-round knockdown had never happened to me in my entire career. As I picked myself up from the canvas and brushed myself down, I thought to myself: *You've got your work cut out tonight, guy.*

My constitution was strong enough to soak up the damage that punch might have done in the longer term, so once I had regained my poise, I thought to myself: *I will knock on your door in the tenth or eleventh round but, boy, am I going to have to take some stick in the meantime.* I had no problem with being in the trenches for a while; after all, in some fights, not least Watson 2, I had lived in there permanently. Calzaghe had very fast hands and an awkward southpaw style, so he proved to be quite a handful. I know how to absorb punishment, take it and give it back, but to his credit he stayed there through to the final bell and took a unanimous decision. This was despite my promised late attack which nearly knocked him out in the final seconds.

After the fight, I went to Joe and complimented him on his performance and made no excuses in the press interviews. In return, the media spoke very kindly about me, which was very welcome. Steve Bunce of the *Daily Telegraph* said the bout was: 'quite simply one of the finest fights in British boxing history.' After a career of being almost universally berated, such appreciative words were warmly received.

I was sitting in the bathroom of my dressing area after the fight, deflated. The eminent businessmen Rory McCarthy and Richard Branson came into the room and I was talking to them, saying 'I can't do this anymore, I just can't.' Branson said to me, 'I can't believe how valiant you were in there, you have inspired the whole country.' At that point, I was buoyed by his comment but could not envisage a return match.

Calzaghe was undoubtedly a good fighter but he struggled to show his 'box-office', which was always going to hold him back. Unfortunately, the nature of the modern game demands that to be gifted, disciplined and technically skilled is not necessarily enough. You must have character, charisma and personality as well. Boxing skills will get you talked about in the boxing press, but charisma will make you, 'box-office', and will get you on to the front pages.

It was notable that the fighting public did not appreciate Naz's apparent arrogance after his own victory that night – ironically, in the wake of my defeat, and brave and gracious acceptance of the loss, the British public warmed to me like never before. Friedrich Nietzsche said, 'The only way to

Marrying Karron on
23 December 1990
was a momentous day
– I felt so lucky.

My mother Ena
and father Irvin.

Above: Muhammad Ali's incredible victories in the boxing ring are dwarfed by what he has achieved as a human being.

Left: As it was in 2001. The West Pier in Brighton would have made a sumptuous home.

Left: Ronnie Davies has been with me through some of my finest and darkest moments. He is an honest man whom I would trust with my children, my mother and my wife. I love this man.

Right: I was delighted when Prince Charles said to me, 'I can't believe how much you've mellowed.'

Above: Congratulating my son Christopher on winning his first race at school.

Right: Enjoying time with my family at home in Hove, with little Joseph.

Left: A moment of contemplation, with John Regan in the background, on a boat going to inspect the West Pier, feeling queasy.

Below: Lost the battle – *the fight*, but won the war – *public empathy.*

Left: I lost out on points against Thompson. I'm on Doctor's shoulders.

Below: My severe eye injury was a proud badge of honour, a battle scar.

Right: Helping to wash oil-drenched penguins in South Africa, three days after my father's death.

Below: Mike Tyson as I know him – a quiet, gentle man.

Below: Presenting a Holy Quran to the President of the United Arab Emirates, Sheikh Zyied, with his son Sheikh Mohammad, the General of the Army of the Emirates.

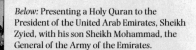

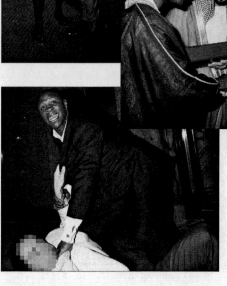

Left: Performing a citizen's arrest in 2002 on a character who had eluded me for over a year.

The Eubanks: (clockwise from myself), Sebastian, Christopher, Karron, Joseph and Emily.

Left: Channel 4's *Celebrity Big Brother* gave me the perfect opportunity to show the public another side of me and to raise money for Comic Relief. Coming out of the *Big Brother* house first, meant the charity got maximum exposure.

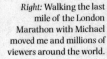

Right: Walking the last mile of the London Marathon with Michael moved me and millions of viewers around the world.

Left: Gladiator, a vicious, undignified, humiliating and terrifying experience. I was ready to fight Benn in 1990 and 1993, but this was only supposed to be a game show.

know a man's true value is his capacity for sticking to his guns.' When asked if I was going to retire now, I said, 'Life is a show and the show must go on.'

Dodging a fighter is a cardinal sin in boxing and is something I can never be accused of, unlike one such character who came on the scene at the end of my era. Roy Jones, James Toney and Michael Nunn, for example. I did not dodge.

Let's use Roy Jones as an example. When people asked me why I wouldn't fight him, I would say to them, 'Never mind the title or my job, a fight like that can take five or six years off my life.' I was well aware of that. He was, pound-for-pound, arguably the best fighter on the planet; in regards to his style, his devastating punching ability, the whole repertoire, he had it.

The rule is that if you are champion of the world for one body, you cannot be the No. 1 contender for another belt. Unless someone was officially the recognised No. 1 contender, I had no professional obligation to face them. With Roy Jones, he was fortunately (and I use that word with the utmost respect) never No. 1 contender. Had he been, I would not have dodged. I would have taken the fight. Would I have won the fight? Highly unlikely. What would have been for sure was that he would have come away from the fight and got hurt, and I would have been hurt probably far more than he was. It would have been a war. Technically we would have been well-matched, so our pure grit would have started to come into play. I believe we both had powerful wills, so I feel that fight would have ended up running on pure instinct. That can be an exceptionally violent occurrence. Interestingly, I was told that Roy Jones was rumoured to have said that the only fighter he had reservations about facing was me. I don't remember my critics saying much about that.

One fighter I was relieved never to see at No. 1 contender rank was the skilful Herol Graham. I made it quite clear at the time what I thought of his gift. That fight would never have happened unless he was No. 1 contender, in which case I couldn't dodge. McCallum and Nunn were quality fighters but not like Herol Graham. You couldn't hit him – he was so elusive, they said in the business, 'you couldn't hit him with a handful of stones.' That was true, he was a grandmaster.

I did say that I would not fight in New York. You see, having learned to fight over there, I knew the hunger of the New Yorkers. They were a peculiar type of beast, very hard, relentless fighters who swear by the 'kill or be killed' mentality. Plus, by living in England, I openly admitted to enjoying being a big fish in a little pond. America is a vast pond, with some very dangerous, large fish in there! I needed to make money and there were fighters in New York who were not No. 1 contenders but were very risky to take on. I don't remember actually being offered a fight in New York. If Barry had come to me with the No. 1 contender in New York, I could not have dodged. Ultimately, I would have become accepting of it. But it would have been a very rough and tough night's work.

So, the ultimate measure of a fighter is not dodging. If you do, you lose your standing, your respect, your honour. Don't dodge the No. 1 contender.

I remember watching Muhammad Ali fight in 1974 and being aware, despite my young age, of everybody talking about this man. As I grew up and became involved in the fight business, I obviously became more acutely informed of what he had achieved both in and out of the ring.

Muhammad Ali was a great fighter as well as a great boxer (there is a difference between the two). He was also a great showman and a mighty tactician. However, all of his incredible victories inside the ring are dwarfed by what he has achieved as a human being. There are many great boxers – Joe Louis for example, a brilliant fighter but he didn't take a stand. Ali took a stand and used his position to do so – the fact that his status was a result of being the master in a business that is the hardest on the planet makes that stand all the more astounding. Speaking up for black people at that time was tantamount to public suicide in terms of his image. Then refusing to serve in the Vietnam war, on religious grounds, was the sign of an ultimate warrior, integrity in its purest form. Standing up to the media and the government, the two most powerful adversaries you can have. That was the sign of a truly great man, someone who sacrificed his own personal desires, and that cannot be compared to fighting George Foreman in Zaire. Yes, that is universally acknowledged as one of the greatest bouts of all time, but it was child's play compared to what Ali has achieved for humanity. His degree of righteous conduct is that rare flame that separates ordinary people from the very, very few greats.

Furthermore, the degree to which he was shunned made no impact on his belief in what was right. He knew his own character and his family's name would be severely besmirched. It was a battle which, in many ways, he couldn't win. Yet, he stuck to his guns. Provided he wasn't assassinated, he was taking a stand for which people would bow to him in 30 years' time – which they do. He is a legend in his own lifetime.

I have been privileged to meet Muhammad Ali three times. The first brief encounter was at the Brit Awards. Then I was on set with him during the presentation of the BBC 'Sports Personality of the Century' awards ceremony. There were various high-profile boxers present, including Lennox Lewis, Frank Bruno, Evander Holyfield, Barry McGuigan and Naseem. They were all talking about what Ali had accomplished in the boxing ring and what the man meant to each champion, but for me this was missing the point, this has no weight compared to Ali as a man. So, I had to make that point. When Ali put his hand on mine, this great man who has Parkinson's Disease, I began to shake and stutter. The programme had to be moved on because it was live, so John Inverdale, the presenter, said, 'It takes Muhammad Ali to shut up Chris Eubank'.

The third time I met Ali was the next day at his birthday party at The Hilton in London. It was an honour just to be invited. I wanted to give him a written message, but only had two of my postcards. I couldn't give him the card featuring the caricature of me, so I used one which pictured me by the side of my truck. I greeted his security guards, then went up to Ali and leant down, put my arm around his shoulder, handed the postcard to him and said, 'Don't worry about the picture on the back. Happy Birthday, this is for you.' I pointed at the five names on the card and read out my words. 'This is what you mean to me: Moses, Jesus Christ, Muhammad, Nelson Mandela, Muhammad Ali. Thank you very much, Chris Eubank.' He listened, then said to me, 'You make me feel so good.'

I gave the card to his wife and prefaced that by explaining, 'I'm not a sycophant or an idiot. This has been my life, these have been my role models. This is what has motivated me, not what a man does in his chosen profession. Truth is what I look up to.'

I am humbled by Ali's very presence. So many people ask the question about whether Ali would have been the best had he been fighting today. This is a nonsensical question in essence, because you cannot mix the eras. Of his time, he was the most talented heavyweight, the most brilliantly stylish fighter. However, before him you had Joe Louis who was a demigod. Before him you had Jack Johnson, who was also a demigod. And you have fighters today who are demigods, their hands move with more or less the same poetry as Ali's. The difference is this – Ali took a stand. Would I have the courage to do that? Would I have the integrity to do that? The point is this: it is incorrect to talk about his achievements in boxing. That was just his foundation, that gave him the stage to become an icon.

Nelson Mandela also took a stand. Twenty-eight years in prison for his beliefs, then released and made the president of the very country that had incarcerated him. This is one of the absolute icons of modern times. People can talk about taking a stand, showing their resolve, but Mandela did this at such a breathtaking level. Again, a legend in his own time, yet he has such humility. When I first met him, he said, 'It is an honour to meet you, Chris.' He can't say that! I was just an ordinary guy honoured to meet Mandela. What am I supposed to say to that? He endeared himself even more with this comment.

Both these men have obviously been intimately involved in the fight against racism. I have my own views and have largely steered clear of becoming overtly involved, in the public eye at least. Obviously, I am married to a white woman, but we have never had any problems, such as the vile letters some mixed couples receive. Even the racists can look at me and see I am a colourful character with emotional intelligence and humanity. If I did receive a letter, it wouldn't even register. My children, to my knowledge, do not have any difficulties at school.

I enjoy living in England. If you have travelled as much as I have, you will know that it is the best country in the whole world, because of its laws and the civility – my father told me that many years ago and he was right. England is a place that has given me my opportunities.

However, the fact is that England colonised so many

countries around the world and the English have, in their time, been a wicked people. A lot of black people take that historical fact and harbour anguish and grudges because of it. I say to the youngsters today, 'Don't look at the people you see walking around as the people who incarcerated your nation. It was their ancestors. Forgive the ancestors and don't hold it against the people you see in society now. Get on with your life, your time is too short to weigh yourself down.' Of course, when black power was very active in the 60s, it was absolutely necessary – they were fighting fire with fire. It was an extreme solution to an extreme problem.

I don't like it when people go around saying, 'I am proud to be black.' I am black. So what? Yes, there is racism and discrimination in the world – accept that some people are idiotic like that. If someone comes up to you and says, 'You can't have this job or get past me because you are of a certain race,' that's pure ignorance. What is wrong about the phrase, 'I am proud to be black,' is that you can only be proud in that way if another race has been telling you you're not as good as their race is. Nelson Mandela said to me, 'Whatever your target in life, don't let anything get in your way. If it gets in your way, don't fight against it, find a way around it, but always keep your eye on the target.' One should fight it correctly.

If you allow ignorance to affect your own attitude, namely by entrenching your pride, then all you are doing is letting those bigots shackle you. Why? Because if you walk around with a chip on your shoulder, feeling like the world owes you something, you will live an unfortunate life. You will always be complaining rather than doing something about bettering yourself and finding a route around those obstacles. If you say, 'My people were enslaved, massacred, mistreated,' of course, there have been some terrible things done, but to linger on the negative does not help. The chip on your shoulder just holds you down. Me? I was always flying, my mind was always free. Do you think I don't come into contact with racism? Of course I do, but I cannot engage with ignorance.

Life would be much richer if only everybody recognised that there is no colour in people. There are good people and bad people. In private, I often ask someone, 'If you have two job candidates of absolutely equal stature, skill, diligence, personality and experience, but one is white and one is black, how do you choose?' The only answer you can give is to toss a coin. So, yes, over the years, I have never publicly taken a stance on the subject of racism, because I can't speak about something that is ignorant or limited. If you can't even see that we are no different, then I am on a completely separate level to you, I would be wasting my breath. I can try and heighten your awareness that we are the colour we are because of the part of the planet that we evolve from, the millions of years of evolution and sunlight. That is all it is. Simple. It has been said that in many years to come everybody will be of mixed race. I am colour-blind towards people; it is the only way.

CHAPTER TWENTY-THREE

A SWEET TOOTH AND SWOLLEN EYES

I do have a sweet tooth, always have. When I was a kid, I used to steal boxes and boxes of sweets – now I buy them. One time I was particularly into Sherbert Dib-Dabs and Curly Wurlys, so I went to this cash 'n' carry and bought dozens of boxes of them. Topics can be a very worthwhile experience too. I prize my selection of confectionery.

One day I was in London for business and took the truck with me. I often stay at The Landmark Hotel near Baker Street and can usually park my truck at the back of the building, where they have allocated spaces for coaches. This one particular day, there were a lot of guests so the coach park was full, meaning I had to find a space for the truck in a side road (which was no mean feat in itself!).

The morning after, I had my breakfast then took a stroll to check up on the truck. When I got there, someone had smashed the window, broken in and taken the television and video I had in the cabin. That was fine. Don't get me wrong, I'd rather it hadn't happened, but I understand that.

As I have said, some people steal for money. I understand where they are coming from, but it still doesn't make it right.

However, as I rummaged around the cabin checking what was missing, I made a chilling discovery. They had taken my strawberry bonbons from the glove compartment. Don't touch a man's strawberry bonbons. *You just don't do that, it is against the rules.* Being as passionate as I am about strawberry bonbons, I had kept them in the glove compartment for about three months, gently maturing. They had ripened beautifully to the point where they were deliciously soft in the middle, something that can only be achieved with careful and experienced fermentation within a glove compartment. This process cannot be rushed. They need to be aged gracefully.

What was even more disturbing was that I thought I also had some blackjacks in there too. I acknowledge that the world is split on this particular chewy sensation, it is common knowledge that they make your teeth go black. However, they are so addictive, so sublime. I wasn't certain there had been some blackjacks in the truck, so I preferred not to think about it because if they had taken my blackjacks as well, that would have been just too much to handle, they must have been desperate men. There is a code of conduct, an honour amongst thieves, don't touch the strawberry bonbons. As for blackjacks, don't even think about it.

I called BBC Radio 1 and said I wanted to report the theft. On a serious note, I was glad of the opportunity to again make my point that, although I understand people stealing material goods, if you hurt someone in the process you must face severe consequences. I reiterated that material goods can be replaced, but you cannot replace strawberry bonbons that have been aged to perfection in a glove compartment for three months.

I also told the police about the strawberry bonbons but they were never recovered.

While I am on the subject of sweets and chocolate, I need to put on record my conspiracy theory about the mighty confectionery bar that used to be called Marathon. This was the best of chocolate bars, the epitome of fine taste, a delicious combination. Then the manufacturers changed the name to Snickers. In my belief, however, they didn't just change the name, they also changed the ingredients. Don't be fooled by all this talk that Snickers is just a Marathon with a different name. They never tasted the same again! I am very perceptive about these things. To add insult to injury, Treats also suffered the ignominy of a name change to the vastly inferior M&Ms. Where's the class? This just does not cut it. M&Ms and Treats should not be spoken about in the same decade, never mind the same breath. Treats was a golden time, it was a magic era, one could say, a way of life. I lived on Treats. So I say this to the makers of M&Ms – if you're reading this, bring back Treats and I will do the advertising for free!

Carl Thompson was a seven. He had true grit, but he was not in the same technical league as myself, he never had my ability or talent, but he had resolve and he was heavier.

I was lined up to fight him on 18 April 1998, at the Manchester Nynex, for the WBO Cruiserweight title, two divisions above my usual weight. The limit was 13st 8lb, and I weighed in 18lb heavier than for the Calzaghe fight.

The press conferences were amiable affairs, with me attending in a straw boater on the HMS Belfast on the River Thames. Thompson and I wanted a better purse, I knew I was the box office draw. So I said to one businessman there, 'Let's do the coin thing.' He said, 'What do you mean?' I closed the door on the journalists and replied, 'I'll flip a coin, £50,000 a time.' Doctor was with me at the time. This fellow agreed and we started flipping this coin. I was on a roll and quickly had him up to a debt of £350,000. It eventually came back down to £150,000 at which point he wanted out. I never saw a penny, he still owes me that debt.

I fought Carl 'The Cat' Thompson in a fight billed as 'Double Trouble'. He was a big man and a former kick-boxing champion. Although you might think the luxury of not having to strip my weight down would be welcome, it was most certainly not. For years I had eaten only once a day, and not in any great quantity even then; here I was being asked to eat three big meals a day. I did not enjoy that at all.

This fight was the first and only time in my career that I did not vault into the ring. I stood by the ropes and waited for the anticipation to build, then just calmly stepped under the ropes. Mainly, I still had that issue with my knees, I didn't want to damage them before I had even started boxing. I would never have them injected again, so I needed to take care. Plus, I felt I didn't need to put on so much of a show. 'I am who I am'. I was always a showman, but that night the vault was not something I felt was needed anymore.

I was later told that George Foreman was cheering me on ringside, which was a great honour. Also, Maximo Perez was in my corner which was a big boost. He was my mentor and I still wanted to please him more than anyone else. Just as all those years ago in the Jerome gym in New York, if he said, 'Subbresso', that recognition meant everything to me.

Despite the weight advantage Thompson held, I was quickly on top. It was a brutal bout – at one point, I almost had to be pushed off my stool to start the next round, such was the sapping ferocity of some of our exchanges. By the fifth I dropped him. I troubled him again in the seventh but, like in the first Collins match, didn't finish the job. I said afterwards, 'The puppeteer stopped working the puppet.' It cost me dearly.

The decision went against me and I couldn't see that. Yes, my eye was severely swollen and bleeding but that was the only damage I had sustained. I felt I had won that fight, anyway. I was absolutely perplexed when they went on to name Thompson as 'Fighter Of The Year'. Even after the defeat, Thompson was still a seven but he stayed in there, and credit to him for that.

I was hospitalised at Manchester Royal Infirmary for nearly 48 hours for observation and treatment on my severely damaged eye. However, when they discharged me, I had a limo pick me up and headed home. The next day, I felt very different. I watched the fight on tape and that reinforced my gut feeling on the night, which was that I had won. I had to try and get that title. The rematch was arranged for only 12 weeks later, a quick return, about which there was a great deal of consternation within the business. Observers said this was with undue haste, particularly in light of the brutality of the first match, which some had likened to Benn 1. However, precautions were taken, such as the BBBC giving me two brain scans which came up perfectly clear.

So many people warned me off the second Thompson fight because my eye had not properly healed yet, but I was not interested. In the press conferences for the rematch, I called my still-visibly bruised eye my 'badge of honour', a proud battle scar. My face is remarkably unmarked for a veteran of 52 professional fights, which some say is a tribute to my defensive capabilities. However, I enjoyed having this scar. As for putting me off a rematch, I didn't even hear the reservations. I just wanted that title.

I had a meeting arranged at Terminal Three of Heathrow Airport with a known promoter before Thompson 2. I was not aware that when I got there, Naseem would be present, having his business to attend to. We were still not talking – for example, I saw him at the Queen's Honours party and such was my refusal to make contact, I lifted my nose in the air when he came over to say hello. I had ignored him for four years, he didn't exist for me because it was unacceptable what he had done.

At Heathrow, I was walking a short distance in front of

Naz when I heard him saying, 'Chris, do you wanna look at my belts? Hey, Chris!' Bear in mind, I had just failed to take the belt in the Thompson 1 fight, so he knew exactly what a disrespect this was. 'Hey, Chris! Do you wanna look at my belts?' I ignored his comments, which he just kept repeating, but then I heard, 'Wanker!'

I stopped in my tracks. This was bullying. Of course, having had the childhood I'd had, I knew that if a bully punches you, you have to punch him back. That is the only way he will respect you. So, I turned around and walked up to Naz, so that we were no more than 12 inches apart, a stand-off. I took his belts off him and threw them across the floor (something I later regretted and said was 'ungentlemanly'). I looked down at him and said, 'Listen, you little mig. What are you doing? You should practise a little more respect.' His bodyguards were all closing in around me (I was alone) and a crowd had gathered for what was, I suppose, an intriguing sight. I pulled my open hand way back and slowly made as if to slap him for his disrespect. In boxing circles, such a slow, telegraphed move is obviously not with actual intent to make contact, it was more a gesture saying: *This is what your behaviour deserves. Don't bully me verbally, don't behave like a child.*

However, despite the blatantly slow, open palm I was showing him, he moved out of the way and threw an open-handed punch, whereby the top knuckle of his little finger clipped my nose. In any circles, let alone professional boxing terms, this was such disrespect. Bear in mind that I was only a few inches from him, he is much smaller and lighter than me and if I had retaliated with a jab, he would have been unable to evade it – someone once analysed my jab and timed the start of the punch to impact at a quarter of a second. It would, quite frankly, have been very damaging, I would have dropped him. This could have been very nasty if I had been the type to not control my impulse.

I was dismayed at his behaviour. *What? First you taunt me, now you lay your finger on my nose?* At that moment, knowing how much emphasis I place on personal conduct and integrity with regards to a fighter's success, I said to myself: *Here is a person who cannot have a fighter's heart.* I am an older man, I have set the course which people like Naz had followed. The reason why fighters like Naseem make the vast sums of money they do now is because boxers like myself opened the floodgates. However, I'm struck by his lack of respect for me. Even when I cannot abide by something one has done, rather than abuse them, I just ignore them. I just thought: *What are you doing? We are not in the playground, we are not seven-year-olds.*

At the time of this airport scene, it was well-known in the business that Naz was strongly religious. Yet, I do not see how his behaviour fitted in with his faith as a Muslim. I tried to think why Naz was behaving like this. Was it jealousy? Envy? Ignorance or perhaps just pure childish behaviour?

I have been watching Naz's career, eager to see if the way he had mistreated me previously might manifest itself – every weakness gets shown up in the ring. For me, it has become almost like a scientific social experiment to watch him. Intrinsically he is a good man, but only a child would taunt someone like that, not least someone who always offered advice and help.

Somewhere along the line, such indiscretions will come around, not necessarily the next fight, or the one after that, but at some point they will. As with all fighters, all people, all walks of life, all businesses, you reap what you sow. Life is a strange thing, in as much as there is usually a price to pay for your wrong-doings. It's not that I want to see Naz fall, but I cannot help but be curious about the concept of Karma – I'm still watching. I remember him saying to me, 'I thought you were a friend and that you would understand.' I said, 'You'd do this to a friend?' At the end of that discussion, he went to shake my hand but I said, 'What? You want to shake this hand? You can't do that. You can't even touch this hand, this is a good hand. Go on!' and I ushered him out of the room. Four years of silence followed.

This is how the situation resolved itself – George Foreman showed me the higher thinking and I acted on his advice. I was staying at the Midland Crown Plaza in Manchester. Mr Foreman and I had exchanged telephone numbers and we later met up in my hotel room, where we spent two hours talking about religion, life, virtues, being an older man, being in the public eye, all manner of things. One of the first pieces of advice he gave me was regarding fans. He said, 'I saw you on the TV today giving out autographs and they got something from you, they went away with their eyes lit up, but you got nothing. That's because you didn't make eye contact with anyone.' I watched the tape and he was right, so from then on, whenever I give an autograph, I try to make eye contact. The fan sees you as a person, not just a celebrity or a puppet, and that is much more rewarding for me as a result.

However, the crucial piece of advice George offered me was regarding Naz. Foreman had seen a press conference for Thompson 1 where several people had shouted me down and had been very abusive towards me. I didn't have a microphone so I could not reply, but nonetheless I remained dignified throughout and never lowered myself to their level.

Speaking to me in my hotel room, George Foreman said, 'I saw how you handled that press conference. I always knew Chris Eubank was a man of good conduct. But seeing that, you went up 20 times in my estimation. You didn't get up and walk out, you didn't shout back, you didn't retaliate or attack, you were calm and rose above it.'

I was, of course, very honoured to hear those words from such a man. Then he came round to the subject of Naseem. He said, 'Naz is just a kid, he needs help. If you've ever liked this kid, if you've ever seen anything of worth in him, then next time you see him, just bring him towards you and *give him a hug.*' That was the first time in all those years that anyone had told me to take the higher ground. All my friends and supporters were understandably still smarting from Naz's words, that was a natural reaction. George Foreman didn't see it like that, he took a very different view, the higher plane. *Hug him and help him.*

I thought about George's words. I recalled way back when Naz and myself had first begun to know each other. I thought he was a good kid. I dwelled on the events and the more I thought about it, the more I knew George was right.

Since that day in 1998, I've been calling Naz and giving him advice. I didn't hug him the first time I saw him after George's advice, it was not appropriate, but the second time we saw each other we made our reconciliation. I said to him, 'The past is the past. Leave that where it is. I will move forward with you.'

In some ways, the advice I give Naz is useless, because you can pass these things on but ultimately you learn best by making your own mistakes. So Naz and myself get on again now, because I dropped it, I rose above it and in so doing I am a better man than before. Naz, in return, has been a help to me in many ways too. He inspires me with his boxing ability. I follow his career with fascination and look to him to become a man of integrity. How he reacts to what was a comprehensive defeat against Marco Antonio Barrera will perhaps demonstrate whether he can go on to become a great fighter.

Naz is still a young man. Some people are not open to the sort of thinking that George Foreman bestowed upon me that night. I have said to Naz, 'You can be short in reality, but stand tall in your mind and you can be bigger than life.' I will watch all this transpire to see if he can make himself a great fighter, maybe even a legend in his own lifetime. He has that potential.

To become a legend, you have to go through stages. If you win the title and do so in a dignified manner, then you are a good fighter. If you then get stuck down on the canvas, drag yourself up and carry on, win or lose, you are a very good fighter. If you lose, then do so with dignity, but if you come back and win, then you are indeed a great fighter. To make yourself a legend in your own time is another matter – to do that you have to win a fight that you can't win.

Winning the fight you can't is very difficult to achieve. Benn did that. He fought Gerald McClellan, got knocked down and battered, yet still won against a vicious opponent. All the odds were heavily stacked against him. At that point, he was a demigod. It must be said that I have heard boxing enthusiasts say that this made him a legend in his own lifetime and I agree.

The second Thompson fight, on 18 July at the Sheffield Arena would be my last as a professional boxer. I trained for this fight at the isolated Hustyns camp near Bodmin Moor, which is owned by a man of respect, Terry Johnson. I invited the press down to see me work out and I enjoyed the distance this gave me from all the distractions of my normal life. I even invited youngsters to watch me train, in order to complete my community service from the fireworks incident. The camp is in a valley, so there was no mobile phone signal at all. Each night, I would walk up to the top of the hill, phone Karron and catch up on the day's news, surrounded by sheep and the smell of manure. Some nights, I was sure these sheep were calling my name, '*Chrriiisss*'.

Distractions and boxing are like oil and water, you need focus. Hustyns gave me isolation, there was nothing to do except train, play dominoes, eat food and be around Terry, who is a good soul to be near. The last time I had trained away from my family had been against the veteran John Jarvis, whom I stopped in three rounds, so I felt this was worth the suffering. I also sparred with Dennis Andries, the veteran former light-heavyweight champion of the world, to get my strength boosted even more.

It was a shame, because for this second Thompson fight, after initially saying I was 'brilliant' in our first match, Thompson seemed more antagonistic towards me, so the amicable atmosphere of the previous clash had dissipated. Some insiders said this was because, although he won the first bout, I won all the acclaim. One headline had shouted, 'Simply The Bravest!'

The fight was being beamed across the United States on ESPN, so the potential stakes for the winner were very high. The crowd reception for me was so warm that it brought tears to my eyes. It was so different for me to enter an arena and have thousands of people chanting, *'Eubank! Eubank!'* This time, despite the brief spell since the last match, I was really on form. I outboxed, outclassed and out-fought Thompson. His weight advantage was again a burden, but I could handle that – after all, his punches were easy to absorb compared to the bombs I had taken in my career, not least from Benn. I felt, as I said, that I'd won our first encounter, but during this second fight, I was without doubt the better fighter. If it had gone to points there was no way he would have won. The first six rounds I boxed very well, something that was widely acknowledged after the fight. However, by round nine, my left eye had swollen badly and nearly closed, after continual jabbing from Thompson. I accept that maybe the eye had not had enough time to recover from the previous bout. I had asked my corner to cut the eye in order to release the build-up of fluids from the swelling, but they wouldn't – I hadn't worked with this particular cornerman before, he was supposed to be good but he wouldn't cut the eye. It was only water and remember, *my health comes second*. I never knew it was illegal to slit your own eye. I just needed to win the fight, 'Slit the eye, I'll win,' I said.

In the corner, the doctor came to look at me and would not allow me to come out for the tenth round. I was amazed and bitterly disappointed. Even if I had lost the last three rounds, I would still have won the fight comfortably on points. That shut eye partly incapacitated me, of course – you can't see particular punches coming – but I was way ahead on all three judges' scorecards. The doctor was disrespectful to me because any fighter who is ahead on points deserves one more round, regardless of circumstances. I had been a world champion, a fighter of genuine worth, so as a courtesy he should have given me that one more round before stopping the fight. When Julian Jackson was fighting Herol Graham, I heard the referee tell Jackson he had three more minutes, then it was over. Jackson knocked Graham spark out with a great punch. It was a huge upset. However, this doctor would not let me out, despite me putting my arm around him and pleading. You can make your own mind up about why. Some people have said certain parties wanted to take me down a peg. He should have let me have one more round.

You couldn't take me down a peg by this point in my career. This is about integrity, I had a true heart through all of the 392 professional rounds I had contested. In the wake of the second Thompson fight, the British public warmed to me in a way they had never done when I was champion for five years. Those two cruiserweight fights, plus the battle I lost to Joe Calzaghe, had won me the respect I had been seeking when I came out of my first premature retirement. Losing with grace and dignity in those final three fights showed my absolute integrity. Although I had taken severe punishment from Benn and Watson, the public did not perceive that I had taken my beating, because I went on to win. People wanted to see how I lost, as well as how I took victory. This is not just a British trait. In order to give you their lasting respect, the public need to see that you can stay the course. I had showed my grit through thick and thin, when times were good and bad. *That Eubank always strutted when he was winning, let's see what he is made of now. How did he lose? Like a man? With dignity? Yes. Then he is the complete package.*

When I hit the canvas in the Calzaghe fight, for example, the crowd who had bayed for my blood for years were shouting, 'No! Eubank, get up! Get up, Eubank!'

They had misjudged me. Whenever I was getting beaten up in the ring, I could have very easily pretended I had twisted my ankle, as many fighters do. I could have taken a shot and stayed down, it would have made my life easier. But my concern was not the public who had seen me quit, my concern was that I had to live with *me*. I could never have done that. That misjudgement (mainly by the press), gave me the opportunity to entertain them, for which I am grateful. However, now they had discovered my true worth. I was never a pretender.

My professional boxing career was over. I knew when I went into the ring against Thompson for the second time that it was all or nothing, win or bust. My last hurrah. As soon as that doctor stopped me from going out for the tenth, I knew, without even thinking, that it was all over. Afterwards, I asked what the British public thought I should do in a phone poll (they decided 2-to-1 for me to continue, while all the phone call money went to charity, of course). But I knew in my heart that the time had finally come to call it a day. My dignity demanded it.

People ask me if I regret taking on a much heavier man. Of course not. I often sparred with much heavier men and that considerable weight difference was of no consequence to me, other than making me work harder. No, that sort of regret misses the point. The Thompson fights were absolutely central to the public perception of me, the media's view of my career, and perhaps most importantly, to my own integrity.

Sometimes you are beaten by a fighter but you have not actually lost. By that I mean you feel you lost the battle but in losing the battle you win the war.

That is the way my cookie crumbled. You can't put your foot into water without getting it wet. Boxing is the same principle. You can't go in and always have it your way. Some days things will go against you and that will tell people the real measure of your person. Even if I had won the Thompson fights, I would have lost eventually. There will always be someone better round the corner. It is like gambling: you win today, tomorrow, you must lose, it is a foregone conclusion. By definition, if you are a winner then at some point you will go into the realm of losing. This is not boxing philosophy, this is life. The point is this: at the very end of the course, it is not actually about the winning and losing. It's about staying the course.

My course had been a long one with many highs and lows. I went through the trial-and-error period to make the grade, then I beat Benn and made the grade. I defended my belt 19 times, then lost the title. I had enjoyed my winning streak, but I did not roll over and slide away spinelessly. I fought on, took my beating and lost with great dignity and bravery. For that, the British public finally acknowledged me for what I had always been – a man of truth, of honour and of integrity. This last concept – integrity – is the key marker. Even if you cannot win, as I have said, stand there and take your beating. For my willingness to do that, the fighters, fight enthusiasts and the general British public respect me. Which is what it ends up being about – The Respect.

My boxing journey had come to an end.

CHAPTER TWENTY-FOUR
SAMANTHA

People often ask me if I miss boxing. In short, no. It is a relief in many ways to be retired. The lifestyle was so spartan, so lonely, so demanding and contained such hardship, it is hard to miss. If you should leave your partner, you will not miss them because the time spent with that person is over for you; if your partner should leave you, then you will naturally want them back – you will miss that relationship.

And yet, it is true that there is an intangible pull that tries to seduce you back into the ring. When I retired after Thompson 2, that was it, finished. However, one of the cleverest things I have done in the last few years (and I've done a lot!) is to start smoking cigars and inhaling. Why is that clever? It is clever because boxing is a far bigger evil than cigars. If you carry on too long in the business of boxing, forget about your health, forget about your damaged knees or potential head injury, you are likely to lose your dignity. If I had depended on my discipline to keep me away from boxing, I am sure I would have gone back already.

Apart from the seduction of boxing, I am concerned by things I see, such as these so-called celebrities who have little merit or substance. Many of these people who are put in the media spotlight are poor role models who haven't achieved very much and should not be given the attention they crave. But I suppose this is the society in which we live. I knew and recognised this, and therefore I started smoking cigars, I used my intellect against that fact. It is no different to me cutting off my right arm, I have disabled myself.

I have been offered 'comeback' fights but this will not happen. Names like Roberto Duran, Thomas Hearns and James Toney have been put forward, there was even talk of Roy Jones. I would not fight these people because my dignity could be challenged and would be brought into question and it is too precious to me. Why come back? I retired just before my 32nd birthday, which in boxing terms meant I was an old man. If the phone rang tomorrow and I was offered £1 billion, then no, I wouldn't do it. My dignity and respect are more valuable. The people who want to see me fight again remember how it was, it will never be better for me.

Take Evander Holyfield. He has fought in some of the greatest contests the business has ever seen, he's beaten Mike Tyson twice after all. Yet, when I saw his millennium year 'comeback' against Ruiz, he'd lost a kind of respect from me. Put simply, he had gone on too long: as the saying goes, 'Take kindly the counsel of the years, gracefully surrendering the things of youth.' If he had retired after Tyson 2, he would have left an abiding, awesome memory in the minds of the people. To go on to that farcical draw with Lennox Lewis, Holyfield has allowed himself to be cajoled back into a business where he has already done his lot. He can't do any more. So many fighters make this mistake.

Why do they come back? For one of three reasons. One, it is truly in your blood, the human animal, which makes you the stereotyped fighter. Two, for fame, which is a flaw in your character which we are all tempted by. And finally, three, for money which is a shame because you didn't put your earnings away the first time and so many of us make this mistake, purely due to being poor businessman and putting trust in others. When I came back after my first defeat it was reported I missed the fame. No, it was because I had not completed my course.

I cannot come back and get in the same ring as Roberto Duran, for example. We have both passed our sell-by dates. To actually stand opposite Duran inside the ropes would be a disrespect to his deserved legend. I am not worthy of stepping into the same ring as a man who, pound for pound, was one of the greatest fighters ever. Duran was an icon and a demigod, so was Thomas Hearns. Plus, they are both my elders – I bow to people like them. When I was an amateur, I would watch fighters like Duran and Hearns in awe – they were from an era before me, I cannot get in there and fight with them. It would be like watching two relics fighting, not two men in their prime. If I did I would be disrespecting them, and in so doing, I would be disrespecting myself.

As well as actual bouts, I have been approached to promote fights and actually have a promoter's licence, but that life does not really appeal to me. I have been involved in a few bouts as a promoter, but it's not something I wish to do all of the time, as it involves me in matters I am not comfortable with. I have also been asked if I would train young fighters. I would make an effective trainer, because I can intimately break down what is in each move, plus I was taught by a great trainer and have competed at the highest level.

Although certain aspects of training would be interesting, I will not do it, for two reasons. Firstly, you can take a kid with obvious natural talent, train him, coach him, guide him through the minefield that is professional boxing, work with him up the ranks until he gets a title shot. Then, at the culmination of all that combined hard work, it might be exposed that he doesn't have the heart. That would be devastating. I don't think I am prepared to give anyone that amount of time who may not be worthy, or of true heart. You can see a good right hand, you can tell if someone has a cast iron chin, you can see good application, obsessive training and good personal conduct. What is invisible, until the moment it is needed, is the heart.

The second reason is that I get more joy out of motivating people. I don't train people in the physical sense, only in the mental sense. Boxing is one of hundreds of trades. Training the mind, talking to people about life – there is no more important and all-encompassing hobby than that.

Now I am retired, most of my days are spent doing charity work, talking to youngsters, visiting educational institutions, doing television and radio interviews and taking part in televison programmes such as *Gladiators* and *At Home with the Eubanks* – I never seem to have a moment to spare. Boxing is often there of course, but that is just the vehicle I use to make my points heard. I have much more time for my hobbies, of course, which have always been poetry, quotation reading and committing poems to memory, chess (which I see as legal fighting) and conversing with people. I love to take up a topic, sit back in a comfortable chair and see where the conversation leads.

One fun job I did after retirement was a show called *Eubank's People* on Talk Radio. I invited esteemed guests such as Naz, Lennox Lewis, Linford Christie and John Fashanu into the studio and we talked about all kinds of things. I really enjoyed it, but they said I talked more than the guests did! My view is this: if someone is telling a story and doesn't elaborate, then I will elaborate for them. I understand good TV and good radio.

I am proud to be an avid charity worker, but I never like to publicise this fact, other than when it benefits the cause in question. I will talk briefly about it here because this is my book. The point is to work for these charities, *whether there is a camera there or not*. So many celebrities cherry-pick certain high-profile charities.

If you can help lots of people, this is very good but you should find it rewarding to help just a single individual as well.

With most charity work, people will say, 'Well, what are you getting out of this?' What I am getting is the payment for knowing virtue; the payment for virtue is virtue itself. My morale is boosted and buoyant. If someone else recognises that I have done a good deed for a person less fortunate, fantastic, but the worthwhile gratification comes immediately in actually doing the deed.

I like talking to youngsters, speaking at universities to raise awareness or money. One fun event is when I work in the trading rooms in the city of London, where I'm on the phone to stockbrokers, trading, buying, selling, raising funds, and being taught the jargon. In return, that stockbroker who has just sold me some shares had a laugh. On top of that, we raise a lot of money in the process.

I enjoy going to charity events and premieres. I went to a bash at The Park Lane Hotel in 1998 for an evening in tribute to Oscar Wilde. It was a big celebrity event, all these high-profile stars chatting to the media and suchlike. A TV interviewer came up to me and said, 'So, Chris, what do you think of Oscar Wilde?' I said, 'Well, I'm sure his mother loves him.' The interviewer thought this was all very profound and I had clearly caught her off-guard. What she didn't know was that at that point, I got away with it by the skin of my teeth. She thought I said loved – my lisp got me out of that one!

Another charity event I helped out with, this time for cancer, was in Dublin, where various celebrities strode up and down the catwalk in designer clothes (I wore my own). There were 40 top models attending, people like Naomi Campbell, as well as various celebrities such as Chris Evans and Christie Turlington. Steve Collins was also on the bill.

There was no friendship between us. After the second defeat, he had always remained bitter – about what? He won both our contests, he should carry himself like a champion. He had never come over to me to say hello whenever our paths crossed.

At this Dublin catwalk show, I saw that Collins was supposed to be going out after me, so I spoke to the person who was organising the running order who agreed it was okay for me to go out last. I was watching the monitor backstage, when this organiser told Collins to walk out for his turn, but he said, 'No. I'm not going.' I just stood there and eventually someone said to Steve. 'You either go now or you don't go at all.' So he had to go. I could see at this point that the situation could have spoiled the event, so I walked towards Steve to say that we should walk out together, but as soon as I approached and said, 'Steve' he stormed off on to the catwalk.

He was about seven yards down the catwalk when I made my own entrance at the head of the walkway. I strode out in jodhpurs, my antique cane, no tie, the full strut. The applause for him had been warm, but the applause for me was deafening – bear in mind, this was in Ireland. Collins looked back when the crescendo of clapping broke, saw it was me and was not pleased. He reached the end of the catwalk and turned to head back towards me, where we met in the middle.

I had my hands behind my back, clasping my cane. Collins walked right up and I thought he was going to shake my hand, so I put mine forward to meet his palm. However, he put his face one inch from mine and snarled, 'So when are we going to fight again, eh? When? When?' I just said, 'No, no,' waved my hand away and walked around him. This was an event for a cancer charity! Why behave like this? He beat me twice, I don't understand what he still craves.

As I have said, it is important that you are a giving person, whether there is a camera present or not, and regardless of whether you raise funds or just boost someone's spirit. As with the theft of my jewellery and that long coat, sometimes people take advantage because I am so quick to help out. However, there have been many more examples where my good intentions are not taken as intended.

For example, I was in Paris with my wife in early 2001 and we were travelling across town in a taxi to our hotel. It was raining hard and there was a lot of traffic. This old woman came towards the car waving her hand in the air, but as we pulled nearer, she slipped onto the wet ground. I stopped the taxi and jumped out, helped her to her feet and said 'Are you okay?' I saw then that she was a very old nun and seemingly could not speak a word of English. I cannot speak nor understand any French, so she gestured to me that she needed to go somewhere. I told her to tell the driver where to go and she could have our cab, as we'd hail another one.

At first the taxi driver would not allow her to get in, mumbling in French something about rules and regulations. Eventually, the only option was to all get in together, so she climbed aboard, out of the pouring rain. We drove to our destination and paid the fare to that point. Then I gave the nun 200 francs and asked the driver to take her where she needed to get to. I turned to the old nun, took one of my caricature postcards out of my bag and gave it to her with a warm smile. I pointed at the card, saying, 'That's me,' and waved her off. The first thing I said to Karron as the nun's taxi sped away was, 'I need another lady like her praying for me.'

Here's a thought. If that nun was ever in a position to have a child, that child might have a child too, who in turn might bear a great-granddaughter for the nun. At the same time, my son may have had a son. One day, my grandson might be travelling through Paris and meet a lady who tells a story of a famous boxer picking her great-grandmother out of the gutter where she had fallen in the rain. In fact, I know my grandson will meet that lady's great-granddaughter, life works out like that. That battered, dog-eared postcard will be passed down through the generations and, somewhere along the line, that story will come back around. That is my honest belief.

That lady may have prayed for me. I have always had one person who has prayed for me ceaselessly every day of my life – my beloved mother. This is probably why I have been as lucky as I have – my mother prays several times every day. They say the harder you work, the luckier you get, but I've had the advantage of someone praying for me.

Another episode where I gained much warmth out of helping someone who really appreciated my actions, was at Harrods. I am fond of Mohamed Al Fayed. We have talked many times about various subjects. When he was criticising those MPs, questioning the sexuality of other powerful people and the like, I said to him, 'These people can assassinate your character, stop talking about them like that.' He said to me, 'If they do anything to me, my spirit will still go to heaven because I am a good man. Then I will descend on them and wipe them out!' Once I came into his office and he said to me, 'Chris, are you gay?' He plays with you like that. He's not intimidating at all, he's just an old boy, an old fox. But then, I don't find anybody intimidating.

In late 1999, Al Fayed asked me if I would open the sales at Harrods with Raquel Welch on 5 January. We had a jovial chat, at the end of which I said, 'Am I attending as a personality or as an acquaintance?' He said, 'Come as an acquaintance,' to which I replied, 'Then there shall be no fee.' We booked the event in.

Three weeks before that store sales opening, I was invited to the 'Children of Courage' Awards at Westminster Abbey. I attend many functions of this nature and the strength of character these young people show in the face of adversity never ceases to amaze me. I always find I come away feeling inordinately thankful for my family's health and love.

The stories I heard that day were deeply moving. There were children who had lost both parents in motor vehicle accidents, children with disabled parents, wheelchair-bound kids and other courageous youngsters. They were all so positive and inspiring, it really affected me. It is at times like these that all the material trappings and complexities of modern life seem so irrelevant.

At the ceremony, Heather Mills, the model who lost her leg in an accident, and has since become married to Sir Paul McCartney, asked me if I would mind being introduced to a girl called Samantha. Heather told me that Sam had terminal cancer. She also informed me that initially the experts had amputated one leg in the hope that it would curtail the disease, but unfortunately that had failed and the cancer had now spread to her stomach, breasts and before long, they suspected, her brain. Medical opinion suggested she had a month to live.

Sam was a delightful and very brave girl. We chatted and shared some tales. Sam's mum, Cathy, then showed me a picture she had taken of her daughter when she was 18, only a year earlier, before the cancer had started to eat into her body. She was gorgeous, a very attractive blonde young woman with the world before her.

At such ceremonies, I have stopped remaining behind for the publicity shots because in the past when I have done such things, the media have accused me of doing anything to get my face in the papers – as if I needed to! Moss Side was perhaps the most extreme example but it had happened several times elsewhere. I would, of course, always sign autographs and take snaps with people away from the newspapers lenses. So, I bade my farewell to Sam and walked away, but I was deeply troubled.

As I walked out of Westminster Abbey, I couldn't get Sam's face out of my mind and her unjust predicament. Suddenly, I was overwhelmed by the adrenaline and passion that the fight business sometimes inspires in you.

Then an idea came to me. I called Mohamed Al Fayed's offices and asked to speak to him but he was not there. I left a message for him to call me urgently and hung up. I didn't expect a call back from him too soon, especially as at the time he was very busy with numerous court proceedings. A little while later, I was eating lunch at a restaurant when my mobile phone rang and it was Al Fayed's secretary, saying he was on the line waiting to speak to me. I went out of the restaurant and, after exchanging pleasantries, the conversation went something like this:

'Can you help me?' I said.

'I will try. What is the problem?'

I told him about Sam and then said, 'Taking into consideration that I waived my fee for the sales opening, would you now agree to exchange part of that payment in order to give Sam the shopping trip of a lifetime and allow her to spend £3000 in your store?'

'Of cause, without hesitation, bring her in,' he said.

I put the phone down and was inspired, fuelled and moving at 100mph. I raced back to the Abbey. Everybody had left by then and had gone to a lunch. The problem was I was given three separate possible locations. I drove around all three of them in my car, but to no avail, I couldn't find Sam or her mum.

I finally found out they were on the motorway heading back to their home in Hertfordshire. I got hold of Heather Mills and fortunately she had a mobile number for Sam's mum. I rang the number.

'Hello?'

'Hey, hello, Cathy, it's Chris Eubank here.'

'Oh, hello! What can I do for you?'

'Is Sam there?'

'Yes, she's here next to me.'

'Listen, turn around and come back to London.' I explained the offer from the Harrods' boss and myself and heard Cathy relaying the story to Sam.

'Yes! Yes! We're turning around right now!'

We stayed in touch by mobile and I drove on ahead to Harrods, arriving 15 minutes early. I spoke to Mr Al Fayed and explained the situation in more depth. To my surprise, he told me that he often made similar offers but that it was usually £250. He went off to a meeting, leaving the instruction with his secretary to call him when Sam arrived.

When she got there, we took her upstairs and Mr Al Fayed came out of his meeting to say hello. He was very tender towards her, told her not to give up hope and promised to speak to his personal doctor about her situation, taking their numbers in the process to pass on to his experts. Then he kissed her on the cheek and gave her a cuddle, before handing over £3000 of vouchers which were redeemable against anything in the store. Cathy (Sam's mother) had told me also that she once wrote to Mr Al Fayed asking for help for a benefit she was arranging. No further questions were asked and a colossal hamper arrived shortly after.

I wheeled Sam around Harrods for nearly two hours. I got into one of my characters – the talkative and gesticulating one – and gave her a royal performance while she shopped. I have many characters, like everybody: showman, daredevil, philanthropist, orator, father, husband, role model, poet, advisor, amongst many others. So I escorted Sam with a colourful show. The first item she bought was a 26″ television with video all-in-one. The assistant informed me that this was the last one and it had already been sold. I said, 'Really? Can I have a quiet word?'

I took this section manager to one side and said with a smile, 'Never mind the wrath of your boss, of whom Sam is a personal guest. If Sam does not get that exact television, you need to be worrying about the wrath of Chris Eubank.' I smiled and he seemed to get the message, the other customers would have to wait. I then explained the actual circumstances to which he said of course (she had not long to live.)

As well as the television, Sam bought an Apple Mac computer and printer, a bunch of videos, £265 worth of chocolates and was still left with £500 of vouchers for a similar spree in the near future. By the end of this excited day, which I will never forget, I was completely calm, I had burnt off all that raging adrenaline and Sam had had a spontaneous adventure.

People have very strong opinions of Mohamed Al Fayed. Remember this: he lost a son and unless you are a parent who has experienced the same, you cannot begin to comprehend what that must feel like. I would rather not even try. He was so warm and caring towards Sam, he was full of genuine affection. He is a loveable, wily, generous old fox.

I got back in touch with Sam shortly after and she told me Mr Al Fayed's doctors had been round to her house, promising to do whatever they could. Mr Al Fayed had also offered to fly Sam and her mother on an all-expenses luxury holiday to New York and Disney World in Paris. She never lived long enough to go on either trip.

CHAPTER TWENTY-FIVE
A HEAVY HEART

My relationship with my father had always remained very strong and close over the years. He travelled between Jamaica and England, and when he was at his house in Ashbury Road, Peckham, I would see him maybe two or three times a week. I always sent him money and we spoke very often. When I was about six years old, I would run up to him and ask for 5p to buy ice lollies, I loved them; well, now the tables were turned and I had worked very hard to be able to buy him a house in Jamacia.

My father was a proud man. He loved telling people about my endeavours in the ring and on five or six occasions he would come with me to television studios, sit in the green room talking to the young ladies, having a good time. I loved my father deeply and I always will.

On 7 July 2000, I was due to do an interview and was lacing my paddock boots up, when my mobile phone rang. It was Peter, who said, 'Dad's in hospital, you'd better go up to London.' I was due to do this interview then travel down to Cornwall to open, of all things, a sexually-transmitted diseases clinic. So, I phoned King's College hospital where my father was being treated and asked to speak to the doctor in charge. I said, 'Is this urgent? How is he?' I just wanted to find out if it was serious, because I am very diligent with my work commitments. Unfortunately, the doctor said, 'Mr Eubank, I think you should get up here as soon as you can.'

So I knew he was really not well. With my sincere apologies, I cancelled the interview I was about to start, then headed for Brighton station. I had missed my train so I drove up to Gatwick, parked in an illegal bay and caught the Gatwick Express to Victoria. It was a bit of a blur, everything was at speed.

I flagged down a taxi, jumped in and started to head towards King's College hospital. All this time I had been trying to call Peter but couldn't get through. When I was just over five minutes away from the hospital, my mobile rang and it was Peter, who said, 'Don't worry, it's too late, he's gone,' then hung up.

So here I was in the back of a taxi and my father is dead. I am with a complete stranger, no family with me, nothing. That is when you really need your brothers. Peter hanging up was just the way he dealt with it. I was, of course, stunned by this news. I put my head in my hands and started to sob. I cried for about three or four minutes.

I got to the hospital and found two security guards outside my father's room to keep the press away (although there were none there). I wiped my face with some tissues that the taxi driver had given to me, then prepared myself to go in, showing a strong face. My father's nephew was there and said, 'He has gone to Jesus now.' I didn't want to hear anything like that, so I asked the nephew to stay outside for a while and let me be with my father undisturbed.

I walked through and my dad was lying there. I immediately thought, *What a beautiful looking man.* I approached his bed and said to him, 'So, is that it?' I put my hand on his forehead and it was just cold, pallid. They had taken his dentures out and when I opened his eyelids, I saw his cataract blue eyes. I just sat there for about 30 minutes. David had left before I arrived, but then after a while Peter and Simon arrived. Peter sighed and sat next to my father's bedside. We just sat there, quietly.

I left the hospital and phoned Terry Johnson, who lives in Cornwall, and told him I would still make the opening of the clinic. Terry kindly sent his private plane to pick me up at Biggin Hill Airfield, which then flew me down for the opening. Although I wanted to fulfil my obligation, it really was more of a selfish thing, I wanted to keep my mind occupied. I couldn't just sit there – I kept seeing my father's face and him lying there in the hospital bed.

So I went to Cornwall and gave as good a performance as I could muster. They knew my father had just died and were very accommodating. I tried to cheer myself up by telling a very tongue-in-cheek poem (keep in mind this is a STD clinic) which goes as follows:

'The portion of a woman that appeals to man's depravity is fashioned with considerable care. And what at first appears to be a simple little cavity is truly an elaborate affair. Doctors who

*have troubled to study the abdomina of certain experimental
dames, they have classified and listed these peculiar phenomena,
they've given them delightful Latin names. There's, let's see, the
vulva, the vagina and the good old perineum, the hymen in the
case of certain brides. There are lots of little gadgets that you'd
laugh at, if you could see them such as clitoris and God knows
what besides. So, isn't it a pity when those common people
chatter about, these mysteries to which I have referred, that they
give to such an intricate and delicate a matter, such a short and
unattractive little word.'*

It went down brilliantly and although I was desperately
sad, I had to try and lighten the proceedings. Terry looked at
me across the room, knowing what I was feeling, and I saw
love in his eyes. I kept my mind occupied again later that
week when my then agent took a call from the International
Fund For Animal Welfare, asking me to fly to South Africa
to help raise awareness of a crisis oil slick that had hit the
country's penguin population. I agreed immediately and
flew out only three days after my father's death. I spent time
washing these poor African penguins that were covered in
crude oil, spoke to the youngsters in the townships and
helped out as much as I could. It was helping me in return,
by keeping me busy.

When I got back from South Africa, I went to see my
father's brother, Uncle Louis, and gave him some money to
take care of preliminary matters. We held a memorial in
England first. I became quite angry with the preacher, talking about Christ, death and sins – it was going on too long. I
actually walked out and was pacing up and down outside,

angry at the service. Then this old lady came and said, 'This is just tradition, you must come and sit down.' So I took her advice and returned to my seat. I needed to hear that from an older person. My mother would have told me the same thing if she had been at the memorial. She was living in Jamaica, but when I phoned to tell her the bad news, she had already found out from another source.

I had sent David to Jamaica to sort out the burial arrangements, as there had been a lot of contention about the exact location. My sister, Joycelyn (I call her Joy), wanted one spot but my father's brothers wanted somewhere else. That was totally wrong, it should have been up to the children. Unfortunately, David was manipulated by one uncle in particular, who is a bully, so he got his way. I left it at that for the sake of peace.

I arrived in Jamaica five days before the burial. The day before the funeral, I was sitting with my mother in a conservatory. It was very hot, all you could do was sweat. At about 2pm, one of my aunties on my father's side, Auntie Blanche, came in and started talking casually to my mother. She said, 'We know what you went through, the beatings, the battering, the wage packets being taken off you.'

I didn't know any of this. I was not part of the conversation, I was just sitting there hearing all this for the first time, the day before my father was to be buried. I'm hearing how my mother was battered and how the twins, Simon and Peter, had to be born in Leeds because she had to get away from my father.

My heart squeezed and became very tight. I said nothing.

At about 4pm, my brothers came back from the house which my father had bought. I wasn't talking to David because he had not sorted out the burial correctly and had also been disrespectful to my mother. I was still shell-shocked by what I had just discovered, so I said to them, 'I was sitting down here earlier and I heard this conversation about Mom being battered by Dad.' They told me they knew that and annoyingly said, 'You didn't know?' I said, 'Well, who told me?'

Peter said it was their relationship and what went on was none of our business, that it was not for us to get involved. I was very angry by now and drawn to raise my voice, so I said, 'But she is our F***ING MOTHER!' I was so irate, I was furious, 'This is our mother!' I was ready to fight, this was my brothers accepting my father's side, the wrong side, the day before his funeral.

I found my mother and said, 'Mum, I held the memorial for Dad in England. I have flown over on the same plane as him, I still love him like I can't tell you, but I have to go now, because I have to respect myself.' I was ready to get on the plane that evening. She said, 'No, you stay here and respect your father.'

There is a saying that goes, 'Honour thy mother and thy father' which I believe has brought me a lot of luck. When I knew my parents were in the wrong, I would just mildly say, 'If that is your view, that's fine, okay, it's not for me, but that's your view.' Personally I would never argue with my parents. Let them be old and be at peace. For example, my father always believed in ghosts and voodoo, he was an uneducated but wise man and certain people took a great deal of money from him because he believed in those things. He used to curse the ghosts out loud in the churchyard to chase them away, which was hilarious. I would say, 'It is not for me, Dad, but I understand.' You must honour your parents.

So I stayed. I could not take my father's side on this one, but I stayed. I am so like him in so many ways, but never like that.

I know one philosophy that states, 'Your mother comes first, second, third, then your father.' You must respect your mother always. NEVER make her cry, NEVER disrespect her. I have always thought that should be strictly adhered to, and say it to my children. *When you become a man, bring me a newspaper and a cigar every few days, I may not need to see you as much as your mother, she has done most of the work, all I have to do is pay.* That is my natural view, it may not be the most fashionable but that is my take on things. I recently (and for the first time in my career) sent a young woman who was interviewing me away for assuming I think the women's place is in the home. She then asked if I was a chauvinist. I was seriously offended because I champion women, especially mothers.

My mother was always first, so when I heard she was taking beatings and working three jobs with four children, I was incensed. Now I knew the full story of why she had left us when I was eight – she had to! What else could she have done? She said to me later, 'I just couldn't take it anymore.' She only lasted as long as she did through her faith in Jesus Christ. For anyone who is asking, 'Why didn't she take you with her to New York?' my response is, how could she? She was an illegal immigrant with no work, she couldn't put four young boys into that position. My father never mistreated us like that, so she knew we would be safe, and she was right, he never did that to us. He only gave us the strap when we were doing wrong. He was a good father.

At this juncture, let me say this. Had I known that my father had been beating my mother, I would still have done the things I did for him and more. I couldn't have done anymore, and neither could my brothers. However, I wish I had taken him with me to more television interviews, radio stations, launch parties, opening nights and so forth. He would have had a good time and it would have been fantastic for me too. If only I had him back, I would do this more so. I love him still. But that one fact I cannot accept. The womanising, gambling, drinking and bad language? I can understand that of men. Beating my mother? No, that I cannot understand or accept.

So I was not at peace at all the day before my father was buried. That said, I did not know what was about to happen. The funeral was to be held in Mount Airey, in the real countryside of Jamaica. When we arrived at the 500-seater church, it was already heaving, with another 500 people who couldn't fit in waiting outside on the grass.

As I had walked into the church, one elder said, 'Yu see dat man de, all Irvin av, a 'im give im.' As I walked in, I noticed two policemen at the door with guns. My sister Joycelyn informed me that, sometimes, Jamaican country folk can get very emotional and do not always use restraint. I had not seen this before, so I didn't think much about it.

There were a lot of young men in the church whom my father had helped and they were crying over the glass panel under which his body lay. I had wanted him dressed in a particular way, his 1940s hat, a pin stripe suit, shirt and tie. Every inch of his 5′ 4″ frame looked immaculate. Of all the people crying in that church, none of them could have loved him more than me. I was his son.

People started getting up to give their accounts. My sister is heavily into the church (she will probably be a preacher one day) and she sang a hymn and then asked all the family to join her up there. I was sitting by where the musicians were playing, in a white shirt with my sleeves rolled up, it was so hot. David didn't stand, he sat where he was in the congregation.

Then my mother gave her account. She said, 'Irvin's gone but thank the Lord for how much we enjoyed him. It is so sad.' She went on to talk about the glory of God and the afterlife, then sat down. The next person was moving to get up and talk by now, but as I was sitting there, I had a raging dilemma burning inside of me.

I am sitting in that church thinking about the truth that I know. It is my father's funeral, he was deeply loved by everybody here and most are distraught that he has gone. I know I am in a part of the world where life can be very cheap. I know how much these people loved him and I know they would take a life over that.

Yet, in my own mind, I am thinking: *I cannot let you go to your grave without having the truth about these beatings come to light. You reap what you sow and if you go down in your grave without this truth being known, then you have not had a true send-off.*

If you love someone you have to tell the truth. I was sick with myself knowing what I was about to do, not because it was wrong but because it was right. The truth and integrity of the correct procedure was so fierce and savage that it turned my stomach.

I kept thinking: *She is my mother, she must have the solace of rectitude being done.* I also agree with the tenet that 'The superior man is a man of truth.' So I asked the fellow who was halfway to the altar to wait a moment, and stepped up there myself. Peter got up and walked out because he knew what I was about to do.

I said to the congregation, 'I am looking to forgive here and my heart is heavy, I am looking to you to help me.' There were a few religious missives from the crowd, because they had misread what I was about to say. Then, steeling myself against the ferocity of the truth I was about to reveal, I said, 'Yesterday, I learned that my mother was battered by my father.' Instantly, there was an electric atmosphere, the tension almost visibly flared up into the church rafters. I continued, 'I came into this news just yesterday. I can't tell you how much I love my father, but this is my mother!'

I wanted to say, 'Also, my heart is heavy because his brothers had no right to dictate where he should be buried,' but the growing wrath of the crowd cut me off in mid-sentence. They shouted me down and stopped me talking. It was mainly the women who were shouting too, which I couldn't understand because so many of them were probably battered wives too. Here I was, taking a stand and they were not recognising that.

I continued above the rising din, 'What? I haven't got feelings, I am supposed to leave now? I am looking for acceptance and understanding, can I not talk now?' The sound of sobbing filled the church by now and scores of people started to get up and leave. I said, 'You're leaving now, what about my mother?' For her part, she was saying, 'Chris! No! No! No!' I walked back to my seat, put my head in my hands and cried.

After about ten minutes, Peter signalled for me to meet him at the far end of the church. He said, 'There are people out there who are looking to kill you. The police are here, go with them now.' I got my jacket and walked out the back and climbed into the back seat of the police car, sandwiched between two officers. As we did, some eight young men started hurling profanities at me. One of them put his head through the police car window, and right in front of the policemen, said he would kill me. We drove off and out of town and, as the police had to return to see if the church was back in order, I stopped a mechanic who was working by the road and asked if he would mind taking me on.

When I arrived back at my mother's house, my half-brother Pes was there and I told him what happened and he replied, 'What is this?' He knew I was right, he is a good man. He said I was right to do what I had done. I packed my things and said, 'I am going to leave before everyone returns from the church.' It was clearly time to get out. If I had gone back to the burial ground with the congregation I would certainly have been killed. I found out later that while they were actually carrying my father's body to be buried, they were planning how to kill me.

As I was about to leave, my mother, sister Joycelyn and half-sister June, came in. My mother walked over to me and hugged me tightly and warmly. She had always prayed for me every day of my life, but now she said, 'I haven't got to worry about you any more. Go on, you are okay.'

When I woke up the next morning, I felt sick, but not because I had done the wrong thing. Facing the truth in that extreme circumstance was truly savage. Compared to any fight I had in my career, no matter how brutal, the courage it took to say what I had in that church was monumental. The most vicious and demanding bout of all-time was a stroll by comparison. It was a scathing test of my integrity. I believe I faced up to that test and met it with the truth.

It was a watershed moment for me. I felt like I was a man in my own right now. I was before, of course, but just like the first Benn fight, this was about cementing what I already knew in stone. Some might say, 'You can't say that at someone's funeral.' No, it is the only thing you can say. The question is, have you got the courage to say it? Plus, I knew I couldn't do it the next day or the day after, I had to do it right then and there. It would have haunted me.

Almost a year later, my mother and Doctor were discussing this episode when she said to me, 'The best day of my life happened in that church.' I was listening to this conversation and when she said this I went to her and hugged her because I never knew how she felt about what had happened.

It is a finished subject now; I don't bring it up in conversation. I will say this though: If my brothers had been men in their own right they would have stood by my side – this was our mother who was being beaten.

The last thing I will say on this matter is this: I can't speak for my brothers, so in a sense this is not really fair, but I want to say it: *No one loved that man more than me.* They may have loved him as much as me, but I loved him so much I had to do what I did.

I haven't been back to Clarendon since.

My father dying was also a pivotal moment in regard to my relationship with my brothers. Although Simon accepts that I am my own man and Peter is beginning to, David still doesn't. The loss of our father means that we are on our own now. Dad held us together in many ways and now he has gone we have to stand on our own two feet. I don't need or want my brothers' acceptance any more. Indeed, when they still try to tell me how to do things, like all those years ago when I was just the bedraggled little brother, I tell them I am not interested, that it is offensive to me. One of the things that has disillusioned me the most in my life is the fact that my brothers are not people I can be next to, I love them, but I don't need their acceptance anymore.

It wasn't until the autumn of 2000 that I finally understood why my brothers never accepted me. For many years, I had wondered if it was jealousy. After all, Simon and Peter had been boxers but I had been world champion. But no, I knew that wasn't it, they were absolutely not jealous. I wasn't world champion when they were berating me in Stoke Newington as a kid. Although they wouldn't admit it, I can see in their eyes that they are proud of my achievements.

One of my close friends, Pepe, told me why he believed they never accepted me and now, in hindsight, I know what the problem was. Pepe said to me, 'It is because you are beautiful.' It was a revelation when Pepe said that to me. He didn't mean physically, but inside, as a person. I have never had any shackles, any chips on my shoulders, I have always tried to help, to be a good person. My brothers are not beautiful like that, if they were then they would not have treated me like they did. They are typical of a certain type of person from the street. I wasn't typical. This is the reason I believe I have been able to transcend my childhood circumstances, progress, then transcend all the situations that confronted me in my career. I always tried to keep my mind on what it is all about – integrity, reason and forgiveness.

CHAPTER TWENTY-SIX
JUST BEING ME

When I was invited into the *Celebrity Big Brother* house in March 2001 by one of the Comic Relief founders, Richard Curtis, I was delighted. I found the whole experience marvellous fun and it was almost as if the house was a microcosm of society, there were so many issues thrown up and highlighted for me in those 36 hours.

The obvious flash point was with Boyzone's Keith Duffy. He seemed quite antagonistic towards me from the first moment. The incident he mentioned where he grabbed my crotch was at the aforementioned charity catwalk event where Steve Collins squared up to me. Keith was there with Collins and some other people in the entourage. Bear in mind, I had only just met Keith when he walked up to me and grabbed my testicles, then when I was obviously offended, said, 'Oh, Chris, I thought we were friends.' I walked away somewhat timidly. What else was I supposed to do? Where I come from on the streets that is the way you pick a fight, if you are immature. A man would use a more masculine, antagonistic method.

I couldn't understand several points here. Firstly, although he had once been on a stage with myself, Nigel Benn and Barry McGuigan a couple of years previously for Comic Relief, Keith and I had never actually met. He should never have assumed such familiarity. If he had walked up and grabbed a woman in the crotch whom he had just met (or indeed at any point) he would rightly be arrested and brought up on charges of sexual harassment. He also brought the question of gay sexuality into it too – again, this was flippant, a gay man with any dignity would not dream of doing that to another man.

The only logical conclusion I could draw from him grabbing me like that was that he wanted me to hit him. If he had done that to Mike Tyson, it would have been the last thing he did before waking up in hospital. However, I was not going to lower myself to his level. In response I put my head down and slunk away, but really I was surprised that he would do that. Obviously he was looking for a fight, and if that is what he wanted, what was I going to do? He can't beat me so he must have been trying to provoke me. But I wasn't going to give up the respect I've earned over the years by slapping him. He wasn't capable of goading me into losing my credibility, he couldn't have understood that I am a pacifist.

Such crudity seems to be generally accepted when in fact it should be treated with disdain. Once, a few years previously, myself and Karron were at the launch of Planet

Hollywood in the West End of London. I am, of course, well aware that my wife is a very good-looking woman whom men find highly attractive. We were talking and having a nice time with one particular celebrity, but when we came to say goodbye, he kissed Karron on the cheek, and then said, 'Oh, let's have another one,' then another and so on. He wasn't actually groping her, but he was making her feel very uncomfortable.

On the street where I come from, we had a way of treating people who behaved that inappropriately. You put your hand over their mouth and pushed them back. This celebrity was being very disrespectful to my wife and me, so I was just about to put my hand on his mouth, when Lennox Lewis walked by. Lennox has always been the same character: never the type of man to try and keep your company, he keeps his distance and his dignity, he is a quiet, softly-spoken guy. He would always nod and say, 'Good performance,' but would not stay around. However, he is also, obviously, a very imposing presence – fortunately for all concerned, this provided sufficient distraction for these lecherous actions to stop. We left without saying another word. I am glad Lennox turned up at that moment, because this man was a powerful public figure and it would have been embarrassing for him.

Going back to Keith Duffy, he showed his lack of dignity later as well when he whistled over me as I was telling Venessa Feltz on *Celebrity Big Brother* how I met Karron. I said to him, 'Hey, Keith, come on guy, I wouldn't do that to you! Come on, don't do it to me.' He apologised and walked off. It was forgotten. I can't abide bad manners in anyone: as an adult, you know when something is rude. I just choose to ignore bad conduct.

Claire Sweeney from Brookside was very, very sweet. She was smiley, bubbly, I really liked her. She coped very well with it all. I liked Anthea Turner, too. She seemed very fragile and uncertain of herself. At one point, she was talking with Vanessa Feltz about how inconsiderate people can be, especially when they don't know the real truth behind a situation. I know from experience that to the personality in question, this can be very hurtful.

To go off on a tangent for a moment, I would like to talk briefly about my cousin, the athlete Diane Modahl, and how her fame and success was damaged by similar misconceptions. The authorities in this country destroyed her career – she had not taken those substances. She was a quality athlete who was proven conclusively to be not guilty of a doping offence. However she was never compensated for her losses, which included her home and income, plus the stress which that caused, and the ban meant that her prime time as a runner had been lost.

Outside of athletics, Diane could have also been making a name for herself as a celebrity, in regard to her career after athletics, but she was so busy and determined in fighting the ban. This country owes her, she was representing her nation, yet those very people took away her vital years. It is a really sad thing to have happened to Diane, they really hurt her.

Back to the Big Brother house. Anthea Turner was hurt

too, albeit on a different level. To exacerbate Anthea's position, I thought it was hurtful for the show's producers to demand we voted each other out. I know those were the rules for the first non-celebrity show, but I thought it was inappropriate for what was a charity event. In my opinion, they should have just let the public make the nominations and choices. Obviously, in regard to the things she'd been involved in over recent years, a section of the general public have a problem with Anthea. I think we were all taken aback by just how sensitive she was to that.

Big Brother had ordered that we did not draw straws or use random ways of nominating. This was unacceptable to me. It went completely against my character and the methodology I have been trying to live by since I was 16. Pulling those pieces of paper as I did was the only way I could nominate, otherwise Comic Relief would be forcing me to not practise consideration. I didn't want to vote against my fellow contestants, it made me feel really uncomfortable.

When Anthea was nominated, it hurt her deeply and at one point, she was crying. She was very sad, and I did not want to see that. I went to see how she was at about 7 o'clock and she said, 'I'm fine, I've packed my bags already.' I said to her, 'Anthea, you are not going anywhere. Don't worry.' How did I know she needn't have worried? I had been into the diary room and, how shall I say it, discussed this with Big Brother.

I actually addressed the mirror in the diary room as Big Sister because there was usually a lady talking to us. They still have the tapes, so my conversation can be verified fully. I said that I was not prepared to see Anthea ejected from the house. I said that if Anthea was evicted by the public, then they should let me go instead. It was not fair to expose her to that kind of upset when she was just trying to raise money for charity. I knew I was much more tough-skinned and comfortable with facing the media if I was evicted. I could not afford to leave Anthea's welfare to chance. I basically said, 'You may want to think very care-fully about who you let go out there tonight.' Let me state quite clearly now that I was voted out, and that Big Brother and Comic Relief has integrity. Nevertheless, I gave them the opportunity to do the right thing, because it was no good to have Anthea leaving, either for her or for the charity. If I had not been voted out, I would have exited anyway. When I came out, I said to the media, 'It would be nice for Anthea, even if she doesn't win, if she gets to stay in for a little longer.' She seemed so raw, she'd obviously had a rough ride. She needed that morale booster. This is the reason Lenny Henry came up to me on the Saturday and said, 'Thank you so much for what you did'. He knew that I forced myself out of the house.

One thing I cannot understand is how celebrities use swear words in public. For one, it is just laziness, it shows a lack of articulation. I am fascinated with communication, whereas profanities just cheapen the beauty of the English language. Secondly, and probably of most importance, it sets such a bad example. When Keith Duffy was using the 'f' word in his public language, the sad thing was that this was making him more popular.

I am undeterred. I will make my stand and be my little individual self and be happy with that. I see these people collecting music awards and saying, 'I effing didn't think I'd effing get this. Thanks an effing load.' I just don't like or understand why they do it, or indeed why people laugh at that. The funny thing is, if I had sworn in the Big Brother house, people would have seen it as unacceptable. I suspect that it is because I choose to be a gentleman, but it still mystifies me how some people get away with it. The same with crudity. When I saw the video afterwards of the other contestants all talking about masturbation, I was glad I had gone to bed. I would not have taken part in that. I was not willing to take part in anything that undignified. Anyone using crudity on television is representing their family values, or don't people think about that?

When I left the house, the first thing I said was, 'Thank you, Big Brother, and the public, for allowing me to entertain you for 36 hours, it was marvellous fun.' The public need to be able to digest you – you should not always be so serious, strutting and snarling. People need to see you having a laugh but this should never be done at the expense of your dignity.

The week following my eviction was so incredibly busy, everyone wanted to interview me. Of course, the tabloids' spin on it was that it was humiliating for me to be sent out first, but they did not know what I knew. Plus, it was not humiliating at all – it was fun. Even for that brief moment, I had been given the opportunity to show the public the real me, without media distortion. So many people said to me, 'If we had known how much flavour and colour was going to leave the house when you were evicted, we would not have voted you out.' If only they knew. Even Jack Dee, the eventual winner, when I left said, 'You know that's the most entertaining man I have ever met.' I think he won because of the psychological game he was playing. He was saying, 'Let me out, I have my bags with me, let me out!' But they wouldn't, the public were saying, no, you can stay, let us see you go crazy; it was a very clever way to play the game.

In addition, I had made well over £115,000 for the charity. When I was in the house, sitting there, I was thinking of all the people watching me and saying, 'That Eubank, who does he think he is? Look at him, in his jodhpurs, why is he wearing a swimming cap? Now he's riding a scooter, what is he about? Get him out! Where's the phone?' Fifteen pence for Comic Relief, thank you so much. Keep dialling. This was really no different to my boxing career – love me or hate me, but have an opinion.

When I think of it, it had to be me who came out first, I don't believe the other individuals had the energy to really push and plug the cause with all those interviews. And, yes, I was offered £50,000 by Chris Evans to break back in (he also offered Comic Relief £10,000 to let me back in) but when you become an adult you should never rain on other people's parades.

The scene where Vanessa chalked all those words on the table really grabbed people's imagination. I wasn't surprised. To people who said that she lost it in there, I would say she achieved her objective. She had the country talking about her. She is a very switched-on cookie and I like her.

For me there was only ever one agenda of importance, and that was Comic Relief. We were nothing more than tools to make money for Aids relief, under-privileged children, famine and medicine in Africa, domestic charities and so on. It wasn't about us, the celebrities. My personal interest was to let the public see the real me, but in so doing, I knew I could provoke, enthral, infuriate, entertain and polarise. That made opinions, opinions made phone calls and phone calls made money. Job done.

People said it was all very tense but I found my time in there to be very restful, there were no telephones, faxes, mobiles, just peace. If I did it again the only thing I would do differently would be to tell people when I was going to sleep. When I went to sleep without saying anything, they took it to mean that I didn't want to participate, but I was just tired. Looking back on the whole experience, it was great fun from start to finish.

Some people do take exception to me. There were people in the Big Brother house sniggering behind my back. I didn't do this and never would. I accept people for the way they are: if that is your character, fantastic: let me get into it, let me appreciate it. The people who sniggered said to me after-wards it was all in aid of Comic Relief and they were playing to the cameras, but I thought it was a little seedy, it was still a snigger.

CHAPTER TWENTY-SEVEN

AT HOME WITH THE EUBANKS

After taking part in *Celebrity Big Brother*, the BBC approached me to take part in a programme with Louis Theroux. He and his camera crew were to follow me around for 45 hours for their programme over a period of 10 days. In many ways this was the pilot for my series *At Home with the Eubanks*. My objective was to show the public that I am an ordinary guy. I have the truck, the monocle, a cane and bike, etc., but in essence I am a family man who is not ashamed of having fun.

I had no control over the edit or the final outcome, but I achieved my objective and created fun, entertaining television. Louis is a very likeable person but you have to understand that he doesn't do this for you; he tries to play you for the entertainment of the public and to put a feather in his cap. Let's not get away from the fact that he will try and make fun of you, find your flaws and expose them. I know my flaws, they are well guarded. The competition is whether you allow him to find them – whether you see it, and are intelligent enough to actually combat it. And I think I thrashed him!

Everything I have been asked to do regarding Michael Watson I have happily done and will continue to do so. So when Geraldine Davis (Michael's PA) asked me whether I would walk the last mile of the 2003 London Marathon with Michael, I said, yes, of course. I've been to charity events, testimonials and interviews but this would be quite different.

Back in November 2002 there was an event that lots of fighters like Lennox Lewis and Frank Bruno turned up to, as well as many other non-boxing celebrities. It was at Grosvenor House and in order to raise money I had my picture taken with people who would pay £10 for the experience and I also sold my autograph for £5. By the end of the night I had raised over £1500 for Michael. Frank Warren wanted to take the money I'd raised and add it to the rest of the money, but I refused. I wanted to hand over my contribution personally.

I didn't really realise how emotional the marathon walk would be; it was very, very moving. I stepped out of the coach at one point and welled up. Michael was being interviewed by a woman at Sky News Live at the time, then she turned to me and said, 'Chris, what do you feel?' and I didn't have any words and I felt ashamed and I said it, and I still couldn't find words and I knew that the word ashamed was wrong, because I meant inspired. She said, 'Why are you ashamed?' and I said, 'Because I'm part and parcel of why this happened, but inspired because of the response and by how much Michael has been able to recover and to do what he's doing.' As far as the human condition is concerned, this was moving, that a person should be able to come back from those horrific injuries and be able to do what he is doing. But, I suppose it was also the fact that the people screaming out his name, the number of people who surrounded him, everyone who walked past as we were walking, just added to the poignant nature of the day. As I said, everything I can do, I do. I've got my track and I'm living my track, and if they need help, then I help.

I have been to Nigeria a number of times now, but what struck me at first was how at home it felt there. My ancestors are from the west of the country and perhaps that was part of the reason I felt so comfortable. I have since taken two of the children there to see where they partly come from and so that they can see how lucky they are; to show them that not everyone in the world is as lucky as they are.

When I first went over there it was to work with the Kanu Heart Foundation to help highlight the fact that there are over 1800 children of all ages, from about two to age 12, who are in need of heart surgery, and the money which is raised is to send the children either to Israel or England. They're trying to raise funds to actually build the hospital in Nigeria where this procedure can be done and obviously the Arsenal footballer, Kanu, has championed this because he had the same problem.

As well as being involved with the Kanu Foundation I was also involved with the Nigerian government with regard to training a number of their best boxers for the All-African games. There was not enough time to arrange everything for the 2003 games, but in the long term, I would like to set up a programme where I would train about six heavy- and middleweights in England, oversee their training schedules, while also giving them lessons in how to become charismatic personalities and how to be media-aware, after all being a good boxer is only part of the equation.

Apart from loving the country, I was also shocked at the negative perception that is given of Nigeria, it is a country of enormous wealth and poverty but it is also a beautiful country with lovely, friendly people.

Before being involved with *At Home with the Eubanks*, I was approached to take part in a one-off series called *Gladiator: Benn vs Eubank* with Nigel Benn. Back in 1995 this same production company had made a documentary about me and Benn called *Clash of the Titans*; they seemed a little obsessed, but it goes to show what an impact we made. People still remember the titanic, brutal fights, the pose, the showmanship I brought to the ring.

This latest venture, however, was far more gruelling both mentally and physically than I expected. I consider myself an accomplished man. You become accomplished by finding out who you are in terms of situations that arise. To look Nigel Benn in the eye, you would have had to come to terms with who you are and what you do. For me Benn, is the most terrifying man I've ever met. In school, there was the kind of kid if you got on the wrong side of, you would just have to fight for no real reason. Even if you beat him, it was just a no-win situation, because there would be too much pain involved in defeating him. To me, Benn is that kid.

The idea of the programme was to have myself and Nigel Benn train as gladiators, in a recently opened gladiatorial school just outside Rome, and take part in a three-round, four-minute bout at the end of a week of hard training. Our trainers, Spartacus and Brutus, would teach us how to use the weapons the gladiators used and we would also have to eat the same food for the full authentic experience. This was a show for television so I was not taking it too seriously. I was keen to inject some humour into the proceedings, so when we were eating squid one day, I'm sitting there and I'm doing it rough, taking my food out of the bowl with a scowl on my face, and, while drinking the water, letting it dribble out of my mouth and I say, 'I do believe they call this calamari, marvellous!'.

It was a game show, but due to its particularly tough nature I don't think the format would have worked with anyone other than boxers: a footballer for instance would not have been hard enough to do this. But Benn was probably happy for the contest – I wasn't, it was an appalling situation they put me in.

We were trained in the use of various weapons and would then have to compete against each other in a series of small challenges which was to culminate in the big fight at the end of the week. For one task we were required to race twice round the amphitheatre with two 25lb sacks in 100-degree heat. At one point I had to put them down and pick them up again because they were so heavy and I lost my grip on the sacks because my palms were so sweaty. During that race, I was behind Benn up until the last few metres and was able to overtake him and win the race, but as I overtook him he let out this roar and redoubled his efforts to win, but I had already won and I had to shout to him, 'I've already won, it's over.' Such was his need to win. I was winding him up all the time in front of everyone to make him angry. He didn't need very much encouragement because he was bubbling over. I said to one of the film crew, 'Can't you see it, he's like a volcano going to erupt.' And sure enough he did.

Three men were attacking us with balls on the end of sticks covered in paint, the point being that you would have to defend yourself against these attackers and if they hit you it would show up as paint on your body. But to add extra spice, me and Benn were together and had to defend each other against our attackers. By the end of it he had more paint on his body than me and started to complain, saying, 'Listen, my legs are red and yours are not – which means, really, that I was protecting your legs more than you were protecting me.' At this point I make a funny gesture to the camera because I can't even believe he's said this and taking it so seriously, when he goes mental, shouting and swearing and then he pushes me. I fronted him up, and was in his face, I wasn't going to be intimidated by him. It was all getting a bit ugly and tense so the trainers and camera crew rushed in to pull us apart. One of the producers trying to keep order said, 'We've got three or four more days of work so let's calm it down, give me your hands, and let's just shake.' Which we did. To further help things along I added, 'But you know, like I do, you got one up because you pushed me, and we're equal now.' And I pushed him. Then he kicked off again and we were kept apart for two days so things would cool down. It was fantastic television.

All this training, however, didn't prepare me for the final battle. I had injured my neck after the second day of training and to be honest I wasn't 100% committed; I was only 75% up for it and for something this intense and physical, against a man like Nigel Benn, that is not enough. The first of the three bouts was with a sword and shield. It was only a plastic sword and a heavy leather covered shield but Benn was coming at me like a madman, slashing and kicking. And the armour we had to wear to protect ourselves was very constricting so it was difficult to manoeuvre. I was thinking, what am I doing here with this man, I don't need this. The second round, with a mace, again plastic, was even worse. Trying to block and counter-attack with my own mace was really difficult added to the fact that my injured neck was restricting me and being attacked by a committed man was more than I was willing to bear.

The final round was to be Greco-Roman wrestling where he held on to the back of my belt and I held on to his, the idea being like Sumo wrestling. I kept thinking that it was going to be such an undignified affair that I didn't really want to do it, and again with my neck restricting my movement I didn't think I could win this event. I had told the producers after the second event that my neck was bad and that I was really thinking about forfeiting the wrestling but I don't think they believed me, they thought it would be matter of pride and I would feel like I had to carry on or lose face. They said, 'Well, if you want to forfeit, then you can, that's your prerogative.' So I did, I hadn't lost face in any way, but I had lost the first two rounds and forfeited the last, so I lost the game. But at least it was the end of an awful experience, for which I should say I was grossly underpaid, considering what I had to endure.

My final word on this game, is this: hey, I lost. I'm very accepting of it, it's no big thing to me but if it makes him happy, then fantastic. At the end of the whole sorry event he walks near me and my wife and to where the camera crew and some of the crowd are, who can all hear and says, 'It's nice to even the score.' My wife was amazed and repeated his words in disbelief, 'Even the score!' I took his soul when I beat him in 1990, he was sobbing on Richard Steele's shoulder. I stopped him then; this was a game, but boxing is the real thing.

The idea for *At Home with the Eubanks* came about following a meeting with Sham Sandhu from Channel 5 in November 2002. My phone rang: it was Karron wanting me to speak to Joseph, who was playing up. Sham was intrigued by the conversation and thought a programme based around my family and me would make great television. When it was

finally agreed, I was delighted and felt like I had been
knighted and really appreciated the opportunity I had been
given. I believe it's because of all the hard work I have put
into my life. I was told that I should be kind, courageous,
considerate, hard and correct; and because I strive for these
things I have been given this opportunity. I also felt that it
was going to be a great opportunity for me to be able to get
across to the public what I was unable to before now. They
would see me not as a sportsman or as the tabloid media
would have me portrayed, but as I truly am. It also gave
me the chance to entertain while also offering my views of
correctness and humanity. I have always wanted to inspire
people and this was the ideal platform for me, while showing
my comic side.

When I first told my family we were going to be taking part
in this programme Karron was at first not convinced, she is a
person who likes a quieter life, she likes to go for long walks
and of course she runs the house which is such a difficult,
full-time job, although having now seen the programme it
is clear that she is extremely comfortable in front of the
camera. But the show really revolves around Karron, I'm
in my element here, I'm used to having cameras in my face,
but her and the kids are normal people going about their
everyday business with a supposedly eccentric husband and
father, the contrast of this gives the programme its humour,
and fun is what it's all about.

The kids were very excited to be on television, they come
round with me and see how people react to me and are quite
used to it, all except Christopher that is. He's older and at

the age where everything embarrasses him and he wants to be a rebel, but he understands, as all the kids do, that it's for their own good and we can't always do what we want in this world.

They filmed everywhere we went and everything we did for about nine months. The film crew were able to go with us everywhere except into the bedroom with Karron and me and to the bathroom with any members of the family. I said they could film everything they wanted, after all I have nothing to hide – I'm not a drunkard, I'm not ill-mannered, I'm not rude, I'm helping other people, why shouldn't people see it? I don't understand privacy.

They filmed the family's interaction round the dinner table or just playing, being in each other's company. They filmed Sebastian playing the drums, the family playing Twister and our holiday to Majorca which highlighted just how important Karron is to the whole family. When we arrived on holiday the villa we were staying in was in the middle of nowhere, the weather was bad and there was nothing for the kids to do, no DVDs or anything to keep them entertained. This was obviously hard work, keeping four children entertained inside, when they were expecting to be outside all the time messing about, but Karron had it all under control and did all the work. At one point the director actually said to me, 'I don't know how you put up with all these children.' I said, 'I don't, Karron does.' Which is a fact – she carries the load.

When she sees how she can influence people, women in particular I'm sure, she will be thrilled. She can influence women with regard to taking care of their bodies, not taking drugs and being a loving mother – being a standard for women. I think that will really empower her and give her satisfaction. She's not dolled up all the time during the filming, she's like, 'Get out of my way, I've got work to do here.' It's not a fly-on-the-wall documentary that has been tampered with to show everything is perfect. And it's the same with me – if you thought I would have helped with the housework just because they were there you would be mistaken, I would be lying to the public, because I don't. For every one time I ever get involved it's like 30, 40 times Karron does it. People may say I'm a chauvinist, but hey, I'm just a man, nothing more, nothing less, but I'm not a liar.

People will obviously draw comparisons with my programme and the American series *At Home with the Osbournes*. I think that I have only seen about ten minutes of the show, the one where Ozzy renewed his wedding vows, which I thought was quite nice. He was obviously emotional or something because his bottom lip was going, but the language used was totally unacceptable and I am not surprised his son Jack is having some emotional problems. I believe that if there is bad language between you and your kids, then your kids will be dysfunctional. They may not be dysfunctional within the family unit, but they will be the moment they have to communicate normally with others outside of the family. They may think it's alright to swear and be disrespectful to those outside the family, which it is not. Manners, conduct, it is very important that this fact is picked up on when people, especially children, watch my programme.

I wouldn't allow my children to watch *The Osbournes* as I don't think they are good role models for my children. My children are warned that when they watch *The Fresh Prince of Bel Air*, that they shouldn't copy that behaviour. I tell them, 'Don't bring that into this house, don't bring that here.' What happens in their friends' houses is fine for them, but in my house we have different boundaries that must be adhered to and if they're not, there is trouble. And the trouble will go on for weeks, trust me! At one point in the series I gave Joseph detention for lying about something he had done, I turn to the camera and say, 'Richard and Judy, *The Sun* newspaper, you're not running this house, I run this house.'

When I was in the ring I was 'box office', I was a showman and although I'm not boxing I still have a flair for the dramatic. The show gives me the opportunity to demonstrate what is obvious: that no man – or rather no person – is only one thing, we are many things. I'm an entertainer who can be philosophical, poetical, a sportsman, paternal. The public will have an opinion about me and I want them to see the good, rather than the bad, the positive rather than the negative, and I am able to get my point across effectively because it's done in a humorous way.

For instance, most of it's humour, but there are particular times when I am asked questions about a particular subject and while my deportment is humorous, my words will be very serious. There are instances where I've got my monocle in and am dressed very well, and they'll say, 'What are your views on sex?' and I'll reply, 'On the subject of sex? Condoms.' And I'll say nothing else and I'll just let the viewers think on that. Because it's not my business what people are doing, whether they are doing it or whether they are not, or if they are cheating on each other. My reply is a humorous way to get the message across.

Well, you can't be serious all the time and I think my series proves that I have the capacity, depending upon the situation, to either enjoy myself or be serious. So far, my life has been a terrifying and amusing journey but it has also been, as an old friend would say, 'Marvellous'.

EPILOGUE

As you have read in this book, no matter where you come from or how humble your beginnings, with perseverance, faith and belief in yourself you can achieve your goals. The key factors will be: focus, application and persistence.

For peace of mind, the following three virtues must be applied and adhered to: integrity (this should be your course in life), reason (this should be your only weapon), and forgiveness (the cleansing virtue).

The true warrior is a creature of irony; for his genuine task is to ensure peace.

CAREER STATISTICS

CHRISTOPHER LIVINGSTONE EUBANK

Born: 8 August 1966, Dulwich, London
Family: Father Irvin; mother Ena; brothers David, Simon and Peter; sister Joycelyn; wife Karron; children Christopher, Sebastian, Emily and Joseph.
Hometown: Brighton, England

Professional Fight Record (Won 45, Drew 2, Lost 5)

No.	Date	Opponent	Result	Location
1	3 Oct 1985	Timmy Brown	Won (4th round), points decision	Atlantic City
2	7 Nov 1985	Kenny Cannida	Won (4), points	Atlantic City
3	8 Jan 1986	Mike Bagwell	Won (4), points	Atlantic City
4	25 Feb 1986	Eric Holland	Won (4), points	Atlantic City
5	25 Mar 1987	James Canty	Won (4), points	Atlantic City
6	15 Feb 1988	Darren Parker	Won (1), TKO*	Copthorne
7	7 Mar 1988	Winston Burnett	Won (6), points	Hove
8	26 Apr 1988	Michael Justin	Won (5), TKO	Hove
9	4 May 1988	Greg George	Won (5), TKO	Wembley

10	18 May 1988	Steve Aquilina	Won (4), TKO	Portsmouth
11	31 Jan 1989	Simon Collins	Won (4), TKO	Bethnal Green
12	8 Feb 1989	Anthony Logan	Won (8), points	Kensington
13	1 Mar 1989	Frankie Moro	Won (8), points	Bethnal Green
14	26 May 1989	Randy Smith	Won (10), points	Bethnal Green
15	28 Jun 1989	Les Wisnieski	Won (2), TKO	Brentwood
16	4 Oct 1989	Ron Malek	Won (5), TKO	Basildon
17	24 Oct 1989	Jean-Noël Camara	Won (2), TKO	Bethnal Green
18	5 Nov 1989	Johnny Melfah	Won (4), TKO	Royal Albert Hall
19	20 Dec 1989	José Da Silva	Won (6), TKO	Kirby
20	16 Jan 1990	Denys Cronin	Won (3), TKO	Cardiff
21	6 Mar 1990	Hugo Corti	Won (8), TKO	Bethnal Green

Wins WBC International Middleweight Title

22	25 Apr 1990	Eduardo Contreras	Won (12), points	Brighton

Defends WBC International Middleweight Title

23	5 Sep 1990	Kid Milo	Won (8), TKO	Brighton

Defends WBC International Middleweight Title

24	22 Sep 1990	Renaldo Dos Santos	Won (1), TKO	Royal Albert Hall

25	18 Nov 1990	Nigel Benn	Won (9), TKO	Birmingham

Wins WBO Middleweight Title

26	23 Feb 1991	Dan Sherry	Won (10), TKO	Brighton

Defends WBO Middleweight Title

27	18 Apr 1991	Gary Stretch	Won (6), TKO	Kensington

Defends WBO Middleweight Title

28	22 Jun 1991	Michael Watson	Won (12), points	Earls Court

Defends WBO Middleweight Title

29	21 Sep 1991	Michael Watson	Won (12), TKO	White Hart Lane

Wins WBO Super-Middleweight Title

30 1 Feb 1992   Thulane Malinga   Won (12), points   Birmingham
Defends WBO Super-Middleweight Title

31 25 Apr 1992   John Jarvis   Won (3), TKO   Manchester
Defends WBO Super-Middleweight Title

32 27 Jun 1992   Ron Essett   Won (12), points   Quinta Do Lago
Defends WBO Super-Middleweight Title

33 19 Sep 1992   Tony Thornton   Won (12), points   Glasgow
Defends WBO Super-Middleweight Title

34 28 Nov 1992   Juan Carlos   Won (12), points   Manchester
                  Gimenez
Defends WBO Super-Middleweight Title

35 20 Feb 1993   Lindell Holmes   Won (12), points   London
Defends WBO Super-Middleweight Title

36 15 May 1993   Ray Close   Draw (12)   Glasgow
Retains WBO Super-Middleweight Title

37 9 Oct 1993   Nigel Benn   Draw (12)   Manchester
For WBC Super-Middleweight/WBO Super-Middleweight Titles
Retains WBO Super-Middleweight Title

38 5 Feb 1994   Graciano   Won (12), points   Berlin
                 Rocchigiani
Defends WBO Super-Middleweight Title

39 21 May 1994   Ray Close   Won (12), points   Belfast
Defends WBO Super-Middleweight Title

40 9 Jul 1994   Mauricio Amaral   Won (12), points   Kensington
Defends WBO Super-Middleweight Title

41 27 Aug 1994   Sam Storey   Won (7), TKO   Cardiff
Defends WBO Super-Middleweight Title

42 15 Oct 1994   Dan Schommer   Won (12), points   Sun City
Defends WBO Super-Middleweight Title

43 10 Dec 1994   Henry Wharton   Won (12), points   Manchester
Defends WBO Super-Middleweight Title

44	18 Mar 1995	Steve Collins	Lost (12), points	Cork

Loses WBO Super-Middleweight Title

45	27 May 1995	Bruno Godoy	Won (1), TKO	Belfast
46	29 Jul 1995	José Ignacio Barruetabena	Won (1), TKO	Whitley Bay
47	9 Sep 1995	Steve Collins	Lost (12), points	Cork

Challenger for WBO Super-Middleweight Title

48	19 Oct 1996	Luis Barrera	Won (5), TKO	Cairo
49	27 Mar 1997	Camillo Alarcon	Won (4), TKO	Dubai
50	11 Oct 1997	Joe Calzaghe	Lost (12), points	Sheffield

Challenger for WBO Super-Middleweight Title

51	18 Apr 1998	Carl Thompson	Lost (12), points	Manchester

Challenger for WBO Cruiserweight Title

52	18 Jul 1998	Carl Thompson	Lost (10), TKO	Sheffield

Challenger for WBO Cruiserweight Title

* TKO – Technical Knock-out

INDEX

A Question of Sport, 20

Al Fayed, Mohamad 359–60, 362, 364–5

Alarcon, Camillo 313

Ali, Muhammed 149, 226, 327–9

Amaral, Mauricio 257, 258

American Express 320

Andries, Dennis 345

Aquilina, Steve 67

Aryeh, Benjamin 55

Aryeh, Nathanial 55–7

Aston Martin Volante 248–50, 253, 295

At Home with the Eubanks 355, 391, 394, 398–401

At Home with the Osbournes 401

Ayling, Andy 232

Bagwell, Mike 46

Barkley, Iran 127

Barrera, Luis 305, 308

Barrera, Marco Antonio 119, 343

Barruetabena, José 284–5

Barry's Matchroom 180

BBC 328, 391

Beaver 22, 68

Beckworth, John 292

Bellenden Junior School 14

Benn, Nigel 44, 94, 96, 98, 100–1, 102, 105, 110, 113, 114–16, 119, 120, 123–33, 137–8, 141, 145, 146, 149–50, 175, 178, 202, 203, 211–15, 220, 237, 243, 248, 269, 273, 306, 338, 344, 345, 347, 349, 378, 382, 394–8

Bennett, Russell 240–3

Blackliners 185

Blair, Tony 245, 246

Bloor, Melanie 94

Boyzone 381

Branson, Richard 324

Breakthrough Breast Cancer 296

Brian, Tommy 20

Brighton 26, 86, 265–7
Brit Awards 328
British Boxing Board of Control 144–5, 154, 270, 276, 305, 314, 338
British Medical Association 240
Bronson, Charles 126–7
Brown, Timmy 45
Bruno, Frank 328, 393
Buckland, Tony 144
Bunce, Steve 324
Burnett, Winston 67, 78

Calzaghe, Joe 109, 321, 323–4, 347
Camara, Jean-Noël 105
Campbell, Darren 185
Campbell, Naomi 356
Cannida, Kenny 46
Canty, James 46
Celebrity Big Brother 85–6, 209, 381, 383–9, 391
Channel 4 209
Charles, Prince 294–7
Chevanne, Carol 46
Children of Courage Awards 360–1
Christie, Errol 106, 145
Christie, Linford 185, 355
Churchill, Winston 297
Clash of the Titans 394
Clifford, Max 292, 309
Close, Ray 206, 207, 216, 219–20, 221, 222, 225, 237, 257, 273
Collins, Simon 95, 97, 98, 118, 131, 150
Collins, Steve 207, 273–4, 275, 276, 277, 284–5, 297–8, 299, 321, 337, 356–7, 381

Comic Relief 381, 385, 386, 388, 389
Contreras, Eduardo 110
Cooper, Henry 146
Correa, Pepe 142
Corti, Hugo 109–10
Cronin, Denys 107–8, 109, 217
Cruz, Dennis 36–8
Curtis, Richard 381

Da Silva, José 107
Daily Express 196
Davies, Geraldine 392
Davies, Ronnie 74–7, 79, 88, 98, 101, 117, 124, 129, 138, 140, 143, 145, 150, 156, 161, 175, 180, 181, 183, 187, 188, 206, 220, 225, 259, 269, 271, 274, 277–8, 313–14, 322, 337
Davy's Street (care home) 19, 20–1
Dee, Jack 388, 389
Doctor 57–61, 110, 184, 268, 291, 336, 379
Dorothy xi–xii, 31
Douglas, Kevin 88
Douglas, Rod 166
Dubai 312, 314–15
Duff, Mickey 88, 270
Duffy, Keith 381, 382, 383, 386–7
Duran, Roberto 205, 352, 353
Durham Prison 285, 289–90
Durite 47

ESPN 345
Esquire 196
Essett, Ron 201–2

Eubank, Christopher (son) 81, 83–4, 225, 399–400

Eubank, Christopher Livingstone
bouts *see under opponents name*
boxing style 44, 60–2, 96–7, 125, 143–5, 156–7, 162–3, 183, 189–90
boxing, begins 30–42, 49
boxing, opinion of 116–21, 167, 267
car crash 169–72, 175–6
care homes, time spent in 17–21
cars, love of 198–201, 247–51, 253, 319
charity work 140, 146, 177–8, 184–5, 243–6, 263–8, 279–84, 284–5, 294–7, 312, 349, 354–65, 385, 388, 389, 393–4, 405
children, relationship with 81–4, 88
circumcision 206–7
correctness, obsession with 187–9, 205, 405–7
diet 24, 31, 75–6, 183–4, 186
dodging fights, accused of 325–6
early life 4–13
fans and fight crowds, relationship with 108–9, 126, 150, 217–19
fight record 409–12
first amateur fight 43
fixed fights, opinion on possibility of 117–19
friendships 247–54, 256–7, 309
'Godspeed' 168–9, 170–2, 174–5, 240

grievous bodily harm, charged with 308–12
image 22–3, 56, 76–7, 83, 91, 94–5, 96–7, 145, 193–4, 208–9, 216–17, 218–19, 303–5, 324, 405–6
injuries 106–7, 138, 165, 337–8, 346
jobs 47–8, 55–7
lisp 94–5
Lord of the Manor of Brighton 303–5
marries 133, 137–8, 141–2
media, relationship with 94–5, 96, 119–20, 121, 122–4, 133, 138–9, 141–2, 143, 145, 150, 153, 161, 163, 165–6, 173, 178, 179, 205, 208–9, 211–12, 218–19, 222–3, 237–40, 244–5, 267, 268, 278, 348
New York, moves to 29–63
post-boxing career 85–6, 209, 243–6, 263–8, 279–84, 284–5, 289–97, 312, 349, 354–65, 381, 383–9, 391, 393–4, 398–401, 405
pre-fight routine 186–8, 204
press conferences 122–4, 146, 154, 212, 274
professional, turns 45–6
promoters, relationship with 89, 101–3, 117–18, 214–15, 222, 269–70, 297–8, 319, 353–4
retires 168, 299–300, 325, 348–9, 351–5
schooldays 13–16, 33, 46–7
shoplifting and robbery xi–xii, 5, 9, 22–7, 52, 67–74

Eubank – *Cont.*
  smoking 5, 15, 30, 31–2
  sparring 181–3, 321
  sweet tooth 333–5
  training 57–63, 74–5, 140–1,
    177–8, 179–85, 354
  wealth and finances 79, 88,
    101–2, 113, 114, 126, 145,
    146, 150, 161, 211, 237–8,
    239, 247–8, 257, 259,
    264–5, 284, 297–8, 320–1,
    336
  weight 270–1, 277, 322–3
  wife, meets 77–8, 80
Eubank, David (brother) 4, 11,
  12, 17, 69, 369, 371, 372,
  375, 379
Eubank, Emily (daughter) 82,
  84, 218
Eubank, Ena (mother) 3–7,
  10–11, 24, 29, 371–80
Eubank, Irvin (father) 3, 4,
  6–10, 11, 15, 17, 24, 29, 89,
  367–80
Eubank, Joseph (son) 82, 84–5,
  402
Eubank, Joycelyn (sister) 4, 5,
  371, 374–5, 378
Eubank, Karron (wife) 77, 78,
  79–81, 82, 87, 88, 125, 133,
  137–8, 141, 187, 201, 215,
  218, 222–3, 242, 283,
  308–9, 322–3, 359, 382–3,
  398, 399, 400–1
Eubank, Pes (half-brother)
  377–8
Eubank, Peter (brother) 4, 11,
  17, 34, 78, 169, 170–1,
  367–8, 369, 371, 372, 376,
  377, 379, 380

Eubank, Sebastian (son) 82, 84,
  141, 400
Eubank, Simon (brother) 4, 11,
  17, 77, 169, 171, 222, 223,
  369, 371, 379, 380
Eubank's People 355
Evans, Chris 356, 388

Fashanu, John 355
Fayegh, Merser Al 314–15
Feltz, Vanessa 85–6, 297, 383,
  384, 388–9
Foreman, George 327–8, 337,
  341–3
Francis, Roy 159–60, 229
Freedom 53
Furlong, Richard 308

Gay 173–5
Geldof, Bob 197
George, Greg 67
Giménez, Juan Carlos 205
Gladiator: Benn vs Eubank 355,
  394–8
Godoy, Bruno 284
Godwin, Earl 303
Graham, Herol 81, 119, 326,
  346
Gutteridge, Reg 105, 158–9,
  160, 213

Hagler, Marvin 202
Hall, Sir John 285, 287
Hamdan, Sheik 314–15
Hamed, Prince Naseem 119,
  254, 256, 323, 324, 328,
  338–43, 355
Hamilton Lodge 312
Harding, Jess 187–8
Harley Davidson 201

Harrods 359–60, 363
Hearn, Barry 101–5, 118, 122, 123, 124, 126, 141, 144, 146–7, 155, 165, 183, 187, 214, 215, 218, 219, 229, 232–3, 237–8, 239, 260–1, 269, 270, 276, 297, 298, 320, 326
Hearn, Susan 218, 237
Hearns, Thomas 45, 113, 155, 352, 353
Henry, Lenny 386
Hide, Herbie 190
Holland, Eric 46
Hollies, The (care home) 18
Holmes, Lindell 205–6, 244
Holyfield, Evander 228, 234, 292, 328, 352–3
Hummer 313
Hustyns camp 344

Ingle, Bernard 255
International Fund For Animal Welfare 370
ITV 96, 110, 122, 211, 254, 255

Jack Pook gym 74, 78, 81
Jackson, Julian 346
Jamaica 3–6, 8, 371–80
Jarvis, John 193, 201, 222, 345
Jeffries, Jim 304
Jerome Boxing Club 34, 38, 337
Johnson, Jack 304, 329
Johnson, Kali 57
Johnson, Terry 245, 344–5, 369, 370
Johnson, Walter see Doctor
Jones, Roy 273, 325, 326, 352

Junior, Frank Santore 144
Justin, Michael 67

Kanu Heart Foundation 393–4
Karib (care home) 19
Kaylor, Mark 145
Kerzner, Sol 258–9
King, Don 103, 214, 215, 222, 229, 248

Landmark Hotel, Baker Street 333
Lawton, Doggie 194
Leonard, Sugar Ray 142, 149
Lewis, Lennox 234, 240, 292, 328, 352, 355, 383, 393
Logan, Anthony 95, 98–101, 105, 168
London Marathon 2003 392
Louis, Joe 327, 329
LSE 290

Madison Square Garden 292
Magri, Charlie 96
Malek, Ron 105
Malinga, Sugar Boy 177, 187
Mandela, Nelson 245–6, 329, 330–1
Marley, Bob 15
Marsden, Amanda 311
Martinez, Andy 38–9
Matlala, Baby Jake 259–60
McCallum, Mike 155, 326
McCarthy, Rory 93, 324
McCartney, Sir Paul 361
McClellan, Gerald 212, 248, 344
McDonnell, Jim 115
McGuigan, Barry 34, 328, 382
Melfah, Johnny 106, 260

Mendy, Ambrose 122, 123, 126, 137
Miles, Keith 77, 79, 80
Mills, Heather 361, 362–4
Milo, Kid 111
MOBO 238
Modahl, Diane 384
Moro, Frankie 103–4
Morris High School, New York 33, 45, 46–7
Moss Side 244
Mullan, Harry 163
Murray, Jim 300

Nasty 22, 24, 73
New York 27–63, 67–8, 102, 121, 181, 225, 248, 274, 326, 337, 374
Newbon, Gary 133, 161, 178
Newton, Max 247, 249–54
Nietzsche, Friedrich 49, 139, 324–5
Nigeria 393–4
Northwold Infants School 13–14
Nunn, Michael 325, 326

Okine, Mr Lord 17
Once Upon A Time In The West 126, 320
Orchard Lodge (care home) 19
Owen, Nick 122
Oxford Union 293–4

Parker, Darren 67
Peckham Manor Secondary School 15
Pepe 380
Perez, Maximo 38, 39–41, 74, 102, 183, 337

Peterbilt 198
Planet Hollywood 382–3
'Pride of Britain Awards' 245
Prince, Mark 321
Prince's Trust 294–6
Pyatt, Chris 167

Queen's Honours party 338–9

Rashid, Mohammed 93
Rawling, John 275
Read, Leonard 'Nipper' 145
Regan, John 88–9, 108, 137, 146, 151, 165, 178, 199, 207, 211–12, 220, 240, 264–5, 273, 286, 299
Regan, Sylvia 151
Richards, Dominic 266
Rocchigiani, Graciano 216–18, 219, 273
Rolls Royce 199, 287
Ruddock, Razor 234

Samantha 361–5
Santos, Renaldo Dos 115
Schommer, Dan 258, 260
Screen Sport 110
Sedaka, Alan 47–8, 55
Sedaka, Maurice 48
Sherry, Dan 142–4, 214, 229
shobins (dances) 22
Simpson, OJ 292–4
Sky 237, 238–40, 247, 263, 278, 284, 297–8, 323, 393
Smith, Darkie 102
Smith, Randy 103–4
SOBRO College of Technology, New York 47
Spanish Golden Gloves 44–5, 106, 229

'Sports Personality of the Century' 328
St Anne's Court, Buckingham 265–7
St Vincent's (care home) 19
Stanford House (care home) 19
Stanley, Benji 243–4
Starrie, David 109
Sticks 22, 24–5
Sting 259
Storey, Sam 258
Stretch, Gary 146–7
Sun 232, 402
Sun City 258–9
Sunday Mirror 222
Sussex University 289–90, 294–5

Talk Radio 355
The Good, The Bad and The Ugly 320
Theroux, Louis 391
Thomas Carlton Secondary School 14
Thomas, Terry 248, 249
Thompson, Carl 118, 335–6, 337, 338, 339, 342, 344, 345–9, 351
Thornton, Tony 202, 203, 204–5
Toney, James 273, 325, 352
Torres, Adonis 35, 38, 175
Tunnel, The 56
Turlington, Christie 356

Turner, Anthea 384–6
Tyson, Mike 109, 119, 128, 225–34, 352, 382

Walworth Road 21–2
Warren, Frank 89, 319
Washington, Desiree 230, 232
Watson, Michael 97, 106, 113–15, 149–64, 165–8, 172, 175, 176, 177, 178, 202, 203–4, 207, 213, 218, 219–20, 222, 273, 274, 275, 276, 277–8, 323, 347, 392–3
Watt, Jim 157–8
WBA 257
WBC 211
WBO 212, 216, 321, 336
Welch, Raquel 360
West Pier, Brighton 267–8
Westdene Primary School 312
Wharton, Henry 268–9, 270–2, 273, 297
Wilde, Oscar 356
Wilkins, Burt 88
Wischhusen, John 232
Wisnieski, Les 104–5
Woodia (cousin) 4, 51, 52, 52
Wyness, Anita 311

Yastrid Hall (care home) 18–20

ZigZag Productions 398

Printed by RR Donnelley at Glasgow, UK